DAVID LAWS
WHO KILLED KITCHENER?

THE LIFE AND DEATH OF BRITAIN'S
MOST FAMOUS WAR MINISTER

Biteback Publishing

First published in Great Britain in 2019 by
Biteback Publishing Ltd
Westminster Tower
3 Albert Embankment
London SE1 7SP
Copyright © David Laws 2019

ISBN 978-1-78590-237-6

10 9 8 7 6 5 4 3 2 1

A CIP catalogue record for this book is available from the British Library.

Set in Adobe Caslon Pro

Printed and bound in Great Britain by
CPI Group (UK) Ltd, Croydon CR0 4YY

MIX
Paper from
responsible sources
FSC
www.fsc.org   FSC® C020471

For Tim Lewis

CONTENTS

CONTENTS

AUTHOR'S NOTE

The last two, previously secret, government files relating to Lord Kitchener and his death on HMS *Hampshire* were finally opened to public view in 2014, ninety-eight years after his death. Even these were released only after a Freedom of Information request from the broadcaster and author Jeremy Paxman. My thanks to the staff of the National Archives for their help and assistance in viewing these files, and the large number of other contemporary Kitchener records they hold, which have been released over the last few decades.

The account in this book is based entirely on facts, and the recollections of those on board HMS *Hampshire*, as well as others who were involved in her mission and in the search for survivors in 1916.

I have set out to tell what is a fascinating tale, and – after decades of controversy – to finally separate fact from fantasy, truth from conspiracy theories. I have sought to do this in as straightforward and accessible a manner as possible. For that reason, I have avoided 'weighing down' the pages which follow with endless footnotes, seeking to cross-reference each fact – that would be too tedious for most readers. Instead, I have provided a detailed bibliography for those interested in further research and enquiry – and for such readers I cannot recommend too highly the recent (2016) Orkney

Heritage Society publication *HMS Hampshire: A Century of Myths and Mysteries Unravelled.*

The account that follows includes many references to the exact time of day at which an event occurred. These timings can never be definitive, and different participants will inevitably have slightly varying recollections, but those given here are the best estimates possible from the documents now available. The timings are particularly important in relation to the analysis of the speed of the authorities' response to *Hampshire's* sinking.

It is important to note that on 21 May 1916, the new 'British Summer Time' was introduced. This was one hour further on than Greenwich Mean Time. In June 1916, the civilian population of Orkney was using this new British Summer Time, but the Royal Navy and the military authorities continued to use Greenwich Mean Time. All the times in this narrative have been converted to Greenwich Mean Time, to avoid confusion.

Where there is a difference between witnesses in the recollection of facts and timings, I have carefully considered the weight of evidence and favoured the version which I think is more convincing. To do otherwise would, again, be tedious for the general reader, who is unlikely to be interested in trivial differences in the recollections of events dating back over 100 years. However, in the few cases where the differences in recollection are of crucial importance for the narrative or for the conclusions reached, I have made these differences explicit. I have also drawn attention to inconsistencies in the accounts available where it is impossible to reach a fair conclusion about the weight to be given to these different versions of history.

But on the whole, after 100 years of doubt, disputes, rumours and conspiracy stories, it is finally possible to tell the definitive story of how and why Lord Kitchener, one of Britain's greatest ever soldiers, came to be the only serving Cabinet minister to die at the hands of the enemy in wartime.

David Laws
Gloucestershire
November 2018

PREFACE

Field Marshal The Right Honourable The Earl Kitchener of Khartoum and of Broome in the County of Kent, Knight of the Order of the Garter, Knight of the Order of St Patrick, Knight of the Grand Cross of the Order of the Bath, Order of Merit, Knight Grand Commander of the Order of the Star of India, Knight Grand Cross of the Order of St Michael and St George, Knight Grand Commander of the Order of the Indian Empire was one of Britain's most popular, famous and successful soldiers – lauded and nationally recognised for his service in Sudan, in South Africa and in India.

Kitchener defeated a 50,000-strong Dervish Army at Khartoum in 1898, wiping out the national stain of General Gordon's death thirteen years before. He defeated the Boers in South Africa and went on to secure a successful peace, in no small part due to his pragmatism and realism. He collected impressive titles: Sirdar, or Commander in Chief, of the Egyptian Army; Governor-General of Sudan; Commander of British forces during the Boer War; Baron; Earl; Field Marshal; Commander in Chief of the Army of India; British agent in Egypt. He was, in his time, a man respected, admired and perhaps feared, by monarchs and the populace, and by friend and foe alike.

Kitchener was also the first serving soldier to become a member of Britain's Cabinet since General Monck in 1660. As Secretary of State for War from August 1914 to June 1916, Kitchener was one of the first of the nation's military and political leaders to correctly anticipate that the 'Great War' would last for many years and require mass mobilisation of men and equipment. He set to work immediately to recruit the 'New Armies', which eventually helped deliver Allied victory, and his image was used in the iconic recruiting posters that are still famous to this day.

But Kitchener was not simply one of those unimaginative, red-hatted World War I commanders who believed in hurling large numbers of men at the well-designed German defences in the west. He was pragmatic about testing the military possibilities in other theatres, not least to reduce the strain on Britain and France's hard-pressed ally, Russia. He had a strategic vision of what was necessary for the Allied nations to prevail which went beyond the limited perspective of many of his senior military colleagues.

As well as being a successful general, Kitchener was also a controversial one. In Sudan, he was accused of turning a blind eye to the massacre of injured Dervish troops. In South Africa, he was accused of using 'methods of barbarism' – concentration camps – to lock up Boer women and children, thousands of whom died of disease.

As the first year of the war passed, the failure to make a decisive breakthrough damaged Kitchener's authority, and that of most of the principal war leaders in each participant country. In 1915, Kitchener was blamed for a shortage of shells and other equipment, and he failed to prevent disastrous campaigns both in the Dardanelles and on the Western Front. In the controversies over First World War Allied strategy, Kitchener was neither a 'westerner' nor an 'easterner'. He always believed that the decisive breakthrough would have to be made in the west, but he could see the argument for ventures in the east if these were designed to diminish German strength, ease the pressure on Russia or protect key British interests. Like many of those who choose to sit on the fence, Kitchener's position was generally rational but often uncomfortable. And when Churchill's Dardanelles exploit failed disastrously, Kitchener could not escape some of the blame.

By late 1915, Kitchener's star was in its descent. He was still respected and admired by the public and by most ordinary servicemen, but support amongst his senior military and political colleagues was draining away. In part, this was due to the difficult and prolonged course of the war. But it was also down to Kitchener's style, character and personal relations. Britain's Secretary of State for War was a complex individual: aloof, stern, antisocial and very private. Many senior officers and most political leaders found him arrogant, secretive and high-handed. At times, as the war progressed, they also considered him out of touch and concluded that he was struggling to cope with the sheer range of his responsibilities.

Kitchener did not naturally build personal or political alliances. Apart from those close to him, he was withdrawn and distant. He spent all his working life in the armed forces and never married. His closeness to a more junior officer, twenty-six years younger than him, caused gossip about his sexuality. In his private life, he enjoyed apparently un-military pursuits such as collecting porcelain and antique furniture, as well as spending time on flower-arranging, not considered an established hobby of the military classes. After his great victory at Khartoum, Kitchener also developed an odd habit of pinching other people's possessions if they appealed to him, even from the houses of close friends – porcelain, again, being a particular favourite. Some hosts even insisted on packing away family treasures before his visits.

But whatever the doubts of those who worked with him, by 1915–16 his very image – through the famous recruiting poster – had become a symbol for and of the nation. Even his critics had to acknowledge the power of his character and his reputation – Prime Minister Asquith's wife, Margot, once allegedly noting that he 'might not be a great man, but he is at least a great poster'.

As his influence waned, his political masters would curtail his authority, but they feared to get rid of him. In late 1915, the Prime Minister sent his Secretary of State for War to the eastern Mediterranean and hoped he could be persuaded not to return. But Kitchener was a stubborn and proud man and was not to be so easily cast aside.

Then, in 1916, while being assailed in Parliament by political enemies who blamed him for the failure to bring the war to a swifter conclusion, he set off on another secret mission. Its purpose was to meet the Russian Emperor, his generals and senior Russian ministers and officials and help to ensure their continued commitment to the war against Germany.

Kitchener never reached Russia. Instead, he set another national record – he became the first and only British Cabinet minister to be killed in conflict. HMS *Hampshire*, the armoured cruiser on which he was travelling to Russia, suffered a catastrophic explosion in stormy waters, just west of the Orkney Islands. She sank in less than half an hour, just one and a half miles from land. Almost all on board were killed.

The news of Kitchener's death spread rapidly in Britain and throughout the world. But who killed Kitchener? It was first assumed that his ship had been sunk by German action – by a torpedo or a mine.

Yet within days of his death, other theories had gained traction

– and many questions were being asked in the press and in Parliament. Had the details of his voyage been betrayed to the enemy? Were the Germans waiting for him? Why was the route taken by his vessel changed shortly before his departure? Why was his ship allowed to sail headlong into the teeth of a massive storm? And why were his escort destroyers sent back to port just an hour or so into their mission?

And then the questions and theories became even more disturbing and extraordinary. Was his ship destroyed by a South African agent or perhaps an Irish terrorist who had planted bombs aboard during maintenance work on the ship? Had Kitchener's body washed up on the Scandinavian shoreline and been secretly buried? Was there a conspiracy in the British government itself to let Kitchener die? Why were the rescue ships sent out only after a long delay? Why was the local lifeboat prevented from going out? Why did British troops refuse to let locals on the Orkney Islands help with the search and rescue of survivors? And what about the messages that were washing up on the shores of mainland Britain, apparently from survivors who had yet to be found?

Why, asked many, including Kitchener's own private secretary, was the government refusing to publish the full details behind the sinking of HMS *Hampshire*, and why were the public and press denied access to secret government papers about the sinking for decades after the war was over?

This book seeks to answer these questions and more. It does not attempt to provide a comprehensive perspective on Kitchener's life and times. That would require a much longer volume than this. Nor is it a detailed attempt to weigh Kitchener's achievements against the criticisms that have been levelled at him. To understand why his death was so important and controversial, it is, however, necessary to look back into his earlier life and shine a light on certain key chapters.

This account looks to uncover the truth about why and how one of Britain's most successful ever military leaders came to meet his end: who killed Kitchener?

I am grateful to Iain Dale, formerly of Biteback, for agreeing to commission this work – my first venture beyond contemporary political writing. My sincere thanks, as well, to my ever-patient editor, Olivia Beattie, and to James Stephens, Ellen Heaney and all the current Biteback team.

Finally, thanks to Theo Rockey for his help in researching this account.

MAP OF THE ORKNEY ISLANDS, HMS *HAMPSHIRE*'S ROUTE AND THE SURVIVORS' JOURNEY

Brough of Birsay

Birsay Bay

Site of HMS *Hampshire* sinking

BIRSAY

Marwick Head

MARWICK

Marwick Bay

Outshore Point

Rivna Geo
Nebbi Geo

• Pallast
• Garson
NORTHDYKE
• Stockan
• Linnahowe

SANDWICK

Bay of Skaill

Garricot

1 land mile

HMS *Hampshire* sinks

• Birsay
• Marwick Head
• Outshore Point
• Floats 1/2 (Rivna Geo, Nebbi Geo)

Bay of Skaill

• Float 3 landing point

MAINLAND OF ORKNEY

Stromness

Kirkwall

SCAPA FLOW

British Fleet

Destroyers leave *Hampshire* here

Hoy Head

HOY

NORTH SEA

Longhope

Tor Ness

Journey of HMS *Hampshire*

10 km

6 mi

Scrabster Harbour

SCOTTISH MAINLAND

THE KILLING

'What is that? A mine, or a torpedo?'

CAPTAIN HERBERT SAVILL, ON BOARD HMS *HAMPSHIRE*,
7.40 P.M., 5 JUNE 1916

Tor Ness, off the most south-westerly edge of the Orkney Islands.
It is 5.45 p.m. on 5 June 1916.

Three warships are battling their way through a force 8 gale,
lurching up and down in the tremendous swell as the waves crash
around them and smash over the front of the ships, sending white,
foaming spray arcing up into the sky. Almost the longest day of the
year, it is still light and will be for another four or five hours in this
northern outpost of the British Isles.

To the right of the ships, the dark, sheer cliffs of Tor Ness are
clearly visible, white waters breaking around their base, and every
few seconds huge and powerful waves crash directly into them,
forcing great blankets of water to soar up into the air. To the left,
there is nothing but the angry and unwelcoming Atlantic Ocean,
stretching away to the distant horizons.

These seas are the roughest most of those on board the three
ships have ever seen, and the winds are strong enough to blow men

on the decks right over if they do not grip on tight. In any case, few are venturing outside for more than a few brief steps.

But though the conditions are now bad, the three ships' captains know that they are soon going to get worse – much worse. Up to now, their journey has taken them westwards, and so they have been able to shelter from the northern winds behind the landmass of the island of Hoy. Now, they are about to leave the protection of the land, head out into the open ocean, and turn north on their designated route along the west side of Orkney.

And as they steer to the north, they face the full blast of gale force 9 winds blowing directly against their path. The wind that a few moments ago was strong is now ferocious. It rips over each of the ships, drives rain and sea water over every exposed inch of steel, and slams the sea into their bows, fighting their progress through the ocean.

It is the coldest June in Orkney for forty years. The air temperature is just 6° centigrade – bitterly cold. Add in the wind chill and it is freezing. The rain sweeps down in squalls.

On board the leading ship – the armoured cruiser HMS *Hampshire* – her captain, Herbert Savill, surveys the scene. Earlier that day, the wind was from the north-east, from where the staff at the Scapa Flow Royal Navy base assumed it would continue. If they had been right, Savill's ship would now be enjoying some protection from the land to the east of him. But *Hampshire*'s captain now realises that the forecasters have got it badly wrong. The wind is now blowing not from the north-east but from the north-west, and the land to the east can offer no protection at all.

Savill uses binoculars to scan the horizon for German submarines – U-boats. With his secret VIP passenger on board, it would be a disaster if his ship was torpedoed. And he knows that in these bitterly cold waters, of perhaps just 9° centigrade, swamped by waves of 25 or 30 feet in height, a man would lose consciousness in an hour and be dead in three at most – whether of hypothermia or drowning. But, Savill concludes, if there is any silver lining from these appalling and unseasonal conditions, it is that a U-boat attack is surely impossible.

Standing on the compass platform from which the ship is commanded, Captain Savill now asks for *Hampshire*'s speed. His orders from Admiral Jellicoe, Commander in Chief of the fleet, are to make 18 knots. His destroyer escorts – HMS *Unity* and HMS *Victor* – should normally be able to keep up with this. But in these dreadful conditions, who knows? *Unity* and *Victor* are only small destroyers, no more than 1,000 tons each – less than a tenth the weight of *Hampshire*. They will find it difficult to maintain their speed in the face of a storm of this force.

Savill looks behind his ship. He can see that *Unity* and *Victor* are already lagging behind, struggling to keep pace. One moment they are visible, on the crest of great waves, the next they surge forward and downwards, and the front of the ships disappear under waves the size of houses. At times, it seems certain to those who watch that they have been swamped and will not re-emerge from the ocean. But they battle on, fighting the currents and the winds, and rise again, casting the frothing waters to left and right. They will not be beaten, but they are borne back ever further away from the ship they are supposed to be protecting.

At 6.05 p.m., Savill receives the message he has been fearing. It is from the captain of *Victor*, Lieutenant Charles Ransome. It is relayed by *Unity*. It tells Savill that *Victor* can make only 15 knots without risking serious damage – bluntly, she cannot keep up. Savill thinks for a moment. He is charged with taking to Russia the members of a secret mission, led by Lord Kitchener, Secretary of State for War and one of Britain's greatest military leaders. He knows the urgency of the mission and Kitchener's desire to keep to the ambitious timetable he has set. He knows that he cannot afford to lose time. But is it really sensible to proceed through these waters, so close to Britain's biggest naval base of Scapa Flow, and therefore a hunting ground for German submarines, without a full destroyer escort? It is a difficult judgement.

Now, at 6.15 p.m., he has made his decision. Savill orders *Victor* to return to port. However, *Unity* is struggling to keep up, too. *Unity*'s captain – Lieutenant Commander Arthur Lecky – now signals *Hampshire* that his ship can make only 12 knots without damage. Savill ponders again. He does not want to lose both escorts. He asks for *Hampshire*'s own speed. He knows his ship is also finding it difficult to maintain the planned pace.

By now, *Hampshire* herself is only making 15 knots instead of the 18 that her captain had ordered. The news is shared with Savill, who now cancels his message to *Victor*. Instead, over the noise of the storm, he shouts: 'Signal *Unity*. Tell her: "I am only going 15 knots. Can you keep up?"'

Savill looks back behind his ship. He can now barely make out *Victor* and *Unity* through the spray and heavy seas. *Unity* does not take long to flash her answer back: 'No.' At 6.18 p.m., *Unity* signals that she can only make 10 knots, not even the promised 12.

Captain Savill knows that he has to choose. He has decided: he cannot risk slowing his own ship any further. At 6.20 p.m., he turns to the signals officer: 'Send this message: "Destroyers, return to base."' But then, almost immediately, he seems to change his mind, fearing to proceed unescorted. He now tells HMS *Victor* to remain with him. But by this time *Victor* has fallen well astern. She cannot close the gap. At 6.25 p.m., *Victor* reports: 'Maximum speed I can maintain without risk of injury is 12 knots.'

Savill's decision is now final. He orders *Victor*, too, to return home. *Hampshire* has now lost both her escorts, after just forty-five minutes of protection and just five miles from port. It is 6.30 p.m.

Hampshire steams on alone, hatches battened down against the rising storm outside. Only the rear hatch is not sealed, to allow limited safe access from the decks. But on this night, few venture outside unless they must, as the Atlantic waves crash over her fore-castle and sweep along her exposed decks.

From the compass platform, Savill quietly watches the destroyer escorts heading back to Scapa Flow. With each minute they are further away, until they finally slip out of sight behind the waves. On *Hampshire*, they are now truly alone. Savill wonders if he has made the right choice.

Fifteen minutes later, at 6.45 p.m., there is a message passed up to Savill from the telegraphists on board. It is from Admiral Jellicoe at Scapa Flow, timed at 6.40 p.m. The Commander in Chief has requested permission from the Admiralty for *Hampshire* to recoal at Archangel in north Russia, and remain there until it is time to bring Kitchener and his party back home. Savill is relieved. At last, some good news. This will save making two dangerous return journeys to Russia – one to deposit Kitchener and another to collect him. Later, at 7.20 p.m., *Hampshire* will acknowledge the order. As the telegraphist types out the message, he cannot know that it is the last telegram *Hampshire* will ever send.

By 6.45 p.m., *Hampshire* is just over a third of the way up the west coast of Orkney Mainland. Soon, to the east, Savill can see the entrance to Hoy Sound, and after this his ship passes Stromness, the second town of the Orkney Islands.

The wind speed is climbing and the wind direction is still almost head on, from the north-west, blowing furiously in the ship's face. The 45-year-old Savill has been in the Royal Navy since 1883, when he joined as a thirteen-year-old cadet, but he has rarely experienced such a storm. Even *Hampshire*, with a top speed of 23 knots, can now manage just 13½.

The watches are still on the lookout for other ships, and their eyes scan the water's surface for signs of U-boats. But the surging seas make it impossible to identify anything on the surface. And surely, on a night like this, no U-boat could successfully mount an attack? With no destroyer escorts, that is now the hope.

To the east, on the starboard side of *Hampshire*, Savill and the others on watch can still clearly make out the harsh Orkney coast a couple of miles away, the waves breaking dramatically on its jutting crags and high cliffs. The closeness of the land offers some reassurance. They are still in sight of safety. Not far away are people, homes, warmth and security. To the port side, there is nothing but open ocean for thousands of miles.

A little further on, to the east, through rain showers and waves, Captain Savill can make out the Bay of Skaill, a smallish cove, about a mile in length and around half a mile deep, with a narrow and rocky beach. It is a place where boats could easily land. To the north of this bay, the shoreline becomes less hospitable, with four miles of steep and rocky cliffs until you reach the gentler inclines of Marwick Bay.

Savill is tempted to go down below now, to join Lord Kitchener for dinner. But with the weather this bad he decides he must stay on the compass platform a little longer. And in any case, will Britain's formidable Secretary of State for War really want to speak to a mere ship's captain? He has a long journey ahead of him. Perhaps he will soon want to attempt some sleep.

It is now 7.20 p.m. *Hampshire* has been sailing for two and a half hours and there, ahead to the east, is the unmistakeable sight of Marwick Head, where, just north of Marwick Bay, huge cliffs rise sheer from the sea to a height of almost 100 metres. The waves sweep in, one after another, crashing onto the cliffs, turning the water into a bright white surf for 200 metres out to sea. They are booming and thundering tonight as they smash head first into the rocks, sending spray upwards in huge sheets.

This is a hard and unwelcoming shoreline, one whose strength and toughness has been shaped from having to absorb, day after day, year after year, century after century, the unforgiving brutality of the western winds and waves. Passing Marwick Head, Captain Savill looks further north towards the land, and can see the Atlantic rollers sweeping into Birsay Bay, less than a mile deep and criss-crossed by rocky ledges. In the bay, just behind the narrow sandy beach, are the squat homes of Birsay village. And behind the weather-beaten houses are visible the ruins of the sixteenth-century Earl's Palace, which lends some sense of grandeur to an otherwise unexceptional place.

Just north of Birsay is a small rocky island, the Brough of Birsay, which can be accessed at low tide from the mainland by a long ledge of rock. This is the most north-westerly point of Orkney's mainland. The first stage of Savill's mission is almost complete. Soon, *Hampshire* will be out into the open Atlantic, far from the British fleet in Scapa Flow, hopefully far away from any watching U-boats. Then Savill can alter his course towards the east and set sail for Russia.

But for now they are still battling the north-west winds. The dark seas are still sweeping over *Hampshire*'s forecastle. Savill checks his position. They are about a mile and a half from the shores of Birsay and two miles from Marwick Head.

Hampshire is a large ship, almost 500 feet, or 150 metres, in length and displacing around 11,000 tons. But this evening, with the hatches battened down against the storm outside and most sailors crowded inside for safety, there is a sense of suffocating claustrophobia. The main deck is crowded and the atmosphere oppressive.

On *Hampshire* is a crew of 735 – including seventy-four under the age of eighteen, with some as young as sixteen. And tonight those 735 have been joined by Kitchener and the thirteen-man party he is taking to Russia, including his loyal aide and personal friend Lieutenant-Colonel Fitzgerald, his close protection officer and a number of servants. Most of the crew are on the main deck or in the engine rooms and boiler rooms – walking about gingerly, as their ship crashes from wave to wave, but otherwise feeling safe and secure and relieved to be away from the freezing air and spray outside.

The engine and boiler rooms are the most claustrophobic places of all, and the lack of space is only compounded by the intense heat and the loud noise of the machinery. Men have to shout to be heard, and just hours into their mission they are already dripping in sweat and covered in coal dust, oil and grime. Down here, the work is toughest and the tension is greatest – the men are keenly aware that if the ship gets into trouble and sinks, they will have furthest to travel to their abandon ship positions on the upper deck. And if they are hit by a mine or torpedo, these men know that they are more at risk than others of instant death, appalling injuries or the horror of drowning. The life of a stoker in His Majesty's Royal Navy is not an easy one.

Now, above the crashing of the waves, the crew can hear the note of the supper bugle and the call to 'stand by hammocks'. *Hampshire* has proceeded unescorted for an hour. It has just passed the landmark of Marwick Head.

Petty Officer Wilfred Wesson, Captain of the Foretop, has gone down to the mess deck to get some warming supper. He is aged thirty-three, 5 feet 7½ inches in height, was born in Hampstead in London and joined the navy aged fifteen. On his right arm is a tattoo of a bird in flight, chasing a fly. His friend and fellow Londoner Petty Officer Thomas Leach is already there, eating his bread and cheese at a table. 'How about Leicester Square, tonight? Do you fancy coming out?' Leach jokes. A few hours into a new and exciting mission, there is a lot of banter amongst the crew. Another petty officer, the heavily bearded, 5 foot 5½ inch, 41-year-old Samuel Sweeney, an old rogue from Ireland, has a few minutes ago been teasing others about the risks of a submarine attack. He is quickly shouted down and now has to leave to take up his position on the forebridge, on the compass platform, alongside the captain.

Meanwhile, making his way slowly to dinner as the ship rolls and groans, is the most important cargo any British vessel has yet been charged with during the Great War: Field Marshal Lord Kitchener, military icon and War Minister, on a mission designed to bolster Russia, Britain's key military ally, and keep her in the war against Germany. Tiny 21-year-old stoker Frederick Sims, carrying a scar on the left side of his chin, passes Kitchener, walking with another officer and heading into the wardroom. Sims can't wait to tell the others that he's just seen one of the most famous Britons alive.

Captain Savill is still on the bridge, guiding his ship through the gale. Savill is now rejoined on the standard compass platform by Petty Officer Sweeney, the Quartermaster of the Watch, who is helping navigate the ship. Sweeney is one of the most experienced men on board, having joined the navy twenty-six years ago, almost to the day. He was then just fifteen years of age. He has had a career of mixed repute – serving some time in custody after deserting in

March 1898 – after which it took the navy sixteen months to track him down.

Sweeney now watches alongside Savill. He relays instructions from his captain to the rest of the crew. There is no unnecessary talking. With the captain on the watch, the small team is on its best behaviour. And perhaps there is something else, too – a sense of nervousness, of anticipation, beneath the sangfroid. They've all seen big seas before, but this is amongst the worst. And although they have only just returned from doing battle with the Germans at Jutland, then they were accompanied by the whole British fleet. Now, they are very much alone.

The ship's engines are presently set to deliver 15 knots and ninety-three revolutions. But with the seas crashing headlong into *Hampshire*, Sweeney can see that the actual speed is still only 13½ knots – well below her maximum. In the boiler rooms and the engine rooms, the stokers and engineers are doing all they can to increase the power. Captain Savill now wants to recheck the knots: 'Give me a new estimate of our speed.' Sweeney hears the navigator shout out that he will know in just a couple of minutes. 'Keep steering north 30 east,' orders Savill. 'Yes, sir' is the crisp response. Sweeney now quietly asks the time from a signalman close to him. 'Three bells' is the reply, indicating the end of the third half-hour period of the 6 p.m. watch. It is now, therefore, 7.30 p.m.

Sweeney is far from the only experienced seaman on board *Hampshire* this night. Leading Seaman Charles Rogerson is on watch on the main deck. He is 5 feet 3 inches, with brown hair and grey eyes. He is only twenty-six years of age but has already served on nine ships before *Hampshire* – including the battleship HMS *Goliath* and five cruisers – His Majesty's ships *Gladiator*, *Edgar*, *Hawke*, *Argonaut* and *Ariadne*. And down below there are men with long service records and deep knowledge too – Warrant Mechanician William Bennett is Officer of the Watch in the ship's engine rooms. Bennett joined *Hampshire* only a few weeks ago. He is an experienced sailor and a tough man – the son of a brickyard labourer, and one of fourteen children, only five of whom survived to adulthood. He joined the navy in 1899, aged eighteen, and has worked his way up from stoker to warrant mechanician – an officer rank. It is a rare achievement. Bennett is respected by the toughest of the ship's stokers, including 24-year-old former gardener Stoker 1st Class Walter 'Lofty' Farnden. The engine room is even more crowded and noisy than usual tonight – the crew are struggling to deliver as much power as possible, and are conscious of the captain's frustration at the slow progress they are making.

Up above, thirty-year-old Shipwright William Phillips, who joined the Royal Navy aged fourteen, is preparing to issue bedding to Lord Kitchener and his small party of military advisers. He is on the after part of the ship, on the main deck.

Most of the crew have now just finished their supper. Some are getting themselves prepared before going on watch at 8 p.m. Able Seaman John Bowman, aged twenty, along with Able Seaman William Cashman, aged twenty-eight, and Able Seaman Richard Simpson – just seventeen years of age but pretending to the navy to be nineteen in order to join up for the war – are standing by hammocks in the gunroom.

Leading Seaman Rogerson is walking back down the ship, from his position as leading hand of the foretop, port watch. He is going back on the main deck, answering the 'stand by hammocks' call. At 7.35 p.m., Rogerson stops off briefly in the canteen. Five minutes later, he leaves the canteen and heads along the mess deck, steadying himself as the ship lurches about in the stormy waters.

Just two miles away, on shore, the bucking cruiser is clearly visible to anyone who dares to be out on such a night. Just after 7.30 p.m., twelve-year-old John Fraser is ushered out of his house by his excited father: 'Come out and see this big battleship passing in these rough seas.'

Nearby, a bit further along the coast, thirteen-year-old Peter Brass is outside, too, looking after the family sheep. He sees the cruiser crashing through the waves and is transfixed.

On *Hampshire*, Stoker Sims has just finished his tea and is sitting at a table on the stokers' mess deck, making small talk with his friends. Sims is on the forward part of the deck, opposite the forehead hatch. He is telling all who will listen about having seen Kitchener earlier. He is fielding the other men's questions, and perhaps adding a little embellishment to his tale.

And then it happens: a sudden, huge, rumbling explosion that rocks the ship, followed by another smaller explosion just afterwards. The men gasp. There are shouts of surprise, and of fear. The ship lurches. For those close to the explosion the noise is deafening, and the shock seems to shake the ship all over. Sims almost immediately feels a blast of hot air sweeping past him, which scalds his face and neck.

Throughout the ship, the lights flicker and then go out, plunging the whole vessel into darkness. Sims and his mates can hardly breathe for the dense fumes. He thinks he will suffocate. There are terrible screams from men who have been badly burnt, or worse. Men rush to escape through the hatches, but these are locked from above. There is pushing and shoving as men bump into each other in the dark.

A flash fire has broken out, badly burning many sailors before they can escape. With the magazine sited so close to their mess deck, there is a desperate surge of men seeking to clamber above and onto the upper levels, away from the smoke and the risk of secondary explosions.

Sims guesses that the explosion has come from the port side, towards the front of the ship. It must, he thinks, be a mine, and by the size of the explosion he wonders if the forward magazine has also been blown up by it. Already, it feels as if the ship is behaving abnormally, struggling to right herself. Is she sinking?

On the main deck, Shipwright Phillips is thrown instantly to the floor by the force of the explosion. Next to Petty Officer Wesson, standing on the mess deck, there is a great rush of air, which blows men's hats off onto the floor. There is already an alarming slant to the floor of the mess deck. And this time it isn't just caused by the waves outside – Wesson notices with concern that the slant isn't correcting itself. At the same time, through the darkness, he can make out a large volume of suffocating smoke spreading along the deck, and there are sparks falling onto the floor, providing at least a modicum of light.

Leading Stoker Alfred Read, a 24-year-old former painter and decorator who joined up in 1912, is on the after end of the stokers' mess deck, on the port side. He hears the explosion and immediately thinks it is a mine. He heads on deck through the galley hatch and goes to the upper deck.

In the gunroom they also hear the massive explosion. It feels as if the ship has slammed down on a heavy sea. Immediately, there is a shout of 'No panic, lads.' Most guess that it is a mine. The young boys on board look shaken. Many are only sixteen or seventeen.

In the boiler rooms and the engine rooms there is calm, but the looks are of panic. They are at the bottom of the ship. If she is going to sink, they risk being trapped in this metal tomb and drowned.

Their strong instinct is to climb immediately up the ladders to the upper deck. But they must await orders. Stoker 1st Class Lofty Farnden is on watch in the port engine room. He is shaken by the enormous explosion, which sounds to him like it came from below the foremost stokehold. In spite of his nerves, he remains at his position.

Up above, on the standard compass platform, Petty Officer Sweeney and every man including Captain Savill hear the explosion too – a rumbling eruption, followed by a smaller one. Almost immediately, they see the after-effects. There are lyddite flames shooting up around them, and then thick, brown smoke – hot and suffocating – coming out from below and billowing up in a large cloud above the ship. The smoke is so thick that for a while Sweeney loses sight of Captain Savill, who is standing just alongside him, the only officer on the bridge.

Savill, choking back the fumes, shouts out, 'What is that? A mine, or a torpedo?' But there is no answer. Only a downward lurching of the ship, which suggests that the centre of her has been torn out by the blast. They cover their faces from the smoke and try to hold their breath to avoid taking in the noxious fumes.

When the smoke has finally cleared, Captain Savill recoils in horror as he sees just how disastrous the explosion has been – he looks forward and can clearly comprehend that they are already sinking, head first, with the waves submerging the bows of the great ship. Before the explosion, the forecastle would successively rise above and then fall below the surface of the sea. Now it has disappeared below the waves. Savill knows that he, his crew and the Kitchener mission are all in mortal danger.

The lights are out but a call to the engine room confirms that the engines are still working, propelling the ship slowly forward. With relief, Savill hears from below the voice of the chief engineer on watch – William Bennett, calm and composed in spite of all that has happened.

The 35-year-old Bennett is now near the forward boiler room. He immediately knows that the explosion is serious. It sounded to him like a dull thud, underneath the middle of the ship. He judges that it was below No. 1 stokehold – on the port side of the ship, between four and six stations, and underneath the bakehouse. For a second he thinks it is a torpedo, but then guesses it is a mine.

Bennett curses his bad luck. He had been on the light cruiser HMS *Arethusa* when she hit a mine off Felixstowe on 11 February 1916, just four months earlier. Six men had been killed, and the engines stopped immediately, water gushing into the back of the ship. Two more men died when their Carley float – a type of raft – had sunk. *Arethusa* had then drifted onto a shoal while under tow and had broken her back. Surely he is not going to have two ships sunk under him in just four months?

Bennett now expects orders from the bridge. But none come. He uses his own initiative, scrambling around in the darkness and managing to light the emergency oil lamps in the engine room. Then he shouts to the chief engine room artificer on watch, 'Keep cool. Carry on your duties. I am going to investigate.' His job is to calm the other men, but he does not feel calm himself – the ship already seems as if she is going down into the water, head first.

The engineer officer on board, forty-year-old Commander Arthur Cossey, now orders the ship's speed to be reduced. The engines are still working, but the driving wind, waves and tide are changing *Hampshire*'s course to bear more towards the land. On the compass platform, Sweeney can see that the ship is changing direction. He shouts to the helmsman, 'Alter course.' But the helmsman shouts back that the steering gear is jammed: 'I can't move it.' The ship has now lost all lights, lost all communication and lost the ability to control her direction. Captain Savill knows they are in serious trouble. And his escorts are by now back in Scapa Flow – two or three hours' sailing away.

Meanwhile, Warrant Mechanician William Bennett is still desperately assessing what can be done to save the ship. Bennett finds the senior engineer. Together, they scramble up through the hatch of the engine room. As he is going up the ladder, at around 7.50 p.m., Bennett thinks he hears one or two further explosions. They seem slightly further aft than the first one. Yellow smoke is pouring out. The noises seem to be coming from the starboard side of the ship, where the battery of small 3-pounder guns is located. Bennett turns to the senior engineer: 'Have we found a submarine?' He guesses that the gunners must be firing at something in the waters. 'No,' is the reply. 'It looks like we've hit a second mine.' Bennett thinks the second mine, if there is one, might have struck the ship between the first and second boiler rooms. Have they now taken a mine strike on both sides of the ship?

At 7.55 p.m., Bennett reports to Engineer Commander Cossey on the quarterdeck. Cossey wants to know if it is possible to stabilise the ship by flooding the back section, to counterbalance the bow, which has already disappeared under the waters. Bennett checks. It isn't possible. The valves at the back of the ship are now clear of the water.

The deck hatches are still mostly battened down – only the one at the rear of the vessel seems to be open. Bennett helps to open another hatch, knocking away the beechwood wedges that keep it sealed. Immediately, forty or fifty relieved sailors emerge and rush away.

By now, Savill has had time to make a quick appreciation of the condition of his ship. He knows that if he is to have any chance of saving lives – including Kitchener's – then he must act quickly and decisively. For every ship's captain, it is the bitterest of moments. But Savill has decided. He turns and calmly issues the instructions. Across the ship, moments later, the order comes through: 'Take up your abandon ship stations.'

Down in the engine rooms, the stokers need no further encouragement. The last thing they want is to be down below in a sinking ship. They queue to climb up the narrow and steep metal steps and are soon on the mess deck. From there, they make hastily for the nearest hatches. Lofty Farnden has stayed in the engine room for five minutes after the explosion. But it is clear that they are losing power and the ship is sinking. He is ordered to leave and join the others at their abandon ship positions.

Leading Seaman Charles Rogerson, on the mess deck, now looks out through the port windows: he is shocked when he sees that they are already under water. The explosion was loud and sounded to him as if it had come from right under the centre of the ship. He knows that they are in trouble.

All the sailors in the back of the ship are now making a rush for the one main deck hatch that leads up to the quarterdeck. Rogerson has to wait for others to get up the ladder, and then he is up too. He rips off the large coat he is wearing and heads for the starboard side of the upper deck, into the starboard battery. From there, he heads for his abandon ship station at No. 1 float, amidships. The sea gangways are already awash with water.

Hampshire is sinking head first into the sea, with her rear end now rising out of the water at an increasingly severe angle. The front end of the ship is totally submerged. There is no panic amongst the crew, but the look of fear in their faces tells that many are not confident of surviving.

Stoker Sims, scalded by the explosion's blast, is now trying to escape above. There is still much smoke and he fears he may suffocate, not least because most of the hatches have been shut from above. Two men in front of Sims push hard on a hatch above them, and it opens – to their relief, it has not been properly clipped down. When Sims and his mates scramble up the 10-foot ladder onto the deck and into the open air, a grim sight meets their eyes. A number of dead and seriously injured sailors are lying there. Blood mingles with sea water around their bodies. Some are moaning with pain. Most are too shocked to speak. Sims can see that even though it is only a matter of minutes since the explosion, the ship is sinking by the bow and listing heavily. He realises that the decks are now at an angle of 30° and notices the rear of the ship lifting out of the water.

Petty Officer Wesson was in the mess room when the explosion occurred. The hatches there were closed. Wesson and those with him now make their way to the only open hatch, at the back of the ship. There is gushing water in the corridors and serious congestion as all the sailors try to make their way up through the single hatch. Wesson heads through the gunroom flat and into the half deck. Word is that the ship has hit a mine on the port side of her foremost engine room. Wesson is in charge of the Carley raft stations to the side of the ship. Here, there are three crude floats, capable of supporting perhaps 150 men in the water while they wait for rescue boats to pick them up. Those on the floats are usually the unlucky ones when a ship sinks – the sailors who haven't been allocated a boat to escape in. Wesson makes his way there.

By now, Shipwright William Phillips has recovered from his fall and he too is heading in the darkness for the nearest hatchway. Men are gradually leaving by the rear hatch to the upper deck. Some, like seventeen-year-old Dick Simpson, then help open other hatches to allow more sailors to get up from below.

Phillips is a little ahead of Wesson. He has just reached the upper deck, where he hears the familiar voice of 28-year-old Lieutenant Humphrey Matthews, the ship's gunnery officer. Matthews is down below, near the bottom of the steps, shouting, 'Make way for Lord Kitchener.' Leading Seaman Rogerson hears the calls too, but cannot see Kitchener in the darkness.

Phillips doesn't wait around to witness the Field Marshal escaping from below. With the seas still washing over *Hampshire*'s forecastle, Phillips is an experienced enough sailor to know that the ship is doomed. He realises, however, that for the first time at sea, he has left his lifebelt in his sea chest. For one moment, he hesitates. Should he go back? But his sea chest is too close to the site of the explosion to risk it. With a lifebelt, Phillips might have been tempted to jump straight into the sea. Instead, he knows his only chance of survival is via the boat he has been allocated or a Carley raft. The rest of the men on board are quickly making their way to their abandon ship stations. Phillips decides to follow suit.

Down below, Petty Officer Wesson now sees the tall and recognisable figure of Kitchener in the gunroom flat and hears the gunnery officer, Lieutenant Matthews, shouting, 'Make a gangway for Lord Kitchener.' Others take up the cry: 'Make way for Lord Kitchener.'

The sailors step back dutifully and calmly to let the War Minister and Lieutenant Matthews come through. Wesson then heads up the ladders himself, gets on deck and helps to knock the seals away from the gunroom hatch. Men are now swarming up through all the hatches in their hundreds. The upper decks are crowded with sailors. Wesson walks along the upper deck to his abandon ship position.

Leading Seaman Rogerson climbs up the ladder just behind Kitchener. He can now see Kitchener with three other officers, all in khaki, without overcoats. They are on the quarterdeck, on the port side of the ship, walking to the rear, near the aft turret. Kitchener is calm. There is no panic. He is pacing up and down, talking to the other officers with him.

Able Seaman Jack Bowman has also made it onto the upper deck. There, he and Able Seaman Simpson can see their captain, Herbert Savill, standing by the ship's galley. Savill is shouting out to Kitchener to get in the boat: 'Come up here!' Rogerson can also see Savill trying to clear a way to the galley, and shouting out to Kitchener to join him on the forebridge, where the galley is located. But the furious wind is blowing away the captain's words. It is clear to Bowman that the ship is sinking rapidly, plunging down head first into the sea. Bowman continues to his abandon ship position on the starboard side.

Petty Officer Wesson also sees Captain Savill's desperate attempts to attract Lord Kitchener's attention. The galley is still hanging on the port side of *Hampshire*, on the third cutter davits – the crane-like arms which are designed to raise and lower boats from the ship. But with power out, it is soon obvious that getting the boat away will be a near-impossible task.

While the rush to abandon ship stations is fully underway, a few men are still fighting to help save the ship. Warrant Mechanician William Bennett, having helped to open the sealed hatches to allow access to the upper deck, now goes back below, to the engine room, fighting against the flow of sailors making their way above. Bennett receives surprised looks as he heads the other way, back down towards danger and death. He cannot get back down to the boiler room itself, as the hatches are sealed to avoid water flooding the upper decks. All watertight doors have now been shut, including those to the mess deck.

Bennett helps to extinguish a fire in the forward magazine and then arrives in the engine room. He is the only man there, in the semi-darkness. He knows that the ship may sink at any moment. He sees that the engine steam pressure has largely failed – the gauges indicate that the pressure is steadily falling away. The engines are still just about moving, but Bennett knows that in a short time the power will be completely gone. There is no more that can be done. It is time to escape. Bennett takes one last look at the empty engine rooms and then clambers up the stairs to the main deck. *Hampshire* is now disappearing into the waters head first, with the back of the ship still lifting out of the ocean. It is a frightening moment as the angle of incline steepens. Then, suddenly, there is a thud from below. The front of the ship has hit the bottom of the ocean, 65 metres down. The vessel groans from the clash of metal with sand, shale and rock – on the seabed are large Norwegian glacier melt boulders, a few metres in height and width. As the waves beat against the ship, the bow is now grinding on the ocean floor, ripping at the ship's metal and gouging out a huge pit in the sand and shale down below.

Bennett now reports to Engineer Commander Cossey the latest situation as he sees it: the engines are still going and the telegraph is set to half speed ahead. There is nothing else he can do. And there is no one else left in the engine room. If he reopens the hatches to get down below, there is a risk that this will just provide an entry point for the waters now seeping throughout the ship. Cossey shakes hands with Bennett, agreeing that nothing more can be done. They know that *Hampshire* has little time left. 'Go to your abandon ship position,' Cossey orders.

Across the whole vessel, the crew are still urgently making their way up to upper-deck level, through the hatches that are now open. Men still queue patiently to climb the ladders. There is no panic, but there is urgency.

Petty Officer Wesson has now made it to his abandon ship station on the starboard side. He can see that desperate attempts are being made to get the boats out – but without success, as the electric power is gone, preventing the lowering equipment from being used.

The wind is howling. Banks of waves crash, one after the other, onto the decks. With the wind chill, it feels freezing. Wesson sees one of *Hampshire*'s boats being lowered with about fifty men in it. The ropes tying it are now cut. Then, disaster. A wave sucks the boat sharply to its crest, and then dashes it against *Hampshire*'s side with tremendous force, smashing the boat to pieces, and leaving just a few survivors struggling in a swirling mass of flotsam.

Wesson knows there isn't much time left. Clouds of steam are emerging from the front engine room on the starboard side. Realising that the boats cannot be lowered, men are now desperately jumping into the swirling seas from the quarterdeck. Some of the jumpers have already been badly burnt from the explosion. Others have wounds that bleed.

Able Seaman Horace Buerdsell, aged twenty and with brown hair and a scar over his right eye, had been on the mess deck when the explosion occurred. He has been in the navy since 1912, having given up his previous job as a wire weaver. He got out via the centre hatch and has made his way to his abandon ship position. The gunnery officer, Humphrey Matthews, who escorted Kitchener, is also there. Buerdsell and others, including Lieutenant Matthews, now jump overboard from the cutter into the icy seas. Buerdsell has no life jacket and it is too late to get one. It is just after 8 p.m.

Sailors are now rushing to get to their stations, by the boats or the three Carley rafts – simple cork-covered devices which can float in the water, allowing some men to stand inside on a wooden platform, waist-deep in water, while others are in the sea, clinging to the sides.

But there are only three Carley floats on board. Those who were allocated space in the boats realise that these cannot be lowered. Some now throw pieces of wood into the water and plunge in after them, hoping this will offer some means of flotation. Some of these men swim. Others soon disappear beneath the mountainous seas. There is a rising sense of alarm and desperation. William Phillips sees a midshipman throw two small chests of drawers into the water and jump in after them. With one drawer under each arm, the man then strikes out in the direction of land – two miles away. Phillips knows that death by drowning or hypothermia is the certain prospect that awaits this sailor.

The Carley floats are now being made ready for use. Able Seaman Bowman finds his, No. 1, amidships on the starboard side. Dick Simpson is there too. The float is designed to accommodate forty-five men inside with twenty-two more in the water, hanging onto rope loops around its side. Able Seaman William Cashman has also arrived, along with Leading Seaman Rogerson. None of them have had time to put their life vests on. The men get their knives out and quickly cut away the lashings that are holding the floats in place. The commander then gives the order to launch them.

Float 1 is on the ship's slips. The men push her off into the sea, diving in after her. Some have lifebelts. A very few have life-saving 'waistcoats' instead. Most have not had time to put theirs on.

Water is now rushing through into the back of *Hampshire*, gradually lessening the angle at which she is pointing downwards. With the waves now close to the ship's upper decks, Able Seaman Cashman is washed off the vessel into the sea and swims as quickly as he can to his float then clambers in. Looking back at *Hampshire*, they can all see the ship sinking forward into the waves, the rear of the ship still above the water's surface and the propellers still turning. Rogerson is on the float now too. He looks back and can see Kitchener and his fellow officers on the starboard side of the quarterdeck.

On board the ship, William Phillips now realises that the boat he has been allocated cannot be launched. He leaps into the sea and swims hard for the large Carley float he can see around 50 metres away. He drags his body over the side and into the centre of the raft – there are already around forty men in it, with more arriving all the time. Phillips has joined Rogerson, Simpson, Cashman and Bowman on Float 1. Others in the water quickly make for the float, scrambling into the centre of it over the cork sides. The middle area of the raft is now full. The only places remaining are in the water, hanging onto the raft's sides.

Petty Officer Wesson decides it is time to launch his float: No. 2, on the starboard side. Lofty Farnden is there with him, determined to get inside as he cannot swim. He has his life jacket on but knows it would not protect him for long in these seas. Farnden looks down with fear into the crashing waves below. Around him, he can see that attempts are being made to lower the galley and a whaler.

Forty or so men crowd around Raft 2, including Stoker Sims, nursing his burnt face and hands. Sims sees a soldier, a servant he thinks, getting into one of the other rafts. He also sees another man in khaki clambering into a small boat. A number of the stokers who were badly burnt by the explosion are brought up from below and placed in Float 2.

With others, Farnden and Wesson now cut the lashings, clamber inside the float and launch it down the sliding platform. It crashes into the rough seas below. It is not the authorised way to launch a Carley raft and with so many men inside it risks damage. But no one wants to dive into the freezing waters.

Sims, though, has missed the float being launched. He jumps into the sea and manages to catch hold of the rope on the side of the float and drag himself inside. He breathes a huge sigh of relief – he is a poor swimmer and knows he could not survive long. One of the men now shouts out, 'We must get clear, or we will be sucked under when she goes down.' The men paddle as best they can, but they are in luck anyhow – the wind and waves are carrying them away from *Hampshire*, in a south-easterly direction.

As they paddle, some of the men burnt and injured by the explosions desperately fling themselves from the sea onto the float. A few are screaming in agony as the salt water inflames their wounds. Able Seaman Buerdsell, who jumped into the water when it was clear the first cutter could not be lowered, now hauls himself on board Float 2. By now, the raft, which was designed for about sixty-seven men in total, has around forty-five men in it and perhaps another forty clinging onto the ropes. It is being tossed around violently but is still being driven by wind and waves away from the ship.

Two floats, carrying as many as 150 or 160 men in total, are now heading away from *Hampshire*. One boat has been lowered and has capsized. Men are diving into the waters. Others wait patiently in or near their boats, still hoping to escape the ship without having to risk the bitterly cold waters below.

Petty Officer Sweeney now makes his way down from the bridge to his abandon ship station. This is Carley float No. 3, the smallest of the rafts, designed for just eighteen men. Sweeney can see the failed attempts to get most of the boats off the ship. But, at last, one boat seems about to get away – the 27-foot whaler is being lowered, full of men. Thank God, thinks Sweeney.

Able Seaman Bowman is now in the apparent safety of No. 1 raft, but, along with the others there, he is already shivering in ice-cold waters up to his chest. He looks back towards the ship and sees the same scene that Sweeney is watching – the whaler has been turned out and men are trying to get it into the sea. It is supposed to have space for just twenty-four men, but it looks seriously overloaded. And then, another disaster. The overladen boat, battered by waves against the ship's side, suddenly cracks loudly and breaks in two, showering thirty or forty screaming men into the icy waters below. It is a shocking sight.

Sweeney also sees the attempts to get the captain's galley away. But if he is to survive, he must now take to his own raft. Other men are there with him, including Leading Stoker Read. Read has seen just one army officer, on the after shelter deck. He is a biggish man, by Read's description, perhaps 5 feet 9 inches. Read did not recognise him. He climbed into the sailing pinnace. Read saw no more of him after that.

Float 3 is now quickly cut adrift and Sweeney and Read put an injured mate into it then throw it over the side. Sweeney, Read and others then plunge 15 feet down into the water after it. They have not had time to put on lifebelts, but they swim for their lives, reach the raft and clamber in.

It takes little imagination to guess what is going to happen next. *Hampshire* is now clearly sinking steadily into the dark and freezing waters. For those still on board, it is a terrifying moment. Many know that they have little chance of survival. The boats were supposed to provide safety for over 600 men. None have so far safely left the ship.

In the sea, there are desperate attempts to get inside the three floats, but these are all now filled up. The lucky ones grab the ropes around the sides and try to keep their heads above the waves. The unlucky soon disappear. The waters are full of hundreds of men, desperately trying to save their own lives.

Some of the ship's crew still clamber into the boats on board *Hampshire*, hoping that when she sinks into the sea they will still be able to float away. And now, as the icy waters of the Atlantic flood through the ship, breaking down doors and washing away anything that stands in their path, the back of the vessel begins to settle down in the water too.

The last to see Lord Kitchener alive is Leading Seaman Charles Rogerson. He spots the 6 foot 2 inch Kitchener standing calmly on the quarterdeck with his faithful friend Lieutenant-Colonel Fitzgerald. The captain is still shouting for Kitchener to go to the boats, but he seems not to hear. He must realise that, as a 66-year-old man, he has little chance of survival in the icy, swelling waters below.

Bennett, the engineer on watch, is still on board but realises that it is now or never. He puts on his life-saving waistcoat and rushes to his own abandon ship station. It is by the picket boat and pinnace. These are boats that he is personally in charge of. There are sixty or seventy men around the boats, waiting to get away. On the upper deck, he sees two more boats filled with men who are hoping they will float away from the ship as she gradually settles in the water. *Hampshire* is now practically on an even keel.

It is now 8.05 p.m. It is still light. The wind is blowing at force 9, sweeping over the boat and tearing at clothing, men and any other obstacles in its way.

Bennett goes round to the sea side of the pinnace. The decks are slippery, covered in water. Men are pushing to get closer as they realise they are fast running out of time. Suddenly, Bennett falls – was he pushed, or had he caught his leg in a rope on deck? He crashes into the waters below, gasping from the shock of their chill. He knows he has to get away from the vessel before she sinks. He swims as fast as the waves will allow. He is now 30 metres or so from *Hampshire*. In the water near him, he can see other crew members – the commander and a midshipman. He heads towards a float he can see some way off in the water; he does not know it, but it is float No. 1.

Able Seaman Bowman is on this float and can see the men in the water desperately trying to swim for the three rafts. He also watches the continuing attempts to get the galley out, but cannot tell if they are successful. When he last sees it, the galley is still suspended from the third cutters' davits. More and more men are jumping from the ship into the waves below.

Bennett is still swimming away from *Hampshire* – swimming, quite literally, for his life. And then there is a crashing sound behind him. He cannot see it, but those already in the Carley rafts can.

Phillips, Bowman, Rogerson, Simpson and Cashman are all in Carley float No. 1, now about 100 metres astern of *Hampshire* on the starboard side, with around sixty men inside and another thirty or so in the water, holding onto the side ropes. Those in the raft now look back in despair and amazement as they see the vast ship which has been their home plunge downwards by the head and perform a complete somersault towards the land, throwing the remaining crew members on the decks and in the boats into the ocean underneath her and crushing the men in the water, close to the ship. It is a deeply shocking sight. Rogerson guesses that Kitchener must now be dead, dragged down with the ship and drowned. There does not seem any way that he could have made his escape in the short time since he was last visible on the quarterdeck.

Those on Wesson's Raft 2, now over 40 metres clear of *Hampshire*, see the disaster too, as do those few on Raft 3, including Sweeney and Read. They see that the boats, crammed full of men, are still tied to the derricks. Then, with a slow lurch, the ship rolls over. Everything that isn't firmly secured on board now crashes around inside the vessel or falls into the water – furniture, food, medical supplies, equipment, ammunition and – of course – men. She goes down bows first and heels right over to starboard, the propellers still going around, slowly, as she plunges into the waters.

At first, Wesson closes his eyes to the unfolding horrors. Then he opens them to see *Hampshire* turning over and drawing down into the vortex with her boats, wreckage and men. For a short while, her keel is visible on the surface, and then she disappears completely. Only the pockets of air, belching back to the surface in places, give a clue to her former presence.

Below the waves, the huge ship is sinking slowly into the Atlantic. Hundreds of items are showering down into the ocean – the advanced guard of the wreck.

Hampshire's four deck-mounted 6-inch secondary guns now fall from their mounts and descend quickly to the ocean floor. They are almost 7 metres long and weigh in at 25 tons each. The huge weight causes them to assume an upright position on their journey downwards through the quiet waters. They fall barrels first, like darts towards the sea floor. As they strike the seabed, the barrels of two guns drive deep into sand and shale, disappearing almost up to their breeches.

Bennett had not got far enough from the ship. He was still only 30 metres or so away as she turned over and he can feel himself being sucked down. It feels like someone has got hold of his legs and is dragging him downwards, downwards, downwards. Ten feet. Twenty feet. Thirty feet. It feels now as if he is almost 40 feet below the surface. Is this the end?

He will not give up. He fights his way back up. He reaches the surface and gasps for air. He catches his breath and looks back to where *Hampshire* has been. Nothing. The great ship has disappeared beneath the waves. She is still slowly descending the 65 metres to the ocean bottom. A huge hole has been ripped out of her underside, behind the bows, as if some giant can opener has been applied to the front 35-metre section of the ship.

All that is left on the surface now is wreckage and a few floating bodies, rising and falling in the waves.

Hampshire has sunk with 749 men on board. She has sunk at the very peak of a force 9 gale in icy seas, with no escort ships anywhere near and no ability to communicate her dire circumstances. She has sunk at 8.05 p.m., just an hour and a quarter before sunset, apparently without being able to safely lower a single boat into the water. Now there are only three Carley floats, designed to keep just 150 men alive in the water for a short period of time to allow rescue vessels to reach them.

The survivors hope that rescue boats are already on the way. They are certain that they will have been seen by the lookouts at Birsay and Marwick Head.

But at 8.05 p.m. on 5 June 1916 not a single rescue boat has even been ordered out. The men of *Hampshire* are alone in a fearsome and freezing sea. No one in authority yet knows of their fate, let alone Kitchener's Cabinet and military colleagues in London.

Floating along in the waves, being driven south-eastwards to-wards the land, is the gunnery officer, Lieutenant Matthews. He had cleared the way for Lord Kitchener to reach the main deck. He will soon be dead, his life-saving collar only partially inflated, his wristwatch stopped at two minutes past eight.

* * *

It is the morning of 7 June 1916, thirty-six hours after *Hampshire* sank. Seven hundred miles away from Orkney, in London, two men are sitting in the study of 41 Cromwell Road, Kensington. Winston Churchill and Sir Ian Hamilton are in Churchill's study, preparing their evidence for the Royal Commission on the Dardanelles – Brit-ain's disastrous attempt in 1915 to break through to Constantinople and undermine the Turkish war effort. Churchill and Hamilton are poring over old telegrams sent by Kitchener, preparing a case to place the blame for the botched expedition on Britain's War Min-ister. If Kitchener can be made to bear the responsibility, perhaps there will be a political way back for Churchill, and the blot on Hamilton's military career will be wiped away too.

Outside, in the street, they hear a noise – shouting. But what is being said? It sounds urgent, dramatic even. Churchill jumps up, rushes to the window and throws it open. A news vendor is passing by, just yards away. Under his arm is a large bundle of newspapers, but it is the words he shouts across the street that catch the atten-tion of the two men and leave them stunned and silent: 'Kitchener drowned! Kitchener drowned! No survivors!'

THE CONSPIRACIES

*'The fact that Lord Kitchener's body has not been recovered
is only one ... of the indications that the official report does
not fully represent the facts. There is no doubt in my mind
that the vessel was destroyed by a bomb placed under the
dining saloon at the time when the guests would be at dinner,
and it was the work of the German secret service.'*

SIR RICHARD COOPER MP, SEPTEMBER 1917

The London Opera House, Kingsway, off the Strand, 12 March
1926.

It is 11.25 a.m. The magnificent theatre, commissioned in 1911 by
Oscar Hammerstein in a short and failed attempt to compete with
the nearby Royal Opera House, is packed: every one of its 2,660
seats is taken. There is a sense of excitement and anticipation, almost
audible through the background hum of a thousand people speaking simultaneously in hushed voices. In the audience are Members
of Parliament, press reporters and interested members of the public.
Unknown to the event organisers, there is also a representative of
His Majesty's Government in the theatre, quietly taking notes.

Whatever their various motivations and interests, these

individuals have come together to attend a mass meeting called on the subject of 'Lord Kitchener and HMS *Hampshire*'. At 11.30 a.m., the proceedings begin with an organ recital. To some, the whole thing seems rather odd. At 11.45 a.m., the music suddenly stops. Three attempts are made to take a photograph of the assembled mass, but the photographer's flashlight will not work.

Then, onto the enormous stage – 78 feet high and 64 feet across – comes Mr Frank Power. Mr Power is forty-four years old. He is largely bald, but with a bit of hair still clinging onto his smooth scalp just above each ear and running round to the back of his head. He wears owl-like, circular glasses. If you had to guess his profession, you might think him a senior clerk in a London law firm. It is a good guess: before he was a journalist, he was exactly this. There is also something funereal about him. He is received with loud and prolonged cheers.

When all is quiet, he starts, portentously: 'Your Highnesses, Your Excellencies, My Lords, Ladies and Gentlemen.' He then calls for silence for thirty seconds to pay tribute to Lord Kitchener and those lost on HMS *Hampshire*. The audience stand as one. There is complete silence. Some of those present look at the ground. Others stare ahead. Many look around at the lavish opulence of this French Renaissance-style auditorium, with its plush stalls and three levels of viewing boxes, reaching right up to a beautifully painted ceiling. The tribute ends with Power speaking again: 'Not unto death, but glory everlasting.' And then the audience sits as one, those in the stall area benefiting from chairs with inlaid mahogany and Rose du Barry pilo velvet upholstery.

The audience has come to hear Power – the author of a series of dramatic and sensational articles in *The Referee*, a Sunday newspaper founded in 1877. These articles have cast doubt on the official government and Admiralty narrative about Kitchener's death – that he was on a secret mission to Russia and drowned when his ship went down, having hit a German mine.

Power starts by paying tribute to the newspapers that have supported his campaign and thanks those MPs who have advised him, including Sir Robert Hamilton, the MP for Orkney and Shetland. His thirty-minute speech begins with a glowing tribute to Lord Kitchener and his career and there are loud cheers at appropriate points in his detailed narrative.

And then his questions come thick and fast: why was Kitchener ever sent on such a dangerous trip to Russia? Is it true that some of his Cabinet colleagues never wanted him to return? Then, even stronger stuff: assertions that appear to directly contradict the official version of events. According to Power, there was not just one explosion on *Hampshire*; there were three. And there is proof, proof on the basis of sworn written statements, of treachery on board the ship, and proof of spies having previously been found on the vessel. And after the ship sank, there were no proper rescue operations. Worse than this, the nearby Stromness lifeboat was prevented from going out – at this claim, there are cries of 'Murder' from the audience.

There is more from Power, as the huge audience listens intently: no proper precautions were taken to safeguard Lord Kitchener; HMS *Hampshire* was an 'unsuitable and even dangerous' ship to use for such a vital mission, and was sent on a route that had not been swept for mines. And a dramatic claim: that rather than drowning when the ship went down, Kitchener and his loyal aide Colonel Fitzgerald escaped on a 'little cockleshell of a boat'.

And then his summing-up: the government failed to hold an inquiry; no one was punished; and there is a cover-up. 'I make no personal charges against any members of the Admiralty, but I am going to say that we shall have the truth.' This statement is met with loud and sustained cheering.

Power continues: the Admiralty must come clean. It must tell the truth. 'Those, ladies and gentlemen, are shortly my charges and I say: let us with our united forces in the name of the nation demand that we have an immediate inquiry.' Loud cheers greet this finale. And then the speech is finished. A short film about the disaster is shown, with organ accompaniment and stage effects. And four survivors from *Hampshire* are then introduced to the audience.

At the end, a resolution is put to the meeting. This calls on the Admiralty to immediately hold a full inquiry. Power declares the resolution carried unanimously. One man protests that the vote was not unanimous. He is drowned out by cries of 'Traitor' and 'Throw him out'.

At the end, a male singer gives a robust rendition of 'Land of Hope and Glory'. And then the meeting ends. The crowd departs. The government official files his careful report.

It is almost ten years since *Hampshire* sank. But the questions and controversies will not go away. And in the filing cabinets of the Admiralty and the War Office are secret papers which will not be released until ninety-eight years after the ship went down. What is it, ask many, that the authorities are so determined to hide?

* * *

On 13 June 1916, Kitchener's memorial service took place at St Paul's Cathedral in London at twelve noon on a cold, grey and blustery day. Everyone who was anyone in the British establishment was there – the King and Queen, the Prime Minister and senior Cabinet ministers, the Lord Mayor. The Royal Engineers and Irish Guards provided the guard of honour. The Archbishop of Canterbury and Bishop of London were present. Outside, the streets were lined with people, come to pay their respects.

The service commenced with hymn No. 27, 'Abide with Me'. It concluded with 'The Last Post' and three verses of 'God Save the King'. That same afternoon, simultaneously and at two-mile intervals from the coast in Belgium to the end of the British lines on the Somme, the British artillery fired off their guns in tribute to their lost war leader – the only British War Minister and the only British field marshal ever to die at the hands of the enemy. In Parliament, in the press, amongst the public and from foreign leaders, the tributes poured in.

But before the period of mourning had even concluded, questions were being asked, and the doubts, the conspiracy stories and the speculation spread with alarming speed. Just two days after the sinking, two British tabloid newspapers were reporting stories about German spies on board *Hampshire*, and a secret plot to kill Kitchener. And then the questions multiplied. In the absence of a body, could Lord Kitchener still, in fact, be alive? And if he was dead, who had killed him and why?

Why was such an important man not guarded more effectively by the greatest navy in the world? And was it not suspicious that the Munitions Minister, David Lloyd George, who was due to accompany Kitchener on the visit, had cancelled at the last minute? What did others in the UK government know about the journey, and was it all a plot to get rid of Kitchener?

The Admiralty was keen to get its own account of what had happened into the public domain. Within two days of the sinking, a court of inquiry had been held in Scapa Flow on the orders of

Admiral Jellicoe. Three of Jellicoe's own senior naval officers took evidence, including from all the survivors. Within just a few hours, the court of inquiry had reached its conclusions.

On 15 June at 8.50 p.m., two days after Kitchener's memorial service, the Admiralty issued a press notice, embargoed for the next day's papers. It was just two pages in length and based upon the court of inquiry conclusions. Its narrative was simple. *Hampshire* had struck a mine in a storm. She sank in around fifteen minutes. Kitchener and fellow officers had been seen on deck but it was not known what happened to them after this. Large numbers of the crew used life-saving belts, which were effective in keeping them afloat. Many of the survivors of the sinking died before they could reach land. And that was it, apart from a half-apology from the Commander in Chief of the Grand Fleet, Admiral Jellicoe: 'I cannot adequately express the sorrow felt by me personally and by the officers and men of the Grand Fleet generally at the fact that so distinguished a soldier and so great a man should have lost his life whilst in a measure under the care of the Fleet.' Nobody was blamed. It had simply been unfortunate that *Hampshire* had hit a German mine. There were no lessons to learn. No one deserving of censure. No mistakes. Indeed, the only issue the official court of inquiry raised for consideration was whether it was worth including a larger number of Carley floats on Royal Navy warships in the future.

Unknown to the public, the inquiry had already uncovered some evidence about delays in mounting the rescue mission – but concerns about the tardy response had by now been quickly swept under the carpet.

For many – in the public, in the press and in Parliament – it all seemed implausible, and too much like a cover-up. And the initial rumours about the 'real story' of *Hampshire*'s sinking were soon backed up by more tangible evidence of unanswered questions, as those who knew a lot or even a little about the background to the sinking started to communicate with each other, the press and then the politicians.

Within days of *Hampshire*'s loss, an anonymous letter addressed to the Secretary of the Admiralty claimed that *Hampshire* had been blown up by a bomb placed inside the ship: 'You will find the iron is blown outward.' The writer warned that German spies were now on most British warships. Another letter to the 'Lords Commissioners of the Admiralty', sent from Stromness on Orkney just days after the disaster, posed a series of detailed questions and implied Admiralty incompetence in failing to sweep the seas of mines and to deploy rescue ships speedily – including the Stromness lifeboat.

It wasn't long before these concerns and others were raised in Parliament itself, where MPs began to pose questions about how and why Kitchener had died and who was responsible. Sir Richard Cooper, the 41-year-old MP for Walsall, former army officer, and chairman of the Cooper, McDougall & Robertson chemical firm, was far from convinced by the government's official account and was determined to uncover the truth. He now began a six-year campaign in Parliament, designed to force ministers to tell the full and true story behind *Hampshire*'s sinking. And Sir Richard seemed to have inside sources of his own.

On 22 June, just seventeen days after *Hampshire* had sunk, Sir Richard was in the House of Commons challenging the Admiralty's account that *Hampshire* had hit a mine. He was also posing other questions that were uncomfortable for ministers and for the Admiralty: had the sea route taken by *Hampshire* been swept of mines? Why were there no escort vessels with *Hampshire* when she sank?

Other MPs joined the search for the truth. Sir Henry Dalziel, MP for Kirkcaldy Burghs and a newspaper owner, wanted to know if it was true that a vessel flying the Dutch flag had been spotted laying mines just before *Hampshire* arrived in the area. And Commander Carlyon Bellairs, MP for Maidstone, drawing on his own naval expertise, pressed ministers on why a court martial had yet to take place, as was customary after a ship was lost. Commander Bellairs considered the hurried court of inquiry little more than a device to cover up the truth.

On 26 June 1916, Major Rowland Hunt, MP for Ludlow, reported a 'very strong feeling in the country' that the government had failed to provide a sufficiently strong escort for Kitchener, while Sir Richard Cooper MP kept up his barrage of sceptical questions. On 29 June, Cooper raised in the House the issue of a supervisor in the Press Bureau who was believed to be a German citizen but who had recently changed his name to Anderson. Could he be responsible for leaking the details of Kitchener's visit to his German spymasters? After all, had not key details about Kitchener's visit been shared with the Press Bureau before Kitchener's departure, on the basis that they must not be revealed to the public?

Ministers worked hard to rebut each allegation. The 'German' in the Press Bureau turned out to be the British-born son of a British citizen, his name having Scandinavian rather than Germanic origins. But for each allegation dealt with, a new one arose. On 6 July, Mr Basil Peto MP was asking in the House of Commons about two employees of the Russian Bank for Foreign Trade in London – one an unnaturalised Hungarian, the other an unnaturalised German. Could their knowledge of munitions shipments to Russia have been connected to *Hampshire*'s fate?

By 5 July, the dogged Sir Richard Cooper was pressing the Prime

Minister himself for a full debate in Parliament. Asquith stuck with the established government position: a formal court of inquiry had been held into the sinking. It was clear the ship had been sunk by a mine. There was nothing more to add, and no benefit to greater openness – not least in wartime.

But Sir Richard was not to be so easily fobbed off. On 6 July 1916, he finally secured his own Commons adjournment debate on the 'Loss of *Hampshire*'. His charges were serious: the government was failing to give the full facts about the sinking; it was suspicious that a memorial service for Lord Kitchener was announced the very day after the ship went down and before it was even established that Kitchener was dead; it was equally suspicious that the Admiralty was sending out individually typed letters to the widows of deceased officers and crew the day after the sinking and before there could be certainty over who had actually been lost.

Sir Richard's charge sheet grew longer: was it true that some of the bodies recovered showed signs of burning by acid? Was one of the survivors currently under Admiralty arrest in connection with the ship's loss? Was *Hampshire* even a fit boat to use to transport a Secretary of State on such a vital mission?

Sir Richard's confidential sources had also alerted him to various suspicious incidents involving *Hampshire*'s crew in the period between December 1915 and February 1916, suggesting there were 'dangerous elements' aboard the ship. Sir Richard wanted to know if the wires on one side of *Hampshire* had been 'maliciously cut' earlier in the year, leading to a failure of the guns in this area of the vessel. And while the ship was refitting in Belfast dockyard from 18 January 1916 onwards, had not two members of the crew been found to be a threat to the ship's safety, with 'strict measures' taken against them? Sir Richard also wanted to know about the mysterious Dutch vessel rumoured to be near *Hampshire* before she went down. And why did two German newspapers – *Berliner Tageblatt* and *Leipziger Nachrichten* – have obituaries of Kitchener ready to print before his death appeared even to be public knowledge?

Sir Richard concluded, provocatively, by suggesting that if the Prime Minister had died under such circumstances, a public inquiry would inevitably follow: 'It does drive one to the conclusion that, in the opinion of the government, Lord Kitchener's death is not worth a public inquiry or a court martial.' There was, at this point, uproar in the House of Commons, and shouts of 'Withdraw'.

The Parliamentary Secretary to the Admiralty, Dr Thomas Macnamara, rose from his place on the green leather-covered government front bench and dropped his speech onto the despatch box in front of him, nodding to the Speaker before beginning his response. He gently rejected most of the claims, or offered to make further inquiries. But the minister had not silenced his critics. Instead, his speech was followed by one from Commander Bellairs – again questioning why a full court martial, on oath, had not taken place. Bellairs pointed out that this was the usual practice following the loss of any Royal Navy ship. His implication was clear: the Admiralty didn't want a court martial, as it was more likely to provide criticism of their actions than the simple court of inquiry held so rapidly after *Hampshire*'s loss.

In the days and weeks after the debate, the Admiralty machine cranked into gear, determined to rebut the serious allegations one by one. Some were easy to deal with; others less so. The letters of regret to relatives were sent on 9 June, not the 6th (though officers' letters were sent earlier, as it seemed initially that none had survived – in fact, Warrant Mechanician William Bennett had reached safety). There were also suspicions raised about the delays in sending personal possessions washed up on shore back to relatives, but this could be simply dealt with: it was fiendishly difficult to identify the owners of most of the items discovered.

But for every answer, there seemed to be at least one new question or allegation. On 29 July 1916, British intelligence reported an intercepted letter from a John Sweeney in San Francisco to a Jeremiah Sweeney in West Ballylinch, Co. Cork. This described various Irish nationalist groups in America, reporting that one of the members knew of Kitchener's journey two days before it was begun and had predicted that neither *Hampshire* nor Kitchener would ever reach Russia. The secret intelligence report concluded with a quote from the letter: 'You know there was a nephew of Tom McDonagh's, a petty officer on *Hampshire*: and he was the man that blew her up.' If this story were true, it could hardly be a coincidence. And the *Hampshire* records showed there was a Petty Officer Samuel Sweeney on board that night. Sweeney had given his place of birth as Fahan, Donegal, in Ireland. Could he be the man in question? Suspiciously, he was one of only twelve survivors.

Soon after, new doubts were being raised as to whether the reported survivors were the only ones to get away. On 13 August, a message written on a postcard and placed in a bottle was found on the shoreline close to Cliffe Fort, an artillery fort built in the 1860s to guard the entrance to the Thames from seaboard attack. The commander at the fort sent the message on to the section commander for the Thames, who rapidly despatched it to the major-general commanding the Thames and Medway Garrison. By 19 August, the letter had reached the highest levels of the Admiralty. In clear, if slightly shaky, black writing, the card was headed: 'To the man who finds this.' It continued over ten lines: 'HMS *Hampshire*. From Seaman W. H. Wilson. Please send help to my islands. May

Orkney Islands. Sincerely W. Wilson.' Could there really still be survivors from the disaster, waiting to be rescued? The Admiralty's conclusion was 'probably a fraud'. But they noted that there were three Wilsons on *Hampshire* when she sank. They included a 29-year-old sick berth steward, William Wilson, whose body had yet to be recovered.

On 29 November, the Admiralty intercepted news reports that another letter had been found in a bottle in the Norwegian Stavanger Ford. The letter, written in English, read:

> HMS *Hampshire*. We hitherto safe but cannot say how long. We are in an open boat but very leaky will not be long. We cannot see land. We know we will be revenged boys will take care of it. We were torpedoed twice and had not time firing before submarine disappeared and we sunk. Five of us are here we are all dogtired by rowing and baling. This is last from us. If it is found send it to Mrs Smit, South Shields.

The note was passed to the British Consul, and the First Sea Lord was informed. There were eleven boys and men with the surname 'Smith' on *Hampshire*.

In March 1917, yet another message in a bottle was picked up in Studland Bay, Dorset. It was soon on the way from the Board of Trade to the Admiralty, where it was carefully read. It purported to come from two sailors aboard *Hampshire*, Skinner and Gage. Their seventeen-word message claimed there had been an 'internal explosion' on the ship. The Admiralty carefully noted that a William Skinner – Stoker 1st Class – had been on board *Hampshire*, but no one by the name of Gage. However, there were two 'Gales'. Could it be that one of these had survived? Neither body had been found.

The Admiralty concluded again 'probably a hoax'. But they could not be sure. Perhaps there were still stray survivors alive?

A fourth message arrived in another bottle found at Dundrum Bar on the Irish coast on 2 September 1917. It was perhaps the easiest to dismiss. Dated 28 July 1917, the message read: 'Friend, should you find this please send help immediately to a survivor of *Hampshire* on some small island north of Iceland. Cannot hold out much longer.'

Some misinformation was painful for the relatives of *Hampshire*'s crew. In May 1917, the War Office received information that an officer named Beck, allegedly a *Hampshire* survivor, was in a prisoner-of-war camp in Germany. The Admiralty made inquiries of Mr William Bex of 135 Sheen Road, Richmond. Had he heard anything from his son, Boy 1st Class William Luke Bex, since his reported death on *Hampshire* aged just seventeen? Mr Bex had not. The Admiralty sent an embarrassed apology.

These individual stories could be assessed and dealt with, but the wider claims proved more difficult to rebut. Why had Kitchener been sent on a dangerous mission to Russia? Were the other members of the War Cabinet trying to get rid of him? Even David Lloyd George, no great ally of Kitchener's, told the Cabinet that they had 'Kitchener's blood on their hands'.

Why did HMS *Hampshire* sail directly into an oncoming storm, through a route unswept of mines? Why did *Hampshire* sail on without escort vessels, and what explained the long delay before rescue ships were sent out to the area where *Hampshire* had sunk?

How was *Hampshire* destroyed? Was there one explosion or more on board? Even the survivors disagreed on this point. Did *Hampshire* suffer a mine or torpedo strike, or did one or more of the explosions come from inside the ship? Had Kitchener been killed not by the Germans but by Irish nationalists or by Bolshevik Russians, who did not want his mission to prop up the Tsarist administration to succeed? Or had news of Kitchener's secret mission been leaked in advance to the Germans? Were there submarines waiting for him?

Was it true, as is now widely claimed, that while in dock for refitting it had been discovered that a secret agent was trying to put a bomb on board? What had happened to Kitchener's body, and why had it never been recovered? Finally, why the secrecy? Why were the Admiralty and the government refusing to publish the results of the official inquiries into the sinking? What had they got to hide?

It was not simply journalists and politicians who were asking the questions. Kitchener's close friend and private secretary Sir George Arthur was demanding answers too. At a minimum, he wanted the proceedings of the court of inquiry to be published. A confidential, internal Admiralty note in January 1924 acknowledged that 'this application from Sir George Arthur cannot be treated lightly'. But they still refused to publish. Sir George would not give up – he claimed to know that there was a second, secret report on his friend's death, which was being suppressed.

It is not uncommon for governments to stall in providing answers to difficult questions on sensitive issues. They hope that the passage of time will cause critics to turn their focus elsewhere. Not this time. The years went by but the questions multiplied. And the claims became ever more dramatic, and in contradiction to the official account.

Viscount Broome, Kitchener's nephew, felt obliged to write to the Admiralty to ask about the veracity of a new story which claimed that Lord Kitchener and two others had survived the sinking and found themselves washed up on rocks. One of the survivors allegedly suspected the other of being a spy and determined to stay close to Kitchener. However, he was eventually persuaded to crawl along the rocks and look for help. When he returned, Kitchener was gone. Instead, there were two dark objects floating in the waves. Had Kitchener really met his death in a hand-to-hand struggle with a spy? Sir George Arthur refused to comment on the story but repeated his calls for more openness.

The concerns raised by MPs and by some of Kitchener's friends were also pursued by the press and the wider media. In 1921, the British Board of Film Censors received a request to approve a film entitled *The Betrayal of Lord Kitchener*. The film caused consternation in Whitehall. It claimed that, during the war, a German lady living in London fell under the influence of a German spy. She allegedly became a German agent and picked up information about Kitchener's visit to Russia through certain British officers whom she knew. She communicated this information to her German spy chief. From there, it was leaked to Admiral von Tirpitz, who despatched a submarine to lay mines in the path of Kitchener's vessel. Disturbingly for the government, Sir George Arthur appeared as himself in some of the scenes in the film, and a well-known and respected book he had written on Kitchener was frequently referred to.

The film was viewed at the offices of the British Board of Film Censors in early April 1921. The matter was being taken seriously across government. Present were three senior staff of the film board, two knights from the War Office – Sir Herbert Creedy and Sir B. Cubitt – a representative from the Air Ministry, two from the Home Office and three from the British War Museum.

A short summary of the film's contents was made and circulated by Home Office officials. The dramatic plot was noted, along with disapproving comments on the film's style: 'a mess of eulogistic letters and press comment, not always couched in classical English'. The conclusion: 'The whole thing is crude, dull, vulgar and inartistic in the extreme.'

The government was determined to block the film's showing, not just in Britain, but overseas. In November, a telegram from the Foreign Office in London to the British Ambassador in Paris instructed him to speak to the French government to stop the showing of the film. And when the film arrived by ship in New York to be viewed in the USA, the importer was not able to take delivery of the package – the US customs authorities had intervened after special requests from the British Embassy.

By April 1922, with the German spy story appearing in UK newspapers, the War Office was forced into issuing an official statement rejecting the claims. The statement admitted that there was a German spy named Elbie Boecker, but it denied the claims attributed to her that she had received 10,000 marks from the German government for having tipped them off about Kitchener's visit. Instead, the War Office noted that Elbie Boecker was sentenced at Marylebone Police Court on 8 May 1916 – long before arrangements were made for the Kitchener visit – and imprisoned for two months for having travelled beyond a five-mile limit imposed on the movements of 'enemy aliens'. She was thrown out of the country after serving her prison sentence, on 29 June 1916.

Still the stories multiplied and became more extreme. In one, a German spy called Captain Fritz Duquesne claimed that he was behind the death of Kitchener: he wrote that he had disguised himself as a Russian nobleman, boarded *Hampshire* with Kitchener and signalled to a waiting German submarine, allowing her to torpedo the ship. He then escaped in a boat and was picked up by the submarine.

In 1923, Lord Alfred Douglas, former lover of Oscar Wilde, accused Winston Churchill of being bribed by Jewish bankers into spreading wartime stories that had made them a fortune. He also alleged that Lord Kitchener had been killed by Bolshevik Jews who had supposedly put a bomb on board *Hampshire* to scupper Kitchener's mission and help clear the way for a Jewish-backed Russian revolution. Churchill sued Douglas for libel. For once, the claims were decisively dealt with: Douglas was found guilty and sentenced to six months' imprisonment.

A decade on from the disaster, in 1926, the government might have hoped it had now dealt with the controversies over Kitchener's death. But they refused to go away. And with the tenth anniversary of *Hampshire*'s sinking now approaching, the claims only grew in number.

The March 1926 public meeting in Kingsway was only one of a series of events that formed part of Frank Power's attempt to challenge the official narrative over the Kitchener death; his campaign had begun as far back as 1921. From November 1925 to August 1926, Power led a determined attempt to reveal the truth about the Kitchener death. There were public meetings. There were films. There were lectures in major towns and cities. There were two books. And there were almost thirty newspaper articles, notably in *The Referee*.

There was also a public display of a dinghy in the shop window of 315 Oxford Street. This 16-foot vessel from *Hampshire* had allegedly been picked up by the patrol trawler *Arisino* close to Hoy Head, at the south-west side of Orkney. There was apparently a body in the bow of the boat – Power claimed this was none other than Fitzgerald, Kitchener's trusted aide. Power had purchased the boat from a yard in Stromness.

In November 1925, *The Referee* led on its front page with Power's dramatic account of Kitchener's supposed escape from *Hampshire* and his later death. The banner headline read: 'The Kitchener Mystery: Survivor's Story of the Field Marshal's Battle with Waves'. It even hinted that Kitchener's last resting place had now been identified.

By January 1926, Power was writing detailed letters to the First Lord of the Admiralty, William Bridgeman, challenging his House of Commons statements on Kitchener's death and claiming support for his allegations from first-hand witnesses. Power cited the editor of the *Belfast Irish News* as backing up his claim that two spies were found on board *Hampshire* when she was in for maintenance in Belfast docks. Apparently, they had been caught running an electric wire from the dynamo to the ship's magazine. This was designed so that when certain lights were turned on, the magazine would blow up, scuppering the ship. Two men were allegedly executed and two more arrested. The story appeared again in the Belfast press, along with claims that the facts were known to all the Belfast media but kept secret at the time by the press censor.

By 11 March of the same year, the British Board of Film Censors was writing privately to the Home Office warning them of a new film entitled *The Tragedy of the Hampshire*. This was, in fact, the rather bland film that Power was to show at his public meeting in the Kingsway Opera House the next day. The film censors had been able to find nothing to object to and pointed out that they could not control or vet the contents of the Power lectures.

For Power, the fate of *Hampshire* and Kitchener was now a full-time preoccupation. On 9 April 1926, he was a speaker at the Ivy Leaf Club in Uxbridge. His speech was heard by around a hundred local residents, including the MP for Uxbridge, Lieutenant Commander Dennistoun Burney, who a week later wrote to the

Secretary of the Admiralty to report its contents. These included claims that *Hampshire's* navigation system was faulty, that as well as a mine there were internal explosions caused by treachery, that soldiers had prevented Orkney residents from assisting survivors and blocked them from sending out the local lifeboat, that *Hampshire* was given no proper escort, and that spies had previously been found on *Hampshire* and had been shot. Many of these allegations had already been made in Parliament.

But now there was an even more dramatic new claim: that Kitchener's body had been washed up in Norway and that the government had allowed it to be buried there, rather than being brought to lie in Westminster Abbey. If true, there would be a national outcry.

So persistent were the demands for greater transparency that the government now decided it needed to clear up the controversy and publish a full account of its own in official form as a White Paper. This was unprecedented. But, first, it had to be sure that it had got all the facts straight – any errors would simply open up new controversies. To ensure the White Paper was as accurate as possible, the Security Service, MI5, was asked to go through its files to see if these could shed any light on the stories of spies on ships, leaked details of Kitchener's visit and a host of other rumours. They could not.

The Admiralty now determined to find other ways to discredit Power's claims. In May 1926, an official wrote to some of the survivors, including Charles Rogerson, whose account of the sinking had appeared in a Frank Power article in *The Referee*. The Power article was based on an interview Rogerson had given in 1916 but seemed to include some new wording. Rogerson had been invalided out of the navy in 1918 with a nervous condition. There was no reply to the Admiralty's letter; Rogerson had died almost two years before.

Petty Officer Wesson, another survivor, also received an Admiralty letter. They tracked him down to 221 Arundel Street, Landport, Portsmouth. Was it true, they wanted to know, that Wesson had claimed that he 'fully expected' Lord Kitchener to have been amongst the '200 men' who got off the vessel and safely reached the shore? Wesson, now employed in a naval institute, claimed that he had made no new statements since his evidence to the Admiralty inquiry in June 1916.

Next on the list was Stoker Frederick Sims, now a conductor on the trams. On this occasion, it was a summons on behalf of the Lords of the Admiralty, requesting Sims come to the Admiralty in Whitehall to give his version of events. There was no answer to the first letter of 1 June. Sims had moved address. But they eventually caught up with him at his new home in West Hendon, London. He offered to come to Whitehall on Monday 28 June, gently pointing out that he would need time off work if it was on any other day. The Admiralty was pleased to oblige and flexible on timing – Sims was asked to turn up any time between 11 a.m. and 1 p.m.

At the Admiralty, a nervous Sims was shown a copy of a letter from him, which had been published in *The Referee* as part of the Frank Power series. This claimed that he saw Kitchener on board before the explosion, and in addition had seen Kitchener and others being put into a small boat just before the ship went down. Sims agreed the first was true, but denied he had ever claimed the second. The Admiralty requested a statement in writing to that effect.

On 19 July, Sims wrote to the Admiralty with a three-page account of his experiences. Yes, he had seen Kitchener and other army officers going to the wardroom on *Hampshire* shortly before the explosion. After the explosion he had seen 'someone in khaki get into a small boat', but he could not say who it was.

The Admiralty wasted no time in replying. On 24 July, Sims received a stern two-page letter seeking further clarification and quoting to him the evidence he had given to the Admiralty board of inquiry. In this he had made clear that he had seen no military officers after the explosion: he had seen someone in khaki getting into a boat but had taken this to be a private, probably a servant. Could he confirm this was still his position? Sims broadly stuck to his original account to the inquiry.

The final survivor to be questioned by the Admiralty was Warrant Mechanician William Bennett, the most senior of the *Hampshire* crew to live. Bennett was now serving on the light cruiser HMS *Constance*. The Admiralty cabled his commanding officer on 10 June asking for Bennett's co-operation in their inquiries. Bennett's captain replied on 10 July, stating that a draft report had been completed by Bennett but recommending a face-to-face meeting at the Admiralty with a shorthand writer present. This took place on 12 July. Bennett gave an extraordinarily detailed report. He considered that there had been multiple explosions. He timed his order to go to abandon ship stations very precisely – at 8.02 p.m. He had not seen Lord Kitchener on board.

The Admiralty was now content, hoping that they had succeeded in aligning the survivors' accounts with their own. However, the most senior survivor, Bennett, was still claiming he had heard as many as three explosions, the second allegedly another mine strike.

And on 13 June 1926, again in *The Referee*, Power claimed to have discovered that Kitchener's coffin had been made in London – well before Kitchener had died. If true, this would be difficult to explain away. On 2 July 1926, a ceremony was due to take place on Orkney to unveil a memorial to Lord Kitchener on Marwick Head, over-looking the sea. Lord Horne, the Minister of War, was to represent the government. It was soon discovered, with horror, that Frank Power also planned to be present.

On 22 June, Lord Horne received a stern letter from the formidable W. C. Bridgeman, First Lord of the Admiralty. It was made clear that in his upcoming speech he was under no circumstances to refer to the controversy around *Hampshire*'s sinking. Nor was he to engage in any way with Power. The letter ended on an uncompromising note:

> Mr. Power is a most unscrupulous and mendacious person, and I do not wish anything that may be said before our report is published to be made an occasion for him to start off again with another batch of mis-statements as a sort of counterblast. I hope I have made myself clear.

Clear indeed. But was anything about *Hampshire* and Lord Kitchener's end really now clear?

Why was there still so much contention about how Kitchener had met his end? Some claims had obviously turned out to be flawed, but could they really all be untrue? Why did there remain, even amongst Kitchener's closest colleagues such as Sir George Arthur, such scepticism about the official Admiralty narrative? And even if it was true that *Hampshire* had struck a mine, what was the ship doing sailing unescorted into the teeth of a force 9 gale through seas that had not been swept for mines? And why were there so few survivors?

What had really happened on that June day? And why were the government and the Admiralty so afraid of the truth that some of their secret files on *Hampshire* were still locked away almost 100 years later?

To answer these questions, and establish who killed Kitchener, we need now to turn the clock back and learn more about this man and the extraordinary life and career that ended on a stormy evening in 1916.

THE MILITARY HERO

'Surely [General Gordon] is avenged!'

QUEEN VICTORIA, *JOURNALS*, SEPTEMBER 1898

The desert. Sudan. One of the harshest places on the planet. Nothing green in sight, only brownish scrubland. Little water. Only dust. Intense sun; furnace-like heat. The year is 1898. The date is 1 September.

Looking from afar, all you can see is a series of bright spots on a sandy and sun-bleached background: a few blue-suited cavalrymen are galloping up a steep hill. They reach the top and look around, shielding their eyes from the ferocious glare of the late morning sun.

In front of them, it appears that there is nothing but desert, stretching away into the far distance, a waste and solitary space. But what is that, beyond the desert, away in the far, far distance? Through binoculars, they can just make out the towers of a town. It can only be Omdurman. If so, behind it will be the great prize that they and their army have come hundreds of miles across parched and dangerous desert to reach: Khartoum, the capital of Sudan.

But then, squinting, the British officer sees a dark smear on the distant horizon – like a forest of thorn bushes. 'Enemy in sight!' shouts a young officer from the advanced patrol. And then the cavalryman realises that this is not, after all, an empty plain. The 'thorn bushes' are actually ranks of crouching soldiers. They have discovered the Dervish Army. But how large is it? The lines of soldiers, still barely visible with the best field binoculars, are long and straight, and behind them come more lines. Thirty thousand? Forty thousand? Fifty thousand? More? It is not just a Dervish Army: it must be the entire Dervish Army.

And then the young officer realises, with surprise, that this is no longer a stationary army. It has started to advance. He glances urgently back over his shoulder, down the hill. Behind him is the British Army – or more accurately, Kitchener's Army of British, Egyptian and Sudanese soldiers – sublimely unaware of the enemy force rapidly heading towards it. He looks from the British forces to the Dervish Army and back. For this brief, lonely moment he is one of the very few amongst those two armies of perhaps 80,000 soldiers who can see both sides as they head towards inevitable collision and massive bloodshed.

He spurs his grey horse and hurries back as quickly as he can, down the hill. At first he trots, and then he breaks his horse into a canter. He has been tasked with alerting the Commander in Chief to the threat ahead of him. What kind of reception will he receive? After all, it was only a few months ago that General Kitchener had personally vetoed his attachment to this army. It was then only through the personal intervention of the Prime Minister himself and War Office that this young soldier had secured his place on this exciting venture. And a Commander in Chief could hardly be expected to relish being told by a Prime Minister which junior officers would fill the ranks of his army.

The heat of a September day in the Sudan desert is intense. The officer knows he must try to preserve the strength of his horse for the battle certain to come. He slows his mount again. It takes him forty minutes to traverse the six miles of desert to reach his own army. Eventually he is there, and he halts for a few moments to rest his horse. From the spur of a dark, rocky hill, he surveys the magnificent scene ahead.

Kitchener's army is advancing in full battle order. Five brigades, consisting of three or four infantry battalions each, are marching in open columns towards Omdurman and Khartoum, flanked on their left side by the river Nile. And on the great river, just abreast of the leading brigade, are heavily laden sailing boats towed by great steam ships. And amongst these many ships are seven or eight gunboats, made ready for action.

Behind the ranks of infantrymen are long lines of artillery, and beyond these are seemingly endless lines of camels, bearing supplies. Meanwhile, on the open desert flank of the army, the Egyptian cavalry and the Camel Corps are providing a shield against surprise attack from the right. It is a stunning sight – the culmination of months, years even, of preparation – to bring a great army across one of the hottest, largest and least accessible deserts in the world. It has required the laying of hundreds of miles of railway track and the fighting of numerous battles to beat off the enemy.

Having taken in the sight, our officer – a lieutenant in the 21st Lancers – now rides towards the centre of the oncoming force, seeking out its leader. There, at the head of the mass of soldiers, leading two horsemen bearing the Union Jack and the Egyptian flag, is a distinct, instantly recognisable figure riding a few feet ahead of his staff – tall, erect, unsmiling. It is the Commander in Chief. The Sirdar. Kitchener himself.

Major-General Sir Horatio Herbert Kitchener is forty-eight years of age. His height is 6 feet 2 inches. Unemotional eyes look out from a stern face, above a large moustache, stretching almost from ear to ear.

The Lancers' officer approaches at an angle, circles behind the General, and draws his horse beside, but slightly behind, his Commander in Chief, saluting as he does so. It is the first time that two great men, who will one day sit beside each other in 10 Downing Street, around the Cabinet table, are to meet: General Kitchener, and our young 21st Lancers officer, Winston Churchill. By character, they have little in common, except for one strong trait of personality: unbounded ambition. Both desire to make their names and be at the centre of events.

Kitchener turns towards the young lieutenant. If he has recognised him, he gives no clue. 'Sir, I have come from the 21st Lancers with a report.' Churchill takes in the sunburnt, almost purple cheeks. The earnest face makes an instant impression. The words are acknowledged with a nod of the head. Kitchener listens, without speaking, to the young officer's calm report of what he has seen of the Dervish Army, the two men's horses crunching the sand as they ride together briefly, side by side. Then, after a considerable pause, there is a crisp response: 'How long do you think I've got?' Churchill replies instantly: 'At least an hour. Probably an hour and a half, sir.'

Kitchener tosses back his head, without saying whether he accepts the young officer's assessment. And then, with a slight bow, he indicates that the brief audience is at an end. The cavalryman salutes, reins back his horse and lets the general and his staff officers ride by.

Kitchener seems absolutely calm. His staff are more excitable.

One observes, 'We want nothing better. Here is a good field of fire. They may as well come today as tomorrow.' As he watches the Sirdar ride off towards the enemy, Churchill mentally recalculates the speeds and distances to ensure that his rushed estimate of the time available to the general wasn't inaccurate. To his relief, it still seems a safe and reliable judgement.

A friendly voice interrupts his thoughts: 'Come along and get some lunch with us.' As Churchill rides back to eat and rest his horse, the infantry has halted at the village of Egeiga and is forming into lines, building a barricade of thorn bushes and biscuit boxes and making a defensive arc, protected from the rear by the broad and fast-flowing Nile. Churchill tucks into a meal of bully beef, washed down with a cool drink. All around him are the excited preparations for battle – a battle expected that very afternoon. Officers shout out commands as units are wheeled into position, stumbling over the rough ground, under an unforgiving sun. The men hear the sound of the gunboats and the artillery opening up a fierce barrage on the town of Omdurman. The gun crews are already taking bets on who will strike the first hit on the Mahdi's tomb, its white dome clearly visible with a telescope through the heat haze.

Few amongst the British Army slept well that night: they had received ominous warnings that the enemy would attack under cover of darkness, reducing the British advantage in weaponry. Every man in camp expected the Dervish Army to descend on them at any time. After all, it was less than two decades since a British Army was overwhelmed and massacred by Zulus at Isandlwana. And they were now just a few miles from Khartoum, where another British force, led by a British general, had been slaughtered thirteen unlucky years before.

But there was no battle that afternoon of 1 September. The

Dervish Army had halted at around the time Churchill was nervously making his report to the Commander in Chief. The Khalifa, the Dervish leader, had contemplated a night attack but had been persuaded by his advisers that the best chance of victory would be to attack the British the next day and then lure Kitchener to attack Omdurman and seek to slaughter his army on the plains of Kerreri.

So, the night passed without incident. Then, at 4.30 a.m., all over the camp, the bugles sounded. The soldiers were immediately awake and soon ready, and by 5 a.m. the 21st Lancers were drawn up outside the encampment. They were ordered to send out patrols to ascertain the location of the enemy. Churchill took six men and a corporal to reconnoitre the ridge between a large hill – Surgham Hill – and the river.

The eight horses trot forward with urgency over the plain and begin to ascend the hill, still in half-darkness. At any moment, the soldiers expect to discover the enemy, or even run into an ambush. What will they find at the summit? Will it already be occupied by the enemy?

Churchill now orders one man to lag back 100 yards, so that at least there will be one survivor if they are taken by surprise. There is no sound but the clatter of the horses and equipment. No one speaks. They reach the ridge unchallenged – a huge relief. Dawn is breaking, the sunlight slowly spreading forward in front of them, lighting up the desert. First they can see 100 yards ahead. Then 200. Now perhaps a quarter of a mile. Nothing. No enemy army is in sight.

The dawn light finally spreads over whole the valley, racing forward across the chilly sands. And then, something is shimmering in the distance: 'There they are!' It is now daylight, and clearly visible around a mile and a half ahead is the Dervish Army – the rays of the morning sun reflecting off thousands of weapons and flagpoles. The enemy front looks even longer than the day before: large masses of men, joined by thinner lines, and behind them are the reserves. Churchill immediately calls forward a cavalryman and sends an urgent message to his Commander in Chief.

A glorious sunrise is now taking place behind the small group of cavalrymen. On any other day, they might have turned to admire it. But not on this day: they stare instead at an army tens of thousands strong, stretched out four or five miles wide ahead of them. It is a once-in-a-lifetime panorama. And suddenly, just before 6 a.m., they realise that this army is once again on the move. And beneath them in the valley they can hear the cheers and roars of thousands of voices – soldiers marching to battle, confident of victory.

Churchill and his scouts advance to meet the enemy – seven men against perhaps 50,000. They halt about 400 yards away from the nearest Dervish troops and fire off a few rounds in anger before wisely retreating back up the ridge. There is a message now from Kitchener: 'Remain as long as possible, and report how the masses of attack are moving.'

Most of the Dervish force passes on either side of their position, behind a line of white banners. Meanwhile, the centre of their army, far out in the plain, has come within range of the British and Egyptian artillery. Two or three batteries, and all of the artillery on the gunboats – at least thirty guns in all – open an intense fire. The first shells fall amongst the Dervish troops, flattening groups of soldiers and sweeping away their standards. Shrapnel bursts tear into the lines of soldiers, instantly killing some and inflicting dreadful wounds on others. The ground is littered with smashed bodies and torn limbs.

But the enemy advance gathers pace, undeterred by the shelling and by its victims. They are racing now towards the British and Egyptian lines. Their advance seems unstoppable. And then

Kitchener's troops open a withering fire. The Battle of Omdurman has truly begun.

They come fast. They come direct. They come without apparent fear, and in enormous numbers. But each wave is met by the volleys of Kitchener's army. Well-aimed bullets rip into the advancing lines of men.

The Khalifa, who has taken over leadership of the Dervish Army after the death of the Mahdi in 1885, has made detailed plans for his attack. And this location is where he wants the battle to be: months before, he claimed that the Mahdi had appeared before him in a dream and told him that victory in a great battle with the British would be his on the plains of Kerreri, outside Omdurman. But the Khalifa's battle plan contains one simple and extraordinary defect: an utter failure to understand the power of modern weaponry against an ill-equipped opponent.

Each of Kitchener's soldiers – British, Egyptian or Sudanese – is armed with the latest Lee-Metford Mark II rifle capable of loading eight bullets at a time. The British artillery has been bolstered by the arrival of additional Maxim machine guns and there is a battery of 5.5-inch Howitzers capable of firing new lyddite high-explosive shells. The Dervishes have guns too, but nothing like this; their old-fashioned Martini-Henry rifles are supplemented by swords, daggers and lances – weapons that have evolved little over the previous thousand years.

It isn't difficult for Kitchener's army to kill. For over an hour, 20,000 British, Egyptian and Sudanese rifles fire, accompanied by eighty guns. The Dervishes charge again and again. But the massacre is almost over by 8.30 a.m. On the ground in front of the British lines, thousands of Dervish soldiers lie dead or dying.

And then Kitchener gives the order to advance – requiring the army to reorganise from its defensive arc and march off, division by division. It is an impressive scene: a well-drilled, professional army at the peak of its preparedness. The 21st Lancers are ordered ahead to reconnoitre the land before Omdurman. They charge a Dervish force, without realising until too late that it is partly hidden in the gullies of the battlefield – but they prevail, in spite of significant casualties, and are later rewarded with three Victoria Crosses for gallantry. Churchill, of course, is in the thick of the action and thrills at his first real taste of battle.

For a while, Kitchener seems to have miscalculated – there are still significant Dervish forces held back, awaiting his advance. They might now catch his force in its rear. But on his right flank the British brigade commanded by Hector Macdonald is ready to face the threat and sees off the Dervishes with more, withering, fire. It is not quite the end of the battle, but whatever individual actions temporarily check the advance of the British, these are mere pebbles in the way of the flood of well-drilled cavalry and infantry advancing in triumph towards Omdurman and onwards to Khartoum.

Some, such as a young Douglas Haig, are later to question the battle tactics. But Kitchener has no doubts. He rides forward on his white charger towards Omdurman, protected in the middle of two Highland regiments, relishing his moment of triumph. For him, this is the culmination of months of meticulous planning, moving his army across the harsh and treacherous deserts of the region. It is also the culmination of years of hope, after national shame.

*   *   *

Kitchener had come to Khartoum to wipe away the stain of defeat that had persisted since Charles Gordon's murder in the Sudanese capital thirteen years earlier. Major-General Gordon – 'Gordon of Khartoum' – was a British officer and administrator sent to Khartoum in early 1884 to secure the evacuation of loyal soldiers and civilians after a revolt had broken out led by the religious leader and self-proclaimed Mahdi – Mohammed Al-Sayd Abdullah – who claimed that he was the prophet of God. But Gordon refused to leave Khartoum and, to the horror of Prime Minister Gladstone, ended up besieged in the city by the Mahdi's forces. Very unwillingly, the British government, which wanted no entanglements in Sudan, assembled a relief force. But this arrived at Khartoum two days too late. The Dervish troops had already entered the city on 26 January 1885, slaughtering 7,000 defenders, including General Gordon. Gordon's head was cut off and presented to the Mahdi.

Kitchener had been part of that relief force, arriving too late to save the general and many of his men. On reaching Khartoum in early February, he found a letter waiting for him from the dead Gordon. In it, Gordon proposed that Kitchener should be a future Governor-General of Sudan. Gordon's death had a huge impact on Kitchener: as one of the last to communicate with him, Kitchener felt a special responsibility to settle the score.

What had happened in Sudan was a major humiliation for the greatest empire on the planet. Queen Victoria was furious about the failure to rescue Gordon and sent an unusually blunt telegram of rebuke to her Prime Minister – the contents of which found their way into the press. Gordon had achieved the martyrdom he seemed to seek, being portrayed as the saintly Christian hero, nobly resisting the Islamic hordes but stabbed in the back by selfish and short-sighted politicians. Stones were thrown at the windows of 10 Downing Street and Gladstone was denounced as the 'Murderer of Gordon'.

13 March 1885 was set aside as a national day of mourning for the 'fallen hero of Khartoum'. The British people, egged on by the British press, wanted revenge – the defeat of the Mahdi and the recapture of the city.

Three months later, the Mahdi was dead from natural causes. The new ruler of Sudan was Abdullah ibn Muhammed, known as the Khalifa – 'the successor'. It was his barbarous rule that eventually prompted the British government to act, reoccupying Sudan.

Kitchener now bore the hopes of the Empire: it had fallen to him to wipe away the stain of 1885. He had patiently assembled an army and built from scratch the railway infrastructure to move it across a great desert, building new track across unforgiving and waterless ground at the rate of two or even three miles each day. With meticulous care, detailed planning and prudent budgeting, Kitchener slowly and surely prepared to crush the Dervish forces. He was now on the edge of a triumph which would for ever secure his place in the history of the British Empire.

Having repulsed the Dervish attack, Kitchener now ordered the advance, sending his troops forward to occupy the town of Omdurman, just a short distance from Khartoum itself. The Dervish militia was over twice the size of the combined British and Egyptian forces. But it was no match for a well-trained and equipped modern army, and it was roundly defeated in the plains before Omdurman, then driven back in chaos towards the town, pursued by the Egyptian Army and the 21st Lancers. By noon, the battle was effectively won.

The Khalifa Abdullah could see that his army was broken. He attempted a last-ditch defence of Omdurman. When that failed, he fled into the desert. The British force now entered the squalid town of Omdurman in the mid-afternoon, picking its way through shattered bodies and debris created by their own bombardment. Kitchener rode to the tomb of the Mahdi – the man responsible for Gordon's death thirteen years before. It was here that Kitchener was almost killed by the fall of a stray shell, but he was unflappable, noting simply, 'It would be a pity to lose our ticket when the day is won.'

The Battle of Omdurman was over. British and Egyptian casualties were a trifling forty-three dead and 434 wounded. The Dervish losses were believed to be around 12,000 killed and over 13,000 wounded. It was, indisputably, a crushing and decisive victory. Gordon was truly avenged. And Kitchener had done it.

That night, an officer friend of Churchill sent a six-word telegraph message to the young lieutenant's mother: 'Big fight. Fine sight. Winston well.' Meanwhile, as others slept, Churchill realised that there were no newspaper correspondents to report the battle, including the bold cavalry charge that he and his Lancers had taken part in. With extraordinary cheek, and his usual taste for the spotlight, Churchill, a serving officer, prepared a long and detailed description of the battle, including his own regiment's charge. He hoped to get it into the newspapers. It was approved by military intelligence. It was passed by the censor. But it was then personally vetoed by Kitchener. Churchill was later to get his revenge in his book *The River War*, a critical account of the campaign in which he condemned what he described as the inhuman slaughter of the wounded, holding Kitchener responsible.

In Khartoum, there was still unfinished business. On 4 September, at around 10 a.m., the gunboats *Abu Klea* and *Melik* moored at the shabby quay that fronted the river by the Governor's palace. Five hundred carefully selected troops, drawn from each detachment which had fought in the battle, arrived and formed up on three sides of the open square of the palace, where Gordon had died thirteen years before, with their backs to the river. They had come to this place to perform a long-overdue service: to commemorate General Gordon's life and death.

Kitchener and his staff stood in the middle of the square, facing the once handsome building, its formerly meticulously maintained gardens now unwatered, untended and returning to parched desert normality. There was silence. From the riverbank, a group of curious locals surveyed the scene. On the roof of the pock-marked and war-scarred palace, near the spot where Gordon was thought to have been slain, were two flagpoles. Down below, in the square, Kitchener raised his hand. The Union Jack was now hoisted, and blew smartly in the breeze. Immediately after this, the Egyptian flag was unfurled too, and raised to top the adjacent flagpole.

A 21-shot salute from *Melik*'s 12½-pounder gun now sounded out across the city, live ammunition flying over the heads of the crowd into the desert beyond. Then 'God Save the Queen' was sung in Khartoum for the first time since the last days of Gordon. Kitchener and his staff saluted smartly and stood to attention. There were three cheers for Queen Victoria, for the Khedive of Egypt, and lastly for Kitchener himself. And then the band of the Grenadier Guards played Handel's 'Dead March' and the chaplain read the Fifteenth Psalm. Finally, the Sudanese band struck up Gordon's favourite hymn, 'Abide with Me'.

It was a deeply emotional moment, and the normally self-controlled Kitchener was not unaffected as first General Hunter and then the other senior officers stepped forward to shake his hand. Appearing choked with emotion, Kitchener turned briefly to Hunter and indicated to him to dismiss the parade. Many thought they saw tears in his eyes.

A few hours later, a telegram arrived, delivered by boat. This announced the award to Kitchener, by Queen Victoria, of a peerage to celebrate the victory. The Queen was delighted, recording in her diary, 'Surely he [Gordon] is avenged.'

A few days later, at Omdurman, the famously frugal Kitchener, who hated waste and extravagance, made out his bill to the government for the entire campaign. The largest item of expenditure was for railway-building, and the total cost of the whole enterprise was just £2.354 million. For this, 700 miles of permanent railway line had been constructed and almost 1 million square miles of Sudan had been brought back under Anglo-Egyptian control. The meticulous Kitchener reported to Lord Cromer in Cairo that he had incorporated Sudan into the British Empire for the price of just £2 2s 6d per square mile – or £1 3s 6d per head of population.

Kitchener's decision to destroy the Mahdi's massive tomb later caused some controversy, which he sought to combat by pointing to the shell-damaged and unstable nature of the building. More controversial was his decision to have the Mahdi's body dug up, the head cut off and the rest dumped into the Nile. For a while, the head was kept by the Sirdar in an old kerosene tin, before being buried in secret at Wadi Halfa.

Back in Britain, there was only joyous celebration. National honour had at last been restored. And the man who had restored it had for ever secured a place in his nation's heart. The long-lasting national affection for this apparently unaffectionate man had begun.

* * *

Kitchener arrived back in Britain on 27 October 1898. A special train carried him to Victoria Station, where he was met by a formal welcoming party and vast crowds. A national tour followed, along with national fame: the Kitchener image now appeared in newspapers, on biscuit tins and on all sorts of memorabilia. A reward of £30,000 from Parliament made Kitchener a wealthy man for the first time. More importantly to him, Baron Kitchener of Khartoum and of Aspall in the County of Suffolk was now a national hero.

Until this moment, Kitchener had looked set to be just another competent officer who had risen rapidly to senior rank without leaving much of a trace in the history books. Born on 24 June 1850 in south-west Ireland, of an English family who were determined to emphasise their Englishness, Horatio Herbert Kitchener was brought up by a stern and somewhat eccentric father, after his mother died when he was only fourteen. Colonel Henry Horatio Kitchener was a former army officer who for reasons of alleged economy and cleanliness refused to sleep between blankets, spending his nights under specially sewn-together sheets of newspaper. Family life was run on a military-like timetable and there was a strong emphasis on discipline for the young Kitchener and his siblings.

Kitchener's father had a distaste for formal education and beyond the early school days tutors were provided for young Horatio and his two brothers, with ambiguous results. Colonel Kitchener hoped that all his sons would pursue an army career, and the young Kitchener crammed for entry to the Royal Military Academy at Woolwich, a training establishment for officers destined for the Engineers and Artillery. He passed out in December 1870 after an unremarkable cadetship. He was regarded as below average for a Royal Engineer officer, and even in those Victorian days of reserve and restraint was considered distant and aloof.

As Kitchener was being granted his commission, in January 1871, the Franco-Prussian War was close to ending. Encouraged by his father, and with a degree of rashness and independence that might not have been expected, Kitchener made his way with a fellow cadet to join the French General Chanzy's Army of the Loire. Kitchener's participation in the war was, however, short and not particularly sweet. He ascended with a French officer in a hot air balloon without proper warm clothing and contracted pneumonia. It took him a full year to recover. As a serving British officer, Kitchener had no permission to be fighting with a foreign military force. On his return to London, he was summoned to the War Office and given a dressing-down by the Commander in Chief of the Army, Field Marshal HRH the Duke of Cambridge. The Duke called him a deserter and a disgrace, but rather qualified the impact of the reprimand by leaving Kitchener with a distinct sense that he might have done the same himself in his youth. It was to be the first, but not the last, time that Kitchener would support the French Army against a German onslaught.

Kitchener's links with the Middle East were established in November 1874 when, aged twenty-four, he was seconded to the Palestine Exploration Fund and ordered to complete a mapping survey of the Holy Land. He was captivated by what was then known as the Near East – an area where he was to make his reputation. He also developed a fondness for warmer climates, and between 1877 and 1914 he avoided spending a single winter in chilly Britain.

For three years, Kitchener and his team worked in the area to the west of the Jordan River, completing detailed maps and a survey of local flora and fauna. It was during this period that his appetite for hard work, thoroughness, mastery of detail and ruthless organisation began to mark him out as exceptional. He also gained a reputation as a somewhat aloof and distant presence – a man who spoke little and seemed to prefer his own company to that of others. It was also increasingly obvious that he was ambitious and was determined to locate himself where the action and prospects for progression were greatest. This eventually led him to Egypt, in 1883, where Britain's power and influence was rising, albeit cloaked in support for Egypt's own government under its Khedive. By now the striking Kitchener moustache was firmly in its place – it was soon to become his hallmark.

Britain's presence in Egypt – buying half the shares in the Suez Canal Company in 1875 and sending in a large military force in 1882 – drew it into intervention in neighbouring Sudan, a vast country almost one third of the size of America. In 1883, Sudan was experiencing a pan-Islamic revolt led by the Mahdi, or 'expected one', who presented himself as the descendant of the prophet Muhammad. The Mahdi was determined on a holy war to expel the 'infidels' from his country.

It was in Sudan that Kitchener was to make his name, taking part in the failed relief expedition of 1884–85 before being appointed in 1886 'Governor-General of Eastern Sudan and the Red Sea Littoral' (a grand title but with responsibility only for a miserable little strip of land). While he held this post, in 1888, he led a small infantry and cavalry action against enemy forces, receiving a nasty bullet wound in the face, which broke his jaw. The wound, and the moderately successful action, received considerable press attention back in Britain. The ambitious Kitchener was only thirty-eight but already a brevet-colonel, an aide-de-camp to Queen Victoria and increasingly well known to the public, the press and senior politicians. He was well on his way to becoming a celebrity soldier. And that was all before his biggest triumph: planning and executing the successful campaign of 1896–98.

After the victory at Omdurman, Kitchener led a small force to a

French fort at Fashoda in the far south of Sudan; the British government feared that the French were about to make a bid to occupy parts of the country. Kitchener helped secure French withdrawal without loss of blood, demonstrating that, when required, he could deploy skills of tact and diplomacy to complement the reputation for ruthless military toughness he had gained at Omdurman.

In September 1898, Kitchener became Governor-General of Sudan. He took a surprisingly progressive position on most issues. He rebuilt the mosques of Khartoum, guaranteed religious freedom for all citizens and attempted to impede Christian missionaries from trying to convert Muslims. He instituted a basic education programme for the populace and established a Gordon Memorial College in Khartoum. He improved the infrastructure, brought in a new system of taxation and reconstructed the capital.

Now that his nation had a new military hero, it intended to make good use of him – and, in turn, Kitchener was determined to be at the centre of events. He had no intention of getting stuck too long in the backwater of Sudan. At first, India was in his sights. But just a year after Omdurman, in October 1899, Britain was at war again, this time in South Africa. Many in Britain expected that the Boer farmers would be crushed by the Empire's highly trained forces in just a few months. In contrast, Kitchener told colleagues that he expected a long and difficult conflict.

Kitchener's expectations soon proved more realistic than the jingoistic optimism of the British press and public. The early stage of the war was marked by British defeats and the besieging of imperial forces in three towns: Ladysmith, Mafeking and Kimberley. For Britain, it was another shocking and humiliating setback, ranking with Isandlwana in 1879 and Gordon's death in 1885. Before long, the Boers had deployed a force of almost 50,000 mobile and well-armed men. The British government decided to take no chances, and sent out not merely more troops but its best generals: Field Marshal Lord Roberts, with a long and distinguished career in India, was to be Commander in Chief, with Lord Kitchener as his Chief of Staff. The two men arrived in South Africa in January 1900.

Within months, the new military leadership and the influx of extra soldiers from Britain and its colonies had converted Boer victories into a string of defeats. All three sieges had been lifted, and the Transvaal had been annexed. At home, the Prime Minister, Lord Salisbury, was so buoyed by success that he called a 'khaki election'. Roberts judged the war to be over by October 1900 and arranged to return to Britain, handing over his post to Kitchener in November and describing the remaining Boer forces as 'a few marauding bands'. Roberts was not the only one who allowed complacency to get the better of him. The British government struck a new medal to commemorate the campaign. On its reverse was a figure of Britannia, holding out a laurel wreath of victory, under which were the expected dates of the conflict: 1899–1900. But the Boers refused to comply with this timetable and fought on for two more years. The British government was forced to strike a new medal, and in the name of efficiency it opted to reuse those medals already struck, manually rubbing out the dates on the back.

To Kitchener, therefore, fell the difficult work of defeating a guerrilla army that was mobile, fought unconventionally and could melt away into the vast countryside of Transvaal and the 'Orange Free State' – the Boer homelands. He applied rigour, energy and detailed organisation to defeat his enemy. He increased the mounted infantry strength to 80,000 by May 1901. He replaced ineffective commanders. He established block houses at strategic points, dividing up the countryside and carrying out sweeps to trap Boer forces. Controversially, he had his soldiers burn Boer farms and establish concentration camps to round up a rootless population. This latter initiative, in which too little attention was given to food, conditions and basic medical care, led to over 26,000 deaths – a majority of whom were children. The Liberal leader, Henry Campbell-Bannerman, described the camps as 'methods of barbarism'.

But in contrast to his harsh and unbending reputation, Kitchener was again a pragmatist when it came to bringing the war to a conclusion. He showed the same restraint and respect for his enemy as at Fashoda, understanding that if unconditional surrender was demanded of the Boers, any peace could be short-lived at best. In March 1901, Kitchener was writing to the British War Minister to urge that reasonable terms should be offered to bring the conflict to an end. He wanted an amnesty for some of the Boer leaders, observing that 'we are now carrying the war on to put two or three hundred Dutchmen in prison ... It seems to me absurd and wrong, and I wonder if the Chancellor of the Exchequer did not have a fit.' Kitchener had personal reasons, too, for wanting a settlement in South Africa. In the same month, he was pressing the Secretary of State for War to make him Commander in Chief in India as soon as the war was over.

Kitchener's task in securing peace was made tougher by the hard-line approach of both the British government and the Governor of Cape Colony, Sir Alfred Milner, who sought an unconditional Boer surrender. Kitchener had at times to display his unconventional powers of political persuasion to change Boer opinion: during the course of negotiations in 1902, he told General Jan Smuts, one of the leading Boer commanders, 'My opinion is that in two years' time a Liberal government will be in power, and if a Liberal government comes to power, it will grant you a constitution for South Africa.'

Eventually, Kitchener succeeded. The Treaty of Vereeniging brought the war to a close – over a year after he had first started arguing for a pragmatic settlement. On 31 May 1902, the 'Kitchener peace' was signed in Kitchener's own residence in Pretoria at just before midnight. Kitchener had accepted what Milner never would: that the Boers would only give up the fight when they realised that self-government was within their grasp. The war that was expected to be over in just months – by Christmas 1899 – had taken almost three years to end. It was a lesson Kitchener would not forget.

The ingredients of victory in South Africa all felt rather similar to the Sudan success: Kitchener had reversed an initial British humiliation; won a war with methods of thoroughness, efficiency and organisation; and proved flexible and pragmatic in securing peace and ensuring a sound basis for reconstruction. But just as the deaths of the wounded and the desecration of the Mahdi's tomb had left an undertone of controversy in Sudan, so had the deaths in the concentration camps of South Africa. Kitchener was developing a reputation for being a harsh and somewhat ruthless warrior who prized victory over all else.

A mark of his achievement, though, is that Kitchener's pragmatism had not merely helped secure an eventual peace: in little more than a decade, South African forces were fighting alongside the British in the First World War. Kitchener had demonstrated that beneath his ferocious and unbending military reputation he was a pragmatist who understood when to be flexible. South Africa, in short, was another significant feather in the Kitchener cap. He had triumphed in Sudan and in Egypt. He had triumphed against the Boers too. He returned home and, after receiving the freedom of Southampton on 11 July, joined a special train to take him to London – the carriages covered in bunting and the engine sporting a huge 'K' attached to the front, surrounded by laurel leaves.

After a brief and no doubt thrilling stop at Basingstoke, to be made a freeman of the borough, he arrived at Paddington Station, where he was met by the Prince of Wales and mobbed by crowds. On the way to Buckingham Palace to meet the soon-to-be crowned Edward VII, the grandstands erected for the coronation were filled with Londoners keen to catch a glimpse of the conquering hero. He was now made a full general and a viscount, with the title 'Viscount Kitchener of Khartoum and of the Vaal in the Colony of Transvaal and Aspall in the County of Suffolk'. This time, Parliament awarded him £50,000 – a huge sum in those times, worth over £5 million today.

But Britain's new favourite general was determined not to rest. He now had his eye on India. The election of 1900 had seen Kitchener's friend St John Brodrick take over as Secretary of State for War. Brodrick had plans to bring Kitchener to the War Office after the South Africa war was won, to help reorganise the army. But Kitchener had other ideas, and exclaimed that he would rather 'sweep the streets' than accept what he saw as a political post.

Kitchener was now on the way to becoming a legend in his own lifetime, and what he pushed for, he generally secured. No one wanted to say no to him, risking his wrath or his resignation. Kitchener lobbied hard, and eventually his incessant pressure secured a promise from Brodrick that he would be handed the plum job of Commander in Chief in India once victory over the Boers was secured.

Lord Curzon, the Viceroy of India since 1899, had supported Kitchener's claim to be the commander of Britain's Indian armies. But he was soon to regret his choice. He and Kitchener were both wilful personalities who were used to getting their own way. India is a large country. But was it large enough for these two strong men to live harmoniously together?

Kitchener arrived in India in November 1902. Within six months, Lord Curzon was writing to the Secretary of State complaining that Kitchener was detached, 'lonely' and unable to accept advice: 'He stands aloof and alone, a molten mass of devouring energy and burning ambition, without anybody to control or guide it in the right direction.'

The tension between the two men came to a head because of the way in which Britain controlled its armies in India. Alongside the Commander in Chief was the Military Member of the Viceroy's Council: an army officer, lower in rank than the Commander in Chief, but in control of the army's finances, transport, supplies and ammunition. With the right personalities, the system could be managed. But this system of dual control could not work with a man such as Kitchener, who expected to have direct responsibility for what he saw as essential parts of the military machine. Kitchener demanded complete control of the army. Lord Curzon refused. Both men threatened resignation. Eventually, after intervention by the Cabinet itself, Kitchener prevailed. In August 1905, Lord Curzon resigned and Lord Minto was appointed in his place. The row had rumbled on for over two years.

In spite of this huge distraction, Kitchener achieved much during his eight years in India: he reorganised the army, founded a military staff college at Quetta and still found time to pursue his interest in gardening. He remained highly competitive, even in small matters. The new Secretary of State for India, John Morley, claimed that Kitchener had a habit of altering the scoreboard when no one else was looking, in order to triumph in games of billiards.

In 1906, a new officer joined Kitchener's staff: Captain Oswald Fitzgerald. At age thirty-one, he was twenty-five years Kitchener's junior, but was to become his master's close friend and companion for the rest of both their lives. Indeed, with the exception of a short period of a few months apart, they were from now on together almost every day.

In 1909, Kitchener was promoted to field marshal – the highest military rank. A year later, he left India. He wanted to be made Viceroy but did not enjoy the support of the Liberal government. Bitterly disappointed, he agreed to take up the command of British forces in the Mediterranean only after direct pressure from King Edward VII; he thought the post was likely to be something of a backwater. But first, he completed a world tour.

In China, the local correspondent of *The Times* was appalled to see Kitchener pocket several pieces of porcelain laid out for his inspection by his Chinese hosts. Nobody dared question his actions. Nor did they when, leaving his command in India, he occupied a special railway carriage that was supposed to be reserved for the new Commander in Chief. Everywhere he went, he was treated as a great celebrity. No one dared question or contradict him.

On his return from the world tour he made a new, and unsuccessful, attempt to be appointed Viceroy of India. And he now declined the Mediterranean command. Instead, he purchased a large property, Broome Park, in Kent, and spent much time over the next five years renovating the house and gardens. The walls of the entrance hall were monogrammed 'KK', for 'Kitchener of Khartoum', and the Kitchener family motto – 'Thorough' – was carved on the fireplace.

In 1911, on a visit to East Africa with his close companion, Fitzgerald, he also decided to buy an estate in Kenya, near the

Uganda railway, where he hoped to live in retirement, during the cold English winters. Fitzgerald also secured a stake in the property, and Kitchener later arranged that his own share would pass to Fitzgerald on his death.

Later in 1911, Kitchener was offered a non-military posting as British Agent in Egypt. It was a country he loved and had lived in for many years. He spoke Arabic and felt genuine affection for the ordinary people of the country. Just as importantly, he hoped that the job might prove a stepping stone to one day becoming Viceroy of India – the ultimate prize he had set his heart on.

Egypt was still governed under the sham arrangement of a 'ruling' Khedive and a General Assembly, allied to the Sultan of Turkey. In reality, it was controlled by Britain – so Kitchener's post was immensely powerful. As ever, he arranged for the faithful Fitzgerald to join him in Cairo. In Egypt, he ruled in regal manner and made major reforms to government and the economy. In 1912, he passed the Homestead Exemption Law, which gave greater freedoms to small farmers. For an imperial ruler, he was very popular with the ordinary Egyptian: on his travels around the country he was often met by banners proclaiming, 'Welcome to Lord Kitchener: The Friend of the Fellah!' Landowners and top officials regarded his meddling as almost socialistic in nature. Kitchener couldn't care less. When he established a new Ministry of Agriculture, he tried, unsuccessfully, to have it paid for through death duties levied on wealthy landowners.

Kitchener also had to cope with rising nationalist agitation in some quarters, and he dealt with this firmly, closing radical newspapers and making a series of arrests. The far-sighted Field Marshal also used his time in Egypt to build constructive links with some of the Arab leaders who might in future be useful allies against

Turkey, at a time when Turkey was increasingly aligning itself with Germany. Kitchener held friendly talks with Abdullah ibn Hussein, the son of the Sharif of Mecca, who would later support Britain in the First World War in exchange for British guarantees of an Arab homeland in the region. In many ways, he was paving the way for the work that Lawrence of Arabia was to undertake in 1916 and 1917.

On 17 June 1914, Kitchener received the news that he was to be made an earl; he was delighted. Two days later, he set off from Alexandria to return to London, receive his earldom and take a short break from his duties. Fitzgerald, again, was at his side. Kitchener was hugely enjoying his work in Egypt, which he now regarded as his spiritual home. He was sixty-four years old and was planning for a few more leisurely and rewarding years in the country, followed by a quiet retirement in England and East Africa. But in Europe, the storm clouds of war were already gathering.

Kitchener would never again set foot in his beloved Egypt.

THE WARSHIP AND
THE SUBMARINE

'Commence hostilities against the German Navy.'

TELEGRAM FROM WINSTON CHURCHILL, FIRST LORD OF THE
ADMIRALTY, TO ALL ROYAL NAVY VESSELS, 4 AUGUST 1914

Tuesday 28 July 1914. The port of Weihaiwei in north-east China – a territory leased by Britain from 1898 to 1930. This is currently the home base of the armoured cruiser HMS *Hampshire*. The port is mainly used as a summer anchorage for the Royal Navy's China Station and has also gained a reputation as a health resort. But the calm and tranquillity of a warm summer evening is shattered by the message that arrives from the Admiralty in London. It is soon read with concern by Vice-Admiral Sir Martyn Jerram, the local commander. The message makes clear that the British government sees a high risk of a conflict with Germany and her allies commencing soon. With German warships deployed throughout the world, no risks are to be taken. All British warships should return to port, take on extra stocks of fuel and ammunition, put to sea and prepare for action.

Within hours, the normally quiet backwater of Weihaiwei is a hive of activity. All crews are on board their vessels. Cranes help to move great stocks of coal on board. Food, water, ammunition, medicine and all the basic items necessary to keep hundreds of men in a state of preparedness for action are quickly rolled up gangplanks and placed in carefully designated positions. Officers and petty officers bark out orders. There have not, as yet, been any formal announcements of what is going on. But a quiet and confidential word exchanged at a senior level is soon shared in confidence with a junior, and so on down the chain of command, until the most junior Boy 2nd Class knows – at least in part – the reason for the sense of urgency. A war amongst the European powers is expected to break out at any time.

After three days of feverish activity, the ships are ready. Their boilers are fired up, ready to power the engines. And then the signal to put to sea is given. It is now 31 July. Just before *Hampshire* leaves port, for an as yet unknown destination, an urgent message is sent to her and all the ships in port from Vice-Admiral Jerram: 'There is a high probability of a European War breaking out soon. The Admiral has confidence that all officers and men will prepare for hostilities with the utmost despatch.'

On board *Hampshire*, there is a sense of excitement but also of shock. Can war really be likely? Are the great nations of Europe really going to fight each other with all the devastating modern equipment of war that is now available? If so, could the war really spread to the distant backwaters of Asia? And if it did, would men who thought they had a cushy number in His Majesty's Royal Navy face battle, injury and even death?

Leading Signalman George Reeve, aged twenty-six, is one of the crew now on *Hampshire* – he joined her only six months ago. Reeve was born in Wakefield in Yorkshire and ran away from home to join the Royal Navy in 1905, at the age of seventeen. His father was furious and felt George had thrown away the chance of ever being a success in life. But he had stuck with his chosen career and served on HMS *Venus, Ostrich, Hecla, Hermes* and even the Royal Yacht *Victoria and Albert* – which he hated, given all the endless drills and naval spit and polish. In 1910, George married Martha Ellen Butterworth – 'Nellie' – and they soon had their first child, a daughter named Winifred, or Winnie for short.

It is now 2 August, two days out of port, and George decides that it is time to write a long letter to his beloved wife, whom he has seen so little because of the obligations of naval service. He and many other sailors on board realise that their lives may soon change dramatically – indeed, they might even be at risk. Loved ones might never be seen again. For these young men, with such limited experience of life, it is a truly frightening prospect.

Finding a quiet place on the mess deck, George obtains a stack of lined writing paper and an ink pen and sits down to write. At the top right of the first page he starts the letter: '23 Mess, HMS *Hampshire*, At Sea, 2 August 1914'. It will be a long letter – nine pages. But he has never known war before, and he feels the need to write from the heart, as if each letter from now on could be his last.

And then he begins:

My Own Darling Wife,

I don't know exactly when I received your letter but it was just before we left Wei-Hai-Wei. I told you in my last letter that there was something in the wind and I didn't know what it was. Well we had to come in and all the ships had to complete with coal as quickly as possible and prepare at once for war. We had not the faintest idea who the war was going to be with ... We have been advised by signal to send all our mails via Suez and that will mean a big gap between the last letter I sent you and this one ... We have had another signal saying that 'Germany has sent an ultimatum to Russia and France to cease preparations for war, and the ultimatum expires in twelve hours', so we should soon know now whether there is going to be anything doing or not. I don't suppose you think that we shall be in it at all out here but there are German, Austrian and Italian ships out here just the same as there are at home ... I can imagine that it will be a time of great anxiety to you just now but look on the bright side of things sweetheart and if anything does happen and you should not see me again please remember that I thank God for having given me the few years I have had of the company of such a sweet woman for a wife and such a darling child and believe me when I say that I love you very very dearly and shall do as long as life shall last. I always want my daughter to think the world of her Daddy as I know she does at present. But enough in this pessimistic strain dear. Very likely the affair will have been settled amiably before this letter reaches you and all cause for anxiety will be over ... It is what I am paid to do, just the same as you are paid to work in the mill dear ... I am very much inclined to think I shall fall in with your suggestion to leave the Navy when my 12 years are done [in 1917] and then I shall be at liberty to go anywhere with you if we have the means to do it ... I am persevering with my shorthand in case that will come in useful ... Well darling I will now conclude, hoping for the best. Please accept my fondest love and kisses for yourself and kiss Winnie for me. Believe me to remain your ever loving husband, XXXX George XXXXXXXXXXXXXXX XXXXXXXXXXXXXXX. Ps: If there is any cause for grave anxiety on my behalf enquire at the Admiralty – they should know something.

He folds the letter twice and tucks it into the small envelope, writing on the name and address 'Mrs. G. E. Reeve, Rough Bank, New Hey, Nr. Rochdale, Lancashire, England' and 'Via Suez'.

But by the time the letter has reached England, the hopes of peace are forlorn ones. There will be no return to civilian life in 1917.

On 4 August, two days after Reeve's letter is written, a second message is sent by the Admiralty in London to all ships of the Royal Navy. It is authorised by the First Lord of the Admiralty, Winston Churchill: 'Commence hostilities against the German Navy.' Germany's decision to attack France through Belgium has brought Britain into the war. The greatest conflict thus far in world history has just begun.

*　　*　　*

Twelve years earlier. 1 September 1902. Elswick, on the river Tyne, Newcastle.

The Victorian era is now over. Edward VII became King over eighteen months ago. Lord Kitchener has returned from South Africa and is preparing for his forthcoming journey to India. And at the Armstrong Whitworth shipbuilding yard, founded in 1847, hundreds of men are preparing to start work on the construction of a new armoured cruiser – the fifth of the six new Devonshire-class ships – estimated to cost around £850,000.

The plans are for a vessel of almost 150 metres in length, with a beam of 20 metres and a deep draught of just over 7 metres. The ship will displace almost 11,000 tons, including over 6,500 tons of protective armour plating. She will carry a crew of around 600, of whom one in ten will be under the age of eighteen. There will also be around seventy Royal Marines on board. If you want to get a feel for what *Hampshire* might have looked and felt like, visit HMS *Belfast*, moored today on the river Thames. *Belfast* is almost the same weight as *Hampshire* was. She is 35 metres longer and has almost exactly the same beam. The Devonshire-class ships, including *Hampshire*, will be powered by two four-cylinder triple-expansion steam engines, each driving one shaft, and producing a total of 21,000 horsepower, allowing a maximum speed of 22½ knots. These will in turn be powered by seventeen Yarrow and six cylindrical boilers. The main armament will be four breech-loading 7½-inch guns, capable of firing 200-pound shells to reach targets almost 8 miles away. Secondary armaments include six 6-inch guns and two 12-pounder guns, as well as eighteen quick-firing 3-pounder Hotchkiss guns and two submerged 18-inch torpedo tubes, one on each beam. *Hampshire's* armoured belt will be between 2 and 6 inches thick.

The ship is designed to carry large quantities of coal. She will also be able to carry 60 tons of drinking water and 160 tons of water for her boilers. There will be around eleven small boats on board, capable of carrying around 600 men in total, to transport the crew to other vessels or to shore or for use in emergencies. The plans also include space for three Carley floats, two large and one small. These are life-rafts, made of copper tubing, surrounded by a mass of cork and covered with a layer of canvas. In the middle of them is a wooden grating, secured to the copper float by netting. The large rafts are each designed to carry about forty-five men, either sitting on the ring or standing on the platform. Another twenty-two men can cling onto the rope loops that are strung around the ring. These rafts are easy to throw over the side of the ship, but they are not designed to protect men for long in the sea. Those standing inside them would be up to their chests in water. Those hanging onto the sides would be submerged up to their heads. Their purpose is to keep men afloat and alive until they are quickly picked up by rescue boats or other ships.

The shipbuilders at Elswick worked hard on *Hampshire* over the next two years, launching her on 24 September 1903 and completing her in July 1905. The new HMS *Hampshire* was a powerful and impressive ship. But within a year the Royal Navy had launched the first of its dreadnoughts. Instantly, ships like *Hampshire* were considered almost obsolete, with the new generation of vessels possessing much more powerful weaponry (12-inch guns) and additional armour. The race against Germany to maintain British naval supremacy had now begun.

Otherwise, these were quiet years for the Royal Navy, patrolling the seas and securing the Empire's trade routes. After commissioning, *Hampshire* was assigned to the 1st Cruiser Squadron of the Channel Fleet, along with most of her sister ships, and then in 1909 she was transferred to the reserve Third Fleet. In June 1911, she took part in the huge coronation fleet review for the new King, George V. And in December 1911, two months after Winston Churchill was appointed First Lord of the Admiralty, she was recommissioned and joined the 6th Cruiser Squadron in the Mediterranean. In 1912, she carried an important cargo from Egypt to Malta and back – Field Marshal Lord Kitchener, by then returned from India.

Later in 1912, *Hampshire* was transferred to the China Station. Most of the crew on board in June 1916 had joined her in Colombo in January 1914, when *Hampshire*'s home base was the port of Weihaiwei in north-east China. By the time *Hampshire* received Churchill's dramatic message in August 1914, she was at sea. The risk of war breaking out had been obvious for some weeks, and HMS *Hampshire* had headed out into the Pacific to attack German communications networks. While on this mission, she sank her first ship – the German collier SS *Elspeth* – and then had to divert to Hong Kong to recoal.

In Germany, plans were immediately accelerated to counter

Britain's naval dominance, and the Kaiserliche Marine – the Imperial German Navy – finalised arrangements to develop a new ocean-going minelaying submarine. While these German plans were being made, in late 1914, *Hampshire* took part in efforts in the South China Sea to find and sink the German surface raiders *Emden* and *Königsberg*. After this mission, she escorted troop ships taking Australian soldiers to Egypt. She then returned to Devonport in January 1915, and from there joined Jellicoe's Grand Fleet at Scapa Flow on 14 February 1915.

In the year before her mission to take Kitchener to Russia, HMS *Hampshire* spent much time on anti-submarine patrols off Scotland. On 1 July 1915, while in the Moray Firth, she had a narrow escape when a torpedo fired at her by the German submarine *U-25* failed to explode. In November, she escorted shipping into the White Sea. And then, after a refit in Birkenhead, she docked in Belfast from 10 January to 16 February 1916 for the resiting of her 6-inch guns.

*   *   *

Late January 1916. Belfast docks. 1.45 p.m. HMS *Hampshire*, a four-funnelled Devonshire-class armoured cruiser, is in for one month of work. Her six 6-inch guns are to be relocated from her main deck to her upper deck. The aim is to improve seaworthiness.

There have recently been some incidents of Sinn Féin nationalists trying to do damage to ships in the docks, so the area is patrolled by armed guards. The sentry on *Hampshire*'s main deck, midships, is patrolling on the starboard side of the ship in the small magazine room, which stores shells for the lighter guns on board. All seems to be in order until the sentry spots something on the floor – some debris, which appears to have been left by a workman. Looking more closely, he sees something else underneath the debris – and, moving closer, he realises with alarm that it is a shell, with its top unscrewed. He leaves the shell untouched and rushes to sound the alarm.

The captain of *Hampshire*, Herbert Savill, immediately calls on the military officer commanding the Belfast Shipyard and Harbour, Major Leathes, to hold an urgent investigation. The culprit is soon identified – he is a former artilleryman who is now working in the shipyard. He admits to the offence. His story is simple: he noticed a fresh batch of shells with a new kind of nose. Out of curiosity, and assuming he could replace the shell before anyone saw him, he unscrewed the fuse. He then heard the sentry coming and panicked, leaving the shell on the floor covered with some debris.

Two detectives come to the ship, with the military officer commanding the shipyard and one of his senior officers. After holding the inquiry, they leave together by car. The workman is cautioned, but otherwise it is a storm in a teacup. But the eagle eyes and ears of others on board *Hampshire* are alert to the incident, and to the unusual comings and goings, including of the two detectives. By the following day, the minor incident has taken on a life of its own. Stories are circulating in the docks that that the sentry had tripped on a small wire on the upper deck. He had followed the wire from the deck inside the ship and from there into the magazine itself, where he found that the wire was attached to a bomb. The wiring from the bomb also connected to an electric light which, if switched on, would blow the ship to smithereens.

There was some further embellishment of the story: two men in British officers' uniforms had been arrested and taken from the ship by two detectives, in a car. The car had travelled to Victoria Barracks in Belfast, where the two bogus officers – no doubt German spies – were shot dead the next morning. In no time, the newspapers were onto the story too, but the wartime censors ensured nothing was printed. It didn't seem like much at the time. But the stories of the 'spies on board *Hampshire*' would echo beyond those January days.

Spy stories notwithstanding, HMS *Hampshire* was, in 1916, a happy ship with a well-regarded captain, Herbert John Savill. *Hampshire* was lightly armoured, and although her guns did not have the range or scale of those on the new dreadnoughts, she possessed one distinct asset: a huge amount of space to store coal. Indeed, she could comfortably take on board 1,600 tons of fuel. This made *Hampshire* an ideal vessel for long-range missions. It also helped seal her fate.

Hampshire's usual peacetime crew had been increased to match the needs of wartime, with just over 700 men on board, many of them very young. The average age of the crew was just twenty-five. Seventy-four were under the age of eighteen. Many of these were as young as sixteen, and some were likely to have been even younger than this: it was common for teenage boys to declare bogus dates of birth in order to join up early. These were still years of empire for Britain and there was a strong sense of patriotism. In May 1916, *Hampshire*'s crew included many men whose very names were an echo of Britain's recent military history. There was Stoker 1st Class Nelson Amey, aged nineteen. There was Private George Inkerman Butler, aged thirty-nine. Butler served alongside Horatio Nelson Cooke, a plumber, aged thirty-seven. And there was Boy 1st Class George Mafeking Evans, aged just sixteen, and no doubt named in commemoration of the relief of that famous South African town on or close to his date of birth.

Already, the war had touched the families of many of those on board. Ordinary Seaman Charles Tuck was typical of the tragedies many had experienced. He had volunteered to join up aged just fourteen. He was now eighteen. His brother had already died at Gallipoli. But amongst the sadness of family deaths, there was good news, too. The 31-year-old petty officer Stoker Frederick Waight had just celebrated the birth of a daughter in February 1916. And many young men had – even in wartime – found their first sweethearts at home.

And in May 1916, George Reeve passed his test to qualify as a petty officer – he was now promoted to become Yeoman of Signals for *Hampshire*. He was proud of his achievement – very proud. Perhaps his father, who had thought he was wasting his talent by joining the Royal Navy so young, would finally be proud of him too. But he didn't want to rub it in too much. On 23 May, he wrote to his delighted 'Own Darling Wife', Martha, rejecting her suggestion that he should inform his father: 'No dear I don't want to send word to Dad, I thought that perhaps you would derive a certain amount of pleasure in informing him…' He assured her that he hoped to be home on leave in September.

In May 1916, it seemed to most of the crew of *Hampshire* that they were set fair for a 'good war', out of the way of the killing fields of western France. The Royal Navy still 'ruled the waves', and the German battle fleet was spending most of its time hiding away in port. Most of the crew held two beliefs about the future course of the war: if the German fleet did venture out, it would be soundly defeated. And, whatever happened, *Hampshire* would safely complete her wartime service. On both counts, these convictions would prove flawed.

*   *   *

The Vulcan Shipyard, Hamburg, 1914. For two years, the owners of this warship-building business have been trying to secure a slice of the highly profitable new orders being placed to build up Germany's fleet of U-boat submarines. In the more frugal pre-war days, there were not so many such opportunities, and the yard had not been successful in its 1912 attempt to win orders. The advent of a world war has changed all that. Germany now needs to accelerate its plans to build the U-boats that can take on the British fleet and deny Britain access to raw materials for its war efforts.

Many of the new U-boats are designed, of course, to torpedo Allied shipping. But German naval strategy now places a strong emphasis on the benefits of minelaying. German light cruisers and torpedo boats regularly lay mines and in the first year of the Great War German mines will sink almost 100 vessels. In January 1916, German mines will also claim a major prize with the sinking of the British battleship *King Edward VII* off Cape Wrath.

On 23 November 1914, the order for a total of ten U-boats was placed with Vulcan. And these were the first of many. From then until the end of the war, the yard would build sixty-nine U-boats of varying types. In early 1915, the German Navy decided to place with Vulcan an order for eight UEI-class U-boats. They were to be speedily designed and built, as the German military did not expect the war to last long. And they would also have a special purpose – as ocean-going, minelaying submarines.

The result of the twin desires for speed and minelaying capacity was to be a rather odd-looking new vessel. She would have a surface displacement of 755 tons and a length of around 60 metres. The submarine was to have a capacity to carry and lay thirty-four UE/150-type moored mines – mines attached to the seabed and so 'fixed' in position. The U-boats were designed and built quickly, with many compromises along the way. For this reason, they weren't popular with their crews, but they had good depth-keeping stability.

They were designed to have a speed of almost 11 knots on the surface and 8 knots when submerged. The U-boats' maximum operating depth would be just 50 metres, and each would have a small crew of thirty-two men. Single external torpedo tubes had to be fitted because there was no room for internal tubes.

These new U-boats were built during 1915 and were available to deploy in early 1916. One such vessel was *U-75*. She came into service on 26 March 1916 and was allocated as her captain a young commander, 31-year-old Kapitänleutnant Curt Beitzen. Beitzen was born in 1885 and had served in the German Navy since 1904, starting his war service in the battleship SMS *Thüringen*. Beitzen then commenced his submarine training in June 1915. *U-75* was to be his first command.

Beitzen was keen to demonstrate the military value of his vessel. He would not have long to wait. In May 1916, the German Navy started to plan for a major engagement: to take on and defeat the mighty Royal Navy. The aim was to tempt the British ships out of their bases, using a provocation by a part of the German fleet. The British fleet would then be led into a trap. If successful, the battle could tip the balance of naval dominance away from Britain, and help Germany to win the war.

As part of the secret German planning for this battle, the mine-laying submarines *U-72*, *U-74* and *U-75* were to head secretly for British waters and lay mines off the Scottish coast, in known shipping lanes. Other German submarines were to position themselves close to British naval bases, ready to sink British warships as they were deployed to meet the German threat.

At Scapa Flow on the Orkney Islands, unknown to his German opponents, British Commander in Chief Admiral Jellicoe was preparing his own plans to entrap and then destroy the German fleet.

Jellicoe was assembling a formidable force of battleships, cruisers and destroyers to take on the Germans in what would be the biggest naval battle of the war – and one of the greatest of all time.

While these two mighty navies made their separate plans to trick and then destroy each other, other crucial war planning was being undertaken. In London and Petrograd, the final preparations were being made for a secret mission of top British ministers and officials to Russia, to help keep Britain's formidable but battered ally in the war. At all costs, they must avoid the Russian Army being destroyed, which would allow the Germans to redeploy their land armies to the Western Front, overrunning the French and British armies and winning the war. At sea and on land, the stakes could hardly be higher.

And as the British and German military commanders finalised their respective plans, the fates of *U-75* and of HMS *Hampshire* were gradually being bound inextricably together.

THE WAR MINISTER

'It is repugnant to me to have to reveal military secrets to twenty-three gentlemen with whom I am barely acquainted ... They would all tell their wives – except Lloyd George, who would tell other people's wives.'

LORD KITCHENER TO FIELD MARSHAL DOUGLAS HAIG,
NOVEMBER 1915

Dover. Monday 3 August 1914. 11.45 a.m. On board a cross-channel steamship.

Ronald Storrs, Kitchener's Oriental Secretary, was due to meet his boss on the one o'clock steamer sailing for France. This would mark the beginning of their journey back to Egypt. Kitchener had been in England on a six-week break. Eventually, Storrs found Kitchener: not in his cabin, but pacing the ship's deck and in a state of some agitation. The boat train from London was late and the captain of the steamer was determined to delay his departure until it had arrived. Kitchener had other ideas: he was ordering that the ship should sail immediately. In Europe, the war clouds were gathering, and he was keen to get back to Egypt before conflict broke out.

Kitchener's aides, Fitzgerald and Cecil, were trying their best to persuade the captain to obey the Field Marshal's order. But they were interrupted by an urgent phone call from London. The caller relayed a message from none other than the Liberal Prime Minister, Herbert Asquith. Kitchener was on no account to leave the country. He was to return immediately to London.

Storrs would never forget the look of shock and horror on his boss's face. Kitchener and his aides returned in gloom to the capital. In the slow-moving train, on a painfully long journey, no one dared speak as Kitchener stared glumly out of the windows. Kitchener knew that a job in the War Office beckoned. But which job? And would he be forced to account directly to a political boss, in Cabinet? The idea horrified him. He was not, as a rule, fond of politicians. These personal concerns weighed heavily with Kitchener. But there was something more than this: he knew that Britain was about to engage in the most dangerous and destructive conflict in its history. Leading our forces at this time would be the greatest responsibility of his life. Hopes for a quiet end-of-career stint in Egypt, or even as Viceroy of India, followed by an extended and peaceful retirement, would have to be put on hold.

The conflict that was to shatter Europe and change the course of twentieth-century history commenced the very next day, 4 August. This was no surprise to Kitchener. Since his arrival from Egypt on 23 June, everything he had heard and read had told him that war could not now be avoided. On Monday 29 June, he read in the morning newspapers of the assassination of Archduke Franz Ferdinand, heir to the throne of Austria-Hungary. He told his companions, 'This will mean war.' On 30 July, Kitchener was advising those of his friends who were in Germany to return to the UK as soon as possible. By 3 August, Germany had declared war on Russia and France.

Germany's secret war plans involved an attack through Belgium, whose neutrality was guaranteed by Britain in a treaty dating back to 1839. Britain was just days from war. Kitchener now made arrangements to return early to Cairo, and he drafted a proclamation to be issued in Egypt should war break out before he arrived. He planned to set off through France to Marseille, then travel by cruiser to Egypt. He spent the weekend of 1/2 August at his country house, Broome Park, in Kent.

But as Kitchener made his arrangements to return to Egypt, an alternative plan was being hatched to keep him in England. On 28 July, Kitchener had lunched with Winston Churchill, by now First Lord of the Admiralty, and with Prime Minister Asquith. Churchill was impressed by Kitchener's grasp of the likely nature of a German attack on France. After the lunch, he made the case to Asquith that his old adversary should be considered for the post of Secretary of State for War. There was a political motive for Churchill's proposal, too, and one that appealed to Asquith. Both could see the value to the Liberal government of having Kitchener at the War Office. The distinguished Field Marshal was popular with both the public and the Conservative Party. Including him in the Cabinet would undermine Conservative criticisms of an all-Liberal war leadership and bolster general confidence in the war effort by placing at its head Britain's best-known and most popular living soldier.

In the press, there was also support for Kitchener to take over at the War Office. And some newspapers even threatened a national outcry if Britain's 'greatest soldier' were allowed to leave Europe for the relative backwater of Egypt at a time of national crisis. Asquith quickly agreed with Churchill that Kitchener was the obvious, and politically safest, choice to be the new Secretary of State for War. So, on 4 August, not long after German units had crossed the Belgium frontier, Kitchener met the Prime Minister in 10 Downing

Street. Huge crowds had gathered in Whitehall, Trafalgar Square and around Buckingham Palace – they were baying for war, and cheered ministers as they entered No. 10. With the noisy crowds audible from outside, Kitchener now agreed to join the Cabinet as Secretary of State for War. However, there were two conditions: firstly, that he would have no parliamentary duties, and secondly that he could go back to Egypt when the war was over. These were quickly accepted. Inevitably, Kitchener also arranged for Fitzgerald – his close aide and friend – to continue at his side as his military secretary.

This was all, of course, a highly unusual arrangement: Kitchener became the first serving soldier to sit in a British Cabinet since 1660. But these were highly unusual times and Britain was faced with conflict on an unprecedented scale. No one understood this better than Kitchener: he was under no illusions about how long-lasting, destructive and costly the European war would be. It would be no walk in the park in some antiquated backwater of Africa. It would be a fight to the death between enormous modern armies, supplied with the very latest equipment – some of which would be superior to Britain's own military technologies.

Kitchener shocked friends and colleagues by telling them that, contrary to the public expectation of a swift and crushing defeat of Germany by Christmas, the war would last at least three years. He had long feared a war against Germany and held a high opinion of the effectiveness of its forces. A couple of years before war broke out, he had told David Lloyd George, then Chancellor of the Exchequer, that the Germans would rapidly sweep away the French Army and 'walk through them like partridges'.

Kitchener had also learnt from the experiences of South Africa, where expectations of swift and crushing victory had soon turned into a three-year slog to a negotiated peace. This new war would be no Omdurman. Kitchener knew it would be necessary to mobilise the full might of the British Empire – and that this would take time.

The Royal Navy was already vast in size and well prepared for war. Over the last decade, Britain had been in a naval race with Germany to build more big battleships – dreadnoughts. It was a race that Britain had easily won. But if the Royal Navy had a clear superiority over the Germans, the balance of power was crushingly reversed when it came to the land forces of these two powers. Kitchener knew that his army was simply far too small to fight the conflict now in prospect. British military planners had focused their efforts on delivering Britain's modest pre-war commitment to support the French, by deploying just six infantry and one cavalry division on the Continent. This might help halt a German advance, but it was hardly proportionate to the efforts likely to be needed to push the expected seventy-eight German divisions backwards to win the war. Indeed, in 1914, the entire British Army, including reserves, totalled a mere 450,000 men – 110,000 of whom were already serving overseas, in places such as India. The Territorial force, whose members were not committed to service overseas, numbered just 250,000, but Kitchener was highly dubious of its capabilities. With these modest land forces, Britain now needed to fight a war both in Europe and potentially across the globe.

On Thursday 6 August at 10 a.m., Kitchener entered the War Office for the first time as its political leader. He had two hours of introductions to senior staff before he was due at Buckingham Palace to be sworn into His Majesty's Privy Council and receive the Seals of the War Office. His private secretary handed him a pen, to give his signature for the official departmental stamp – but it wouldn't work. The great man sighed: 'What a War Office! Not a scrap of army and not a pen that will write.' Kitchener knew that he had taken on a mammoth task.

If Kitchener had doubts about his army, the nation had no doubts about his leadership. He had wiped away the stain of Gordon's death. He had defeated the Boers in South Africa. He had entrenched British rule in India and in Egypt. His image was one of British resolve and assurance. His formidable personality seemed to be what the country now needed.

But Asquith and his closest colleagues knew they were taking risks. The PM confided to his diary that the appointment of a high-profile, determined and unbending soldier to one of the most important offices in the government was a 'hazardous experiment'. Lloyd George, still Chancellor of the Exchequer, had doubts too. How well would Kitchener fit into a Cabinet of professional politicians? Lloyd George would later write:

> He was sitting in council with men belonging to the profession with which he had wrestled all his life, and for which, in his heart, he had the usual mixture of military contempt and apprehension. His main idea at the Council table was to tell the politicians as little as possible of what was going on and get back to his desk at the War Office as quickly as he could decently escape.

Kitchener now sat around the Cabinet table with the ambitious young officer who in 1898 had delivered him the message warning of the approach of the Dervish Army; an officer whose deployment to Sudan Kitchener had personally tried to block: Winston Churchill, First Lord of the Admiralty. After the victory at Omdurman, Churchill had published a well-regarded account of the 'River War'

– well regarded by all but Kitchener, who was explicitly blamed by Churchill for the 'stern and unpitying spirit' which had led to 'acts of barbarity' by his army, including the slaughter of wounded Dervish troops. It was a serious charge. Nor had Kitchener forgiven Churchill for – in the same book – severely criticising his decision to blow up the Mahdi's tomb, dig up his body, cut off the head and throw the rest of the body into the Nile. Churchill had described this as a 'wicked act'. The two men now needed to work closely together. Could they? In the short term, the answer was yes. The war created an immediate, unifying, common purpose. But would it last?

On 6 August, the government approved a massive increase in the size of the regular army – to 500,000 men. Recruitment posters started to go up around the country from the very next day. Kitchener saw clearly the need for a massive expansion in troop numbers and in munitions production. Within weeks, he had warned the Cabinet of his estimate of the likely length of the war and set out his advice that an army of at least a million men was required, allowing Britain to deploy seventy divisions into the field. Many at the top of government and in the military were shocked – but Kitchener was proved right, and by the war's end 5.7 million men had served in Britain's forces.

With the benefit of hindsight, it now seems obvious that the war would be long-lasting and that there would be a need for troops on a scale that Britain had never deployed before. But Kitchener's views weren't shared by everyone – it was not just the public and the press that dared hope that the war would be 'over by Christmas'. General Sir Henry Wilson, Deputy Chief of Staff to Sir John French, Britain's Commander in France, wrote from the front line that Kitchener's 'ridiculous and preposterous army of twenty-five corps is the laughing stock of every soldier in Europe'. He argued that 'under no circumstances could these mobs take the field for two years ... Then what is the use of them?' Wilson even claimed to think that Kitchener was mad, and joked about his 'shadow armies for shadow campaigns at unknown and distant dates'. But it was Wilson who was badly out of touch with the evolving realities of a world war.

Kitchener's strategic wisdom extended to accurately guessing the likely nature of Germany's war plans. He correctly anticipated the German thrust through Belgium, but failed to persuade the French Commander in Chief, General Joffre. Unable to convince Joffre, Kitchener sought to avert the danger he could see by suggesting that the British Expeditionary Force should be concentrated at Amiens, where it would be less exposed to a German thrust through Belgium. But Sir John French argued strongly for sticking with the existing plan, and Kitchener gave way again – which he would later regret.

In the early stages of the war, Kitchener sought to support and stabilise the British front, rocked by the speed and success of the early German advances into France and Belgium. He also insisted that Sir John French should continue to co-operate closely with the French Army rather than exclusively prioritising the safety of his own force.

Meanwhile, calmly accepting the early setbacks on the Continent, Kitchener started detailed preparations for the recruitment and training of the 'New Army' or 'Kitchener Army', which he planned to put into the field in 1915 and 1916. By then, he hoped Germany's resources would be beginning to diminish. He also decided to keep the New Army separate from the existing Territorial units, which had enlisted only for home defence.

On 15 September 1914, the distinctive recruiting poster drawn by

Alfred Leete, with Kitchener's moustachioed face staring out, appeared on the front cover of the magazine *London Opinion*. Before long, the now iconic poster of the Field Marshal, eyes looking straight ahead, his distinctively stern yet reassuring face glaring directly outwards, was displayed across the land. There were different versions, but a common theme. The first finger of the right hand pointed straight out at the observer: 'Your Country needs YOU'. It did, and they came forward. Nothing like it had been seen before. The Kitchener factor was delivering. But Kitchener, always a strong royalist, personally intervened to ensure that later versions of the poster included the addition of 'God Save the King'. He had no wish to get beyond himself.

The first recruitment target was for an extra 100,000 men. This was achieved in a month, and the men were quickly formed into six new divisions. But it was only the start. It helped that Kitchener's military reputation was so high, and that he was seen as a soldier and not as a politician. Britain's armies still relied upon voluntary enlistment – and this was a fundamental principle for many of the country's most senior politicians. During this great national emergency, Kitchener called for volunteers to fight – and three million eventually answered his call.

The new recruits soon received a personal message from the stern but respected Kitchener, which he urged should be kept in their pay books. This put a high priority on the standards of personal behaviour and restraint for which the Field Marshal was himself so well known. It also included the perhaps optimistic guidance that 'in this new experience, you may find temptations both in wine and women. You must entirely resist both,' but ended in stirring terms: 'Do your duty bravely. Fear God. Honour the King.'

The British Army needed not just extra men but rifles, machine guns, grenades, artillery, bullets, shells, planes, ships, medical equipment, uniforms and vast supplies of food and drink. The planning to secure these resources would be on a scale never previously faced by any British government. Kitchener immediately set about putting the required measures in place. His predictions for the war's longevity were soon borne out by developments both on the Western Front and in the east, where Germany was now fighting Russia.

After a brief war of movement, the two huge opposing armies dug in on the Western Front and sought ways to break the stalemate that the new weapons of war – machine guns and barbed wire – seemed to have delivered. On the Eastern Front there was far more movement of forces, but it was soon clear that neither army would achieve a speedy knockout blow.

In the west, the last major German attempt to advance on Ypres was made on 17 November 1914 – after that, bolstered by the arrival of winter, the Western Front stagnated into four years of trench warfare, disturbed by the occasional major engagement in which, for the expenditure of hundreds of thousands of lives, small advances of a few miles would be made. This prospect deeply disturbed Kitchener, who was the first to see the risks of prolonged and expensive stalemate.

The inertia in the 'fortress' west soon led to consideration of whether British and Allied forces should attack the Central Powers at a weaker point, perhaps in the east. Turkey's entry into the war in November 1914 marked the beginning of a long-running debate in government as to the extent to which British forces should be deployed in the eastern Mediterranean. Churchill favoured offensive operations against Turkey, which he argued would bring other Balkan nations into the conflict on the Allied side and enable a military thrust into the more weakly defended southern flank of the Central Powers.

By November 1914, Churchill had initiated a debate in the War Cabinet over a possible British landing on the Gallipoli Peninsula, with the British fleet sailing through the Dardanelles to dictate terms to the Turks in Constantinople. Churchill was not the only senior minister who was looking to other fronts than France to break down Germany and her allies. On 1 January 1915, David Lloyd George circulated a detailed memorandum to the War Council pointing to the stalemate on the Western Front and making the case for interventions in the east. Lloyd George argued for transferring troops from the west to the east – specifically to the Balkans, to attack Austria-Hungary and Turkey, preferably in alliance with Serbia, Romania and Greece. Kitchener opposed this plan without support from Italy.

Kitchener actually felt conflicted. He could not see any immediate prospect of a breakthrough in France or Belgium and he was a supporter of some action in the east, not least to ease pressure on Russia. But at this stage he did not see that he had adequate infantry resources to successfully execute an attack on Turkey. If anything, he preferred a landing in Syria, to cut Turkish lines of communication. He was, in part, thinking of the best way of protecting his precious Egypt. To achieve anything of value in the Dardanelles, he judged that he would need a force of 150,000 men – resources he considered it too risky to release from France.

Meanwhile, the pressure on Russia was rising – Germany was transferring forces from the Western to the Eastern Front, and the Turks were pressing hard in the Caucasus. The Russian government begged the UK and other Allied governments for action. On 2 January 1915, Kitchener received a letter from Grand Duke Nicholas himself, calling for a diversionary attack to relieve Turkish pressure. On the very same day, Kitchener wrote to Sir John French, the British Commander in France, noting that the German lines in France looked like a 'fortress that cannot be carried by assault'. Kitchener asked French for his views on alternative theatres in which Allied attacks might be made.

Kitchener and the British government felt a duty to help their largest ally – after all, Russian troops had invaded East Prussia early in the war, to try to ease the pressure on the French and British after the initial, disastrous retreat from Mons. The British War Council met on 7 and 8 January to consider the options. Kitchener was particularly worried that the stalemate in the west might allow the Germans to shift more of their best troops east, to knock Russia out of the war. He understood that Russia, with its huge land and human resources, was a key part of the Allied strategy to wear down Germany and win the war.

The view that Churchill, and to a less extreme extent Kitchener, held about the need for military action in the east was not a strategy remotely supported by Sir John French, who saw any diversion of resources from the 'main' front in France as a risky distraction. Inevitably, France's General Joffre took the same view.

From the beginning of the war, there had been tension between Kitchener and Sir John over military strategy. Kitchener thought little of French's abilities, and French saw Kitchener as an unhelpful presence, second-guessing his leadership in the field. In November 1914, Kitchener had unwisely shared with General Joffre his thinking that he might replace Sir John French with another commander. Joffre felt he had the measure of Sir John and did not wish to see him removed for an unknown quantity. So he arranged to leak the information to Sir John as a warning. This helped abort Kitchener's plans and for ever soured relations between Britain's two most senior military leaders.

Kitchener was keen, then, to assist Russia, but he could not see how. Kitchener's military advisers and his generals in France were insistent that no troops could be spared to help in the Dardanelles: they joked that the Germans would gladly furnish transport vessels to carry British troops away from the front line in France to the 'backwaters' of the 'Near East'. Kitchener gave Sir John French assurances that France remained the priority.

The idea of a demonstration by the navy at the Dardanelles now arose. Churchill had initially been sceptical that this would be effective without the deployment of Allied troops. Instead, the First Lord of the Admiralty had pursued his own plan to distract the Germans by occupying one of their islands off the North Sea coast. This eccentric idea had little Cabinet support.

Churchill now warmed to the idea of a naval-only strategy to bombard the Dardanelles and break through to Constantinople. The plan had been considered by Admiralty staff on previous occasions and rejected. But the War Council felt under pressure to 'do something'. On 13 January, its members agreed to a proposal advocated by Churchill for naval action to bombard the Gallipoli Peninsula, with Constantinople the end objective. It was certainly bold. At its most optimistic, and if regional allies joined the fight, it could help knock Turkey out of the war and strengthen the supply lines to Britain's Russian ally. But was it remotely likely to succeed without the commitment of huge numbers of ground troops? Many in the Cabinet and in the senior ranks of the British military were dubious. Even if British battleships could break through the straits under the guns of Turkish forts, how could they take Constantinople by themselves? And would the straits be closed again after the ships had sailed through, locking up significant naval assets? If the Greeks were able to send land forces, that might help. But in the absence of this, any operation would hold great risks.

For Kitchener, Churchill's plan had two clear attractions: first, it meant we could 'do something' in the east to help Russia. But it also meant that there would be no need to redeploy troops from the west – not, in any case, until the Russian spring offensive and the arrival of the first of the New Armies had reduced the pressure in France. Kitchener, therefore, signed up to Churchill's navy-only plan. It was a strategy that promised massive returns from limited investment. If this all seems too good to be true, that is because it was.

Kitchener felt deeply conflicted between the western and eastern strategies. He well understood the need to relieve pressure on Russia, as well as diverting Turkish troops away from a possible attack on his beloved Egypt. And Russia was now also proposing to deploy an army corps to take part in the assault on the Turkish capital. Kitchener also thought Sir John French too optimistic about the chances of a breakthrough in the west, and too parochial in his focus on the Western Front.

But Kitchener doubted that large numbers of British troops could be safely diverted away from France, fearing in part that Russia's increasingly fragile military position might free up German divisions for a breakthrough in the west. Quite simply, until the New Armies could be deployed, the British Army wasn't big enough for major military operations on two fronts.

Kitchener appreciated the difficulty of breaking through in the west, but he saw this as the main theatre which would decide the war. For Kitchener, 'eastern enterprises' were always subsidiary in priority: they could help relieve pressure on Russia and protect our interests in the Near East, but not much more. For Churchill and Lloyd George, however, the British forces deployed on the Western

Front were too many, and the prospect of a major breakthrough in the east was much greater – and they believed this could help bring an earlier end to the war. With Churchill and Lloyd George arguing for the east to be given priority, and Sir John French and his generals arguing for the west, Kitchener was caught in the middle. He was neither a 'westerner' nor an 'easterner'. He had good reasons for trying to straddle the fence. But this was not always an easy position to maintain.

Churchill then successfully pressed his scheme on the War Council. The First Sea Lord, Lord Fisher, and other senior naval staff were dubious but did not speak out. Instead, Fisher waited until the initial naval bombardment had begun, and then wrote privately to Lloyd George, warning bluntly that 'Rashness in War is Prudence, and Prudence in War is Criminal. The Dardanelles futile without soldiers!'

Lloyd George continued to lobby for his own scheme of landing troops at Salonika, but Kitchener was less keen on this plan as it would clearly require significant ground troops. No sooner had the scheme for a naval-only action in the Dardanelles been signed off than Kitchener found himself under pressure to send troops to both the Dardanelles and Salonika. He blocked attempts to send the 29th Division – the last regular division, which was being trained in England. Kitchener was being heavily lobbied by Sir John French to release this division to serve on the Western Front, and in February 1915 the British government had received a remarkable message from General Joffre, Commander of Allied Armies in France, arguing that without the back-up of this division he could not guarantee the safety of Allied lines in France. The battle for influence between the westerners and easterners was now in full flow. Kitchener was caught in the cross-fire.

On 19 February 1915, the War Council met and discussed whether troops could be sent east to support operations in the Dardanelles or Salonika. Kitchener warned that the situation in Russia had 'greatly deteriorated in the last week or two'. If the Germans could inflict a decisive defeat on their eastern foe, they might 'bring back great masses of troops very rapidly to France'.

The preliminary naval bombardments in the Dardanelles Strait started that same day, with the main attack by British battleships taking place on 18 March. At the end of this latter day of intense bombardment, three major Allied warships – one French and two British – were destroyed and three more were seriously damaged. The navy made clear that they could not succeed without troops: their plan to break through without ground forces was exposed as fundamentally flawed.

Kitchener was now drawn in to supporting Churchill's disastrous Gallipoli campaign of 1915–16, which tied down large Allied forces for minimal gain. 'You get through. I will find the men,' he assured the First Lord of the Admiralty. He did, and the Gallipoli campaign eventually cost the Allies 250,000 casualties. It was the biggest mistake of Kitchener's long career.

In March 1915, Sir Ian Hamilton was appointed as Commander of Military Forces in the Dardanelles. He and Kitchener knew each other well: he had been Kitchener's Chief of Staff in South Africa in 1901–02. The 29th Division was now also sent east. They were joined by the Royal Naval Division, the Anzac Corps and a French division. What started as a naval engagement, with the bombardment of Turkish guns and forts, now became a major landing of British and other Allied troops. On 25 April, the assault on the Gallipoli Peninsula began; around 30,000 men landed on the first day alone. But within weeks it was clear that the breakthrough had not been achieved and Hamilton was requesting yet more troops and ammunition.

The troops were too late and – initially at least – arrived in insufficient quantities. By now, the Turks had seen the danger and responded. Hamilton's attacking force grew to 75,000 men but faced 84,000 Turkish defenders. Allied planning was also poor: when Hamilton had left for his new command in mid-March, none of his administrative staff were available. Worse still, the sum total of intelligence information made available to him comprised a 1912 handbook about the Turkish Army, a pre-war drawing of the Dardanelles forts and an inaccurate local map.

Back in London, Kitchener was now dealing not just with concerns over the Gallipoli campaign but with a growing outcry about alleged shell shortages on the Western Front. In some parts of the press and Parliament, there were now mutterings that Kitchener needed replacing. He had, of course, rightly planned for a long war and for a significant increase in the output of equipment and ammunition. But from pre-war output, the rise in demand was almost exponential.

During the three-year Boer War, around 273,000 rounds of artillery shells were fired by the British forces. During merely the first six months of the Great War, the comparable figure was one million rounds. The figures for 18-pounder shells are even more striking. In the pre-war period, 3,000 such shells were produced each month. By January 1915, this figure had climbed to 93,000 and by May 1915 to 400,000. By October 1915, the total produced had climbed to over one million shells.

It was not just shell production that needed to be increased dramatically. Before the war, both Britain and Germany had deployed around two machine guns per thousand men. But the worth of these modern weapons was soon obvious, and an immense increase in demand followed. German factories immediately responded to the challenge. Kitchener, meanwhile, ensured that British manufacturers were asked to produce to their capacity. As this was limited, additional large contracts were placed in America. Kitchener also struck a deal with the US Bethlehem Steel Corporation in October 1914 to produce a million complete rounds of field gun ammunition within a year. And US orders were placed for two million rifles, which were due to start arriving in July 1915. But it was May 1916 before any were delivered.

The truth was that this 'Great War' was consuming arms and ammunition in quantities that would previously have been regarded as unthinkable. Kitchener and the War Office had actually responded rather well to the rising demands for equipment and troops. But the war was now over a year old and initial hopes of a quick victory had been dashed. It was inevitable that in all countries people would look around for someone to blame, and some weakness to focus on.

There was a shortage of labour and both in the UK and overseas there were many orders that were not being delivered on time. Kitchener had bluntly admitted as much in March 1915 in the House of Lords. The internal rows in government over munitions supply rumbled on throughout early 1915, pitching Lloyd George, the emotional, energetic and impatient Chancellor of the Exchequer, against Kitchener, the measured, calm and secretive War Minister. The two men could hardly have had more different characters. Lloyd George respected Kitchener but found his unwillingness to share information frustrating: 'the curious mixture of sagacity and opacity that constituted the make-up of this extraordinary man', as Lloyd George would later describe it.

Asquith now tried desperately to avoid the tensions between these two senior ministers leading to the resignation of either. He knew that both were essential to the stability of, and confidence in, his government. On 8 April, he announced that a new Munitions Committee would be established under Lloyd George's chairmanship. Lloyd George's initial delight faded when he realised that the committee would still be wholly dependent on Kitchener's War Office for all its technical information. Getting information from Kitchener was rarely a straightforward process. At a Cabinet meeting on 19 April, Kitchener and Lloyd George clashed head on, the War Minister sharply criticising Lloyd George for telling the Munitions Committee the number of soldiers sent out to France that month. The row that followed included a threat of resignation from Kitchener and the lecturing of his Cabinet colleagues over their alleged security failings. The implication that Cabinet ministers could not be trusted to keep secrets was hardly likely to build bridges between Kitchener and other senior members of the government.

Kitchener was also under pressure from his commander in France, the aptly named Sir John French. French was planning an offensive aimed at breaking through the German front in northern France on 9 May. Kitchener was sceptical. But, pressured by Sir John French and General Joffre, and with the Russians desperate for some sort of diversion, he now approved the plan.

The British objective in the flat and poorly drained terrain was the Aubers Ridge, an area of slightly higher ground. Unfortunately, the fortifications opposite the British lines had been well augmented before the attack, and the offensive was an unmitigated disaster. No ground was won and no advantage gained. British casualties on the first day alone were 11,600 men, and by the battle's end this figure had climbed to 32,000, on top of perhaps 102,000 French dead and wounded.

While it was bad planning, bad tactics and poor leadership that were largely responsible for the losses, Sir John French decided to shift the focus of criticism onto ammunition shortages and to blame his boss, Kitchener. French, seriously worried about his own position if he had to accept the blame, sent his military secretary on a mission to London to give opposition leaders and other influential MPs secret information on the supply of shells. It was a dangerous tactic. French's staff placed before Bonar Law, the Conservative leader, and David Lloyd George, Asquith's colleague and rival, a carefully selected correspondence about alleged shell shortages designed to exonerate Sir John French and shift the blame to the War Office and Kitchener. This was all leaked to *The Times* and appeared under the byline of Colonel Repington, a media ally of Sir John's.

French now joined with Lloyd George and the press baron Lord Northcliffe in trying to get Kitchener removed from the War Office. Northcliffe even wrote to French with advice on how to damage Kitchener: 'A short and very vigorous statement from you to a private correspondent (the usual way of making things public in England) would, I believe, render the Government's position impossible...'

What Sir John and his staff chose not to leak was the cable he sent to Kitchener before the battle, claiming that his ammunition supplies were 'adequate'. Kitchener was dubious about the 'shells shortage' excuses, noting that Joffre and the French Army had almost unlimited supplies of shells and huge reserves but still could not effect a breakthrough. But Northcliffe's papers, *The Times* and the *Daily Mail*, now kept up their own assault on Kitchener over the issue. However, on 21 May 1915, the *Daily Mail* overreached itself, with headlines about 'Lord Kitchener's Tragic Blunder' and a call for his resignation. There was a significant public backlash, and copies of both Northcliffe newspapers were burnt on the floor of the London Stock Exchange.

It was not just Kitchener but the government itself that was now being rocked by the failures in the Dardanelles and France, and by the press campaigns over shell shortages. The inability of the navy to break through in the Dardanelles had particularly damaged Churchill, and led to mutterings in Parliament about his judgement. When Lord Fisher, the increasingly volatile and unstable First Sea Lord, resigned his post over the Dardanelles adventure in mid-May, blaming Churchill for the failures, Asquith felt obliged to form a coalition government with the Conservatives – and drop Churchill from the Admiralty.

The reconstruction of Asquith's government was successfully achieved, but it did nothing to improve the situation on the front lines. It did, however, weaken the advocates of an eastern strategy, by removing Churchill and restricting Kitchener's authority, with the establishment of a new Munitions Ministry under Lloyd George. For the first time in his career, Kitchener's wings had been clipped. But he accepted his loss of control over munitions supply. He had much else to occupy him. He remained deeply concerned by a German breakthrough against the Russians. Did this argue for retaining forces in France, he wondered, or for doubling up in the Dardanelles? The Russian Grand Duke was clear: he wanted more British troops sent to Gallipoli. But although the British government was sending significant reinforcements to the east in July 1915, Turkish strength in the region had also increased markedly, to fifteen divisions. Worse still, the promised Russian corps had to be diverted to help hold up General Hindenburg's new German offensive against the Tsar's forces.

In early 1915, the British had looked east to avoid a costly stalemate on the Western Front. Now, after the eastern strategy had been implemented, the costly stalemate in the west was merely complemented by a similarly costly stalemate in the east. On 18 July 1915, Kitchener noted in a memorandum to General William Robertson, Chief of Staff of the British Expeditionary Force: 'Joffre and Sir John told me in November [1914] that they were going to push the Germans back over the frontier; they gave me the same assurances in December, March and May. What have they done? The attacks are very costly and end in nothing.' Now, he was beginning to have the same fears about the Dardanelles.

When, in August, Hamilton sent a request for an additional 95,000 troops, both Kitchener and the Cabinet had had enough: they declined the request and decided that an Allied attack in France would be the best way to relieve pressure on Russia. The Russians, meanwhile, were retreating in disorder, Warsaw had fallen to the Germans, and in Petrograd there was even talk of revolution. Kitchener was concerned that Russia might be forced to make peace with Germany. Against this bleak background, he now gave his permission for a British attack at Loos in September 1915. This may have honoured a private assurance that Kitchener had given to Joffre in early July, when the British minister wanted French support for the action in the Dardanelles. Again, it was not a strategy that he judged would lead to a successful Allied breakthrough. In both the west and the east, Kitchener was now supporting military actions he did not believe could succeed but which he felt were better than doing nothing.

The Battle of Loos commenced on 25 September. It was the biggest British attack of that year, and the first time the British had used poison gas. It also saw the first large-scale use of the New Armies – before Kitchener had really wanted these deployed. The

British and French tried to break through German defences in Artois and Champagne. But it was another total failure. British forces sustained almost 60,000 casualties in the two short weeks of battle – over twice the German losses of around 26,000. It was now the end of the line for Sir John French – a disaster too far. His replacement was only a matter of time.

As well as the continuing failures in France, thousands of lives were now being expended in Gallipoli for little obvious gain. Kitchener had had a good start to the war. Unlike many politicians and other senior officers, he had correctly predicted the conflict's longevity. He was the poster boy – quite literally – for recruiting extra men to form the New Armies. He put in place the early orders for new guns and ammunition. He was cautious about overcommitting Britain's small army to France, and rightly anticipated the likely direction and force of the German attack. He recognised – again, earlier than most – the risk that the war would get bogged down in a battle of attrition on the Western Front. Therefore, he saw the key importance of considering other theatres of conflict, not least to help keep Russia in the war.

But by late 1915, the tide was flowing against Britain's favourite military leader. In part, this was simply a reflection of the fact that Kitchener was leader of the war effort, and the war effort was not delivering the hoped-for results. The same pressures were facing war leaders in every country. In all his career to date, Kitchener had been lucky, or skilled, enough to be the right man in the right place at the right time. But Kitchener's luck had run out. He was now in the wrong place at the wrong time – still at the helm after a full year of war, with the problems and failings all too visible and with victory a long way off.

But there was something more to Kitchener's declining influence than the problems of war strategy: a failure of personality. When things were going well, Kitchener's distant and haughty character seemed not to matter. Indeed, it protected him from scrutiny. And in the military, the tradition was for senior officers to manage through orders and instruction, rather than debate.

But Kitchener was no longer in an exclusively military role. When he joined the Cabinet in August 1914, he became a member of the British government – a government whose members expected to be kept informed about, debate and decide on major issues. Whether he would admit it or not, Kitchener had now transitioned from the military to the political world. He needed to persuade Cabinet colleagues. He needed to cajole and explain. He needed to address criticisms head on. He was wholly unequipped for all these tasks. He found debate and consultation with mere politicians distasteful. And as the war became more difficult, these politicians wanted more consultation, not less. Kitchener's relations with senior Cabinet colleagues now deteriorated rapidly.

With Churchill, his relations had been on shaky ground since he sought to veto the young man's attempts to join his 'adventure' in Sudan. But with Churchill's political career now in tatters over the Dardanelles, the former First Lord of the Admiralty was looking for someone else to shift the blame to – with Kitchener heading the list. Relations with David Lloyd George were also increasingly strained. The personalities could hardly be more different: Lloyd George open, warm, garrulous, emotional; Kitchener closed, cool, taciturn and stern. In his war memoirs, Lloyd George compared Kitchener to 'one of those revolving lighthouses which radiate momentary gleams of revealing light far out into the surrounding gloom and then suddenly relapse into complete darkness'. The longer the war went on, the less acceptable these qualities became.

Kitchener would often duck questions in Cabinet and refuse to discuss military plans with his senior colleagues. He may have had some good reasons for keeping military secrets close to his chest; the Cabinet could be remarkably leaky. In late 1915, Kitchener told Field Marshal Haig, 'It is repugnant to me to have to reveal military secrets to twenty-three gentlemen with whom I am barely acquainted ... They would all tell their wives – except Lloyd George, who would tell other people's wives.' His Cabinet colleagues could hardly, however, be expected to share his lack of confidence in their discretion.

On other occasions, ministers wondered if Kitchener's unwillingness to discuss the details of military developments was designed to mask the struggles of an ageing man trying unsuccessfully to juggle too many responsibilities. When the War Council met on 8 October 1915, Kitchener seemed unaware that the armies of the Central Powers had invaded Serbia the previous day – even though the War Office had received a telegram telling them of this. Lloyd George, in particular, was appalled and angered by this apparent loss of focus. Others were too, Sir Edward Carson passing a piece of paper to Lloyd George at the Cabinet meeting on which he had scrawled: 'K does not read the telegrams – and we don't see them – it is intolerable.'

The public still adored him. The press still respected him. But in the corridors of No. 10, in the lobbies in Parliament and in the War Office, the whispering campaign had begun: 'He has to go.' For the first time in his career, Kitchener, and not his enemies, was truly in the firing line.

By autumn 1915, Asquith's government was in danger of falling due to a row about whether conscription should be introduced. This was a dispute that divided the Cabinet and was, for some senior politicians, a matter of principle, and possibly of resignation. Kitchener continued broadly to favour a voluntary approach. Now, for the first time, it was not only Kitchener in the firing line. The Prime Minister was too. The successive controversies over French defeats, shell scarcities, the Dardanelles and conscription looked as if they might be used to attempt an even bigger change than the removal of the Secretary of State for War. On 17 October, Asquith wrote privately to Kitchener:

> I should like you to know that what is now going on is being engineered by men (Curzon, Lloyd George and some others) whose real object is to oust you. They know well that I will give no countenance to their projects, and consequently they have conceived the idea of using you against me. God knows that we should both of us be glad to be set free. But we cannot and ought not…

Lloyd George now increased his agitation against Kitchener and the direction of the war effort, writing to Asquith in blunt terms on 31 October, and threatening resignation unless the management of the war was improved. To relieve the pressure, in early November 1915, Kitchener was asked by Asquith to travel to the Dardanelles to make his own appraisal of whether the Allied forces should be withdrawn. During Kitchener's absence, Asquith would take over direction of the War Office. Asquith, now under intense pressure from Lloyd George and others, but neither willing nor able to remove Kitchener, explained in a private note to Lloyd George, 'We avoid by this procedure the immediate supersession of K as War Minister, while attaining the same result.'

Just before the end of the Cabinet meeting on 4 November, Kitchener quietly left the table to make final preparations for his visit to the eastern Mediterranean. He nodded discreetly to Asquith as he left. Some thought – or hoped – that he was gone for good.

Lloyd George – confirming some of Kitchener's suspicions about him – recounted the episode to his mistress, Frances Stevenson, who wrote in her diary:

> Not a word spoken! He might have been going out to lunch. He knew as well as anyone that it was for good he was leaving, but not a sign of his countenance or demeanour gave evidence of this ... D [Lloyd George] says he felt a lump in his throat ... Personally, I think it is rather a cowardly thing the PM has done.

But Lloyd George himself felt differently, noting that when the war started Kitchener was 'practically military dictator and his decisions ... were final'. But 'gradually one mistake after another committed by the military ... lowered his prestige and weakened his influence, and there was a general feeling that his usefulness had been exhausted'. Lloyd George was clear, in his war memoirs, about what the Cabinet now hoped for:

> There was a mute hope that once Lord Kitchener went to the Mediterranean, and especially if he returned to Egypt, the sphere of his greatest triumphs, he might find it worthwhile to remain there to direct the great forces accumulated in the western Mediterranean, in Egypt, Gallipoli, and either Salonika or Alexandretta.

As Kitchener left the Cabinet, another of its members pushed a note across to Lloyd George. On it was written, 'Malbrouck s'en va-t-en guerre. But will he return?"

---

* 'Marlborough has left for the war' – the title of a popular French folk song.

Kitchener had been sent on a foreign mission designed to get him out of the country. Many in the Cabinet hoped that he was gone for good. Kitchener himself was well aware of the risks, and was concerned enough about the weakness of his position to take his Seals of Office with him on the journey, hoping this would avoid his being sacked while abroad.

Out in the Mediterranean, he received a warm reception from troops on the front line, which considerably cheered him up. He made a careful assessment of the benefits of fighting on at Gallipoli and the possibilities and risks of evacuation. He also needed to weigh the wider implications of freeing up Turkish troops to attack both the Russians and Egypt. In particular, Kitchener worried that a British defeat in Gallipoli – as an evacuation would certainly be seen – might cause the Arab nations to shift to backing the Germans and Turks, which could be fatal to British interests. It could also threaten the Suez Canal.

By November 1915, Kitchener had nevertheless concluded that an evacuation of the peninsula was inevitable. For the Cabinet, he set out in secret cables the detailed measures that would be necessary to secure the safety of Egypt – as always, a high priority for him. He then insisted on returning to London, rejecting suggestions from the War Committee that he should oversee the evacuation of Gallipoli and from Asquith that he should stay on to address directly his concerns about the security of Egypt. He was not going to be so easily pensioned off.

But on the way home from the east, the manoeuvring was clearly getting to him. Unwanted and undermined, he confided to the British Ambassador in Rome – an old friend – that he might resign. To his friend, he looked exhausted and isolated. By 30 November, Kitchener was back in London. He signed the register at the wedding of Asquith's daughter, and then shortly afterwards – in 10 Downing Street – offered his resignation to her father – conscious of the blow that retreat from Gallipoli implied. Asquith immediately rejected the suggestion and Kitchener returned to the War Office.

Kitchener was still too big a fish to be sacrificed. And perhaps Asquith realised his own position was too weak to survive the departure of the poster boy for the war effort. Astutely, Kitchener told Haig in early 1916, 'Rightly or wrongly, the people believe in me. It is not therefore me that the politicians are afraid of, but what the people would say to them if I were to go.'

But changes at the top were being made elsewhere: Sir John French was relieved of his command in France and replaced by General Sir Douglas Haig. And in January 1916, Asquith negotiated a dilution of Kitchener's powers: he remained as War Minister, but General Sir William Robertson took over as Chief of the Imperial General Staff, with a direct reporting line to the War Committee. Asquith wanted to continue to use Kitchener as a figurehead but to diminish the actual power he exercised. It might all have been enough to prompt Kitchener's departure. But Kitchener was not by nature a quitter. And Robertson respected Kitchener and was determined to make the new arrangement work. Other powerful forces also served to protect him, including King George V, a strong supporter.

The promotions of Haig and Robertson strengthened the hand of the westerners against those on the War Committee who wanted to continue to pursue solutions in the east. From now on, the focus of Allied efforts would be in France and Belgium. Not that this led quickly to any greater success. In February, the French attacked at Verdun; by the end of June, they had incurred over 300,000 casualties.

In April 1916, Kitchener gave his approval to Haig's great offensive plan on the Somme, though he was dubious of its chances of success and would have preferred smaller, attritional, attacks, with a main offensive later in the year or in 1917. It was at this time that Kitchener became a convert to the cause of tank development, after attending secret trials of the new weapon. He gave orders for forty tanks to be constructed and for the training of crews.

By early 1916, the objective set by Kitchener on 6 August 1914 – that Britain should be able to deploy seventy divisions into the field – had been met. It was a stunning success, and a tribute to his early understanding that this war would be quite unlike anything that had gone before. The voluntary system of recruitment had delivered two million men within a year. Now, in January 1916, after intense political debate, a new Act was passed imposing universal service on all men of military age, with some exemptions. But before conscription was legalised, the voluntary approach had yielded three million recruits.

In spite of this achievement, the failures of 1915, which continued into early 1916, meant that criticism of Kitchener's conduct of the war continued to be made from some quarters both in the press and in Parliament. By the middle of 1916, these attacks had reached a new peak, focusing in particular on the lack of ammunition and equipment. On 21 May, Sir Ivor Herbert, a Liberal MP, introduced a motion of censure in the House of Commons. Technically, this proposed that the Secretary of State for War's salary should be cut by £100. It had no binding effect, but was designed to be a vote of no confidence in Kitchener. To lose the vote would mean resignation and quite possibly the end of his career.

The Commons debate took place on 31 May, at almost the exact moment that the greatest naval battle of the war, the Battle of Jutland, was beginning in earnest. Several MPs spoke against Kitchener – most notably, Winston Churchill. But Asquith robustly defended his colleague, who as a non-MP could not speak in the Commons. The Prime Minister might have been tiring of Kitchener and had acted to reduce his influence, but he was determined to be loyal to an important colleague and one whose reputation was still important for the British war effort. Asquith told a packed Commons:

> There is no other man in this country, or in this Empire, who could have summoned into existence in so short a time, with so little friction, with such satisfactory, surprising and even bewildering results, the enormous armies which now at home and abroad are maintaining the honour of the Empire. I am certain that in history it will be regarded as one of the most remarkable achievements that has ever been accomplished; and I am bound to say, and I say in all sincerity, for that achievement Lord Kitchener is personally entitled to the credit.

The vote was decisively in Kitchener's favour. He had survived. But during the debate, to help win the support of wavering MPs, H. J. Tennant, the Under-Secretary of State for War, promised that Kitchener would personally meet MPs on 2 June 1916 to answer questions on the conduct of the war. Kitchener was no great speaker and no diplomat. His critics hoped that he would fall flat on his face and that his performance would raise new doubts about his fitness for office. His supporters crossed their fingers and hoped for the best. Kitchener himself carefully prepared his speech to defend his record and win over MPs.

The meeting was originally planned to take place in the War

Office. But so many MPs wanted to attend that it had to be moved to Parliament itself. Kitchener would no longer be defending himself on home turf. On the morning of 2 June, at around 11.15 a.m., he left the War Office for Parliament. On the pavement, a photographer captured the moment of departure. Kitchener looked grim-faced and nervous. Ten minutes later, he arrived at the Committee Room corridor – the longest corridor in Europe. He headed for Committee Room 15, one of the largest. It was now 11.30 a.m. The room was packed – standing room only. Two hundred MPs had turned up to hear him.

In military uniform, Kitchener addressed the crowded room. He read from a carefully prepared speech, stuffed with detailed statistics, to refute the claims being made against him. He was modest and self-deprecating: 'I feel sure that Members must realise that my previous work in life has not been of a kind to make me a ready debater.' He was also calm, well briefed, detailed and confident.

The speech was a robust defence of his record as Secretary of State for War: the recruitment of the New Armies and the procurement of vast quantities of new equipment. It also addressed head on the criticisms made of him: on the supply of machine guns, artillery and ammunition; on compulsory service; on the number of men employed supporting front-line troops. There were one or two diplomatic, but carefully crafted, digs at Winston Churchill, who was still throwing stones from the sidelines – claiming, for example, that too many of the British troops in France were being wasted in support functions.

When Kitchener finished his wide-ranging speech, he was received with loud and warm applause. There were then questions – which he met with a directness and openness that disarmed his critics. He seemed to many of those present like a new Kitchener

– demonstrating humility and candour, from a man who usually preferred secrecy and evasion.

At the end, there was a vote of thanks, seconded by the very MP who had moved the motion to cut Kitchener's salary just two weeks before. The vote was resoundingly carried. And then it was all over. Kitchener breathed a sigh of relief. It had been a masterly performance, and of such significance that the King himself wrote to Field Marshal Haig in France to pass on news of the unexpected triumph.

The next day, Saturday 3 June, Kitchener spent the morning at the War Office before lunching with the King, who passed on his own congratulations. Kitchener needed to discuss with the King an important mission which would now, once again, take him away from the country for a few weeks. He had continued to devote considerable personal attention to the Eastern Front and to sustaining Russia in the war. With the pressure in Parliament having abated, he now planned to travel to Russia to meet the Tsar.

Having briefed the King on his mission, Kitchener then motored down to his country home, Broome Park in Kent. He spent the day putting the finishing touches to a sunken rose garden. He must have felt both happy and relieved. It was almost two years into the conflict and he was still at the head of the War Office, having seen off his critics. If Russia could be sustained, then eventually the German Army would be worn down, and the New Armies he had created would surely deliver victory – perhaps in late 1917 or early 1918. Meanwhile, the sea voyage to Russia would provide time to relax, away from the day-to-day pressures of the war. And in Russia itself there would be work, but also dinners, a meeting with the Tsar and top military commanders, and all in a country in which Kitchener was still feted as a great military leader and ally.

On Sunday 4 June, he took care of a number of personal matters, including selling some shares in a Canadian munitions firm which had recently been awarded a government contract, and signing some legal papers relating to his property in East Africa, where he was looking forward to spending the winters during his future retirement.

He had a final exchange with Mr Weston, the manager of his Kent home: 'I shall be back in around a month. I'm looking forward to seeing the Rose Garden in full summer bloom.'

THE BATTLE

'Raise steam for Fleet speed, and report when ready to proceed.'
ADMIRAL JELLICOE'S MESSAGE FROM THE BATTLESHIP HMS *IRON DUKE* TO ALL SHIPS OF HIS GRAND FLEET, 30 MAY 1916

Saturday afternoon, 3 June 1916. In Britain, Lord Kitchener is in his country house in Kent, preparing for tomorrow's journey to Scotland – the first stage of his mission to Russia.

But here in Heligoland, the small, and for eighty-three years British-administered, islands to the north-west of the German mainland, a submarine is nearing the islands' German naval base. Her captain scans the horizon with binoculars. They are close to home now, but they aren't taking any chances. Their mission has already been traumatic enough and they know they are lucky to be returning alive.

The crew can see the islands at some distance, with their 70-metre rock cliffs, and now as they come closer, they can also make out the submarine harbour and the defensive guns sited to protect one of Germany's key naval bases. The concrete gun emplacements can be made out, along with some of the 364 mounted guns defending the base – including 142 mighty 17-inch guns, which can be rotated backwards so as to 'disappear' behind a protective parapet.

The submarine makes her way carefully through the defensive minefield with its ten rows of naval mines. From the shore defences, they are watched continuously as they progress towards the submarine harbour. The lookouts can see that the returning submarine is the oddly shaped *U-75*, a specially designed minelaying vessel.

Captain Beitzen and his crew are relieved to be home. They have only been away for ten days, but it seems so much longer. It has been quite a maiden mission. But they have completed it successfully and lived to fight another day.

*   *   *

In May 1916, the naval war in the North Sea was on the verge of entering a new and critical stage. After almost two years of 'phoney war', both naval leaders – Britain's Admiral Jellicoe and Germany's Admiral Scheer – were under pressure to land a decisive blow on their opponents. German planning was slightly more advanced, and in early May, the Kaiser's navy finalised the details of a major engagement to take on and defeat the much larger Royal Navy. As part of the planning for this mission, the minelaying submarines *U-72*, *U-74* and *U-75* were to head secretly for British waters and lay mines off the Scottish coast in known shipping lanes. Other German submarines were to position themselves close to British naval bases, from where ships of Jellicoe's Grand Fleet might be deployed to meet the German threat.

Admiral Scheer had decided to send his battlecruisers to bombard the east coast town of Sunderland, in the sure knowledge that Jellicoe and his deputy, Vice-Admiral Beatty, would be forced to come out and give chase. In Scheer's plan, German submarines, and the mines some had laid, would be lying in wait for Jellicoe and Beatty's forces. After this, the German fleet planned to engage Beatty's battlecruisers, which were based near Edinburgh, at the Firth of Forth. They would draw them into a trap before Jellicoe's Grand Fleet could make its way down from Scapa Flow. Scheer planned to deploy Zeppelin airships to scout ahead of his ships and ensure that they were not, in turn, caught in a British trap. The German hope was that the British losses might be so large as to even up the two opposing navies – giving the smaller German fleet a real chance to break the Royal Navy stranglehold on the seas.

But the British had their own, rather similar plan. Under pressure from the Admiralty for failing so far to land a serious blow on the Germans, Jellicoe had decided that on 2 June he would try to tempt Scheer and the German High Seas Fleet out into the open North Sea. In a mirror image of the German plan, Jellicoe's bait would be a couple of light cruiser squadrons, which would be waved under the enemy's noses. Meanwhile, Jellicoe would seek to hide his battleships out of sight until the Germans had committed their forces, when he would pounce. They were two different plans, but the strategy was basically the same. Who would act first? Who would fall into the carefully laid trap? And who would prevail in any battle?

The German operation was initially planned for 17 May but was then postponed to 29 May to give time to repair a damaged German ship. Bad weather then intervened, and Scheer decided to amend his plans still further – to a less ambitious sweep into the Skagerrak, the strait running between the south-east coast of Norway and the northern coast of Denmark. The purpose, though, remained the same – to tempt British ships into a trap.

As part of Scheer's plans, eighteen German submarines would be deployed to attack the British. *U-72*, *U-74* and *U-75* were sent to lay mines off the Firth of Forth, the Moray Firth and Orkney respectively. *U-75* received her orders on 21 May from Hermann Bauer, Commander of U-boats for the High Seas Fleet. She was to lay mines off the north-west coast of Orkney Mainland, off the Brough of Birsay – a few miles from Britain's premier naval base at Scapa Flow. The mines were to be laid in a line at right angles to the coast, to target merchant vessels and warships, which German intelligence had established were using a north–south route down the west side of Orkney, just a couple of miles off shore. *U-75*'s orders set out clearly the intelligence basis for the mission: 'According to a reliable source, a warship route runs from the north to Scapa Flow a few miles from the Brough of Birsay (west side of the Orkney Islands).'

The orders were precise about where the mines should be laid:

Mine warship route from Scapa Flow north along the west side of the Orkney Islands, 2 to 3 nautical miles from the coast abeam Marwick Head. If it is for mine technical reasons not possible to place the barrier perpendicular to the course, then lay it in direction NE–SW, so that it is effective against ships coming down from the north-west. Depth setting 7 metres under high water.

A back-up option was provided in case this location proved impossible: St Magnus Bay, the base for auxiliary warships, to the west of Shetland. But *U-75* was ordered to focus on her main minelaying mission and not be distracted by trying to torpedo second-order targets, such as merchant ships. If she found an Allied warship, that would be different – she could engage such a high-priority target.

U-74 sailed first, from the naval base at Wilhelmshaven, on 13 May. Her sister vessel *U-72* sailed ten days later. And, finally, in the early morning of 24 May, *U-75* slipped her moorings at Heligoland and set sail. There was no one to cheer her off – civilians had been relocated to mainland Germany when the war began.

U-75's captain, Curt Beitzen, set course for the Orkney Islands. He must have hoped he was on a relatively routine mission, but from the very beginning things did not go to plan. The submarine started taking in water through her exhaust pipes and urgent repairs were required, slowing the journey and costing Beitzen a full day. *U-75* continued north during these repairs.

He did not know it, but Beitzen's sister ships, *U-72* and *U-74*, were also plagued with bad luck. *U-72* was forced to abort her mission because of an oil leak, which was leaving a dangerous and all too obvious surface trail. *U-74* had a far worse fate: she blew up and sank with the loss of the entire 34-man crew on 17 May, while laying her sensitive mines.

Oblivious to the fate of her sister vessels, *U-75* pressed ahead. On the morning of 26 May, they had reached the coast of Norway. From there, Beitzen set course for an area north of the Shetland Islands. Unknown to Beitzen, that same late May day, the Admiralty sent a message to the Commander in Chief of the Home Fleet, Admiral Jellicoe:

Secret: Lord Kitchener is proceeding to Archangel with a mission … Party leave London on Monday 5 June, arriving Thurso forenoon of 6th, cross to Scapa Flow and arrive at about 1 p.m. as Lord Kitchener wishes to see Fleet before sailing that evening. You should detail a Cruiser to take Mission from Scapa Flow to Archangel Bar and report name of vessel proposed.

The next morning, 27 May, at 1.57 a.m., Jellicoe replied, 'Propose *Hampshire*.' By noon, the Admiralty had approved his choice of ship. The fates of *Hampshire* and *U-75* would from then on be inextricably intertwined.

On *U-75*, Beitzen had calculated precisely the time when he needed to reach the west of Orkney to lay his mines when the tides and the darkness were favourable. But with a day lost due to the required repairs, he had to make haste, with both diesels running at full power. On this occasion, Beitzen's Germanic efficiency failed him. The skies were overcast and there was frequent fog. This made observation to establish the vessel's position difficult. As a consequence, it turned out that Beitzen had miscalculated his submarine's position by some 17 miles, and he ended up arriving off Orkney twenty-four hours too soon. It was an embarrassing error. He was now compelled to keep his submarine out of harm's way, and hope that he was not spotted from the shore or by patrolling British ships.

On 28 May, *U-75*'s crew spent a tense day resting a few miles away from a large part of the greatest navy in the world. Then, that night, the crew spotted what looked like a blacked-out warship just 1,500 metres away. Beitzen's orders allowed him to attack warships but not lower-value merchant vessels. He decided not to attack. Visibility was too poor.

At 1.10 a.m. on 29 May, Beitzen was finally ready. He gave the order: 'Submarine dive.' *U-75* set a course for her planned minefield. After a short while, Beitzen looked through the vessel's periscope. This time he was on course – he could just make out the area of land at Noup Head, right at the north-west corner of the Orkney Islands.

Beitzen steered away further to the west of the land, determined that he and his small crew of thirty-two would not be spotted. By around 6 a.m., he had worked his way to the minelaying area, just a couple of miles off Marwick Head. He had made his approach from well away from the land, to avoid detection from the watches on shore. At this time of the year, the sun was already up by around 3.30 a.m., so he knew he needed to be careful. But Beitzen was determined to accurately establish his location, and he brought the submerged *U-75* in to just a little over half a mile from the shore. On board, his young crew watched nervously.

Eventually, Beitzen was convinced that they had reached the correct area. He took *U-75* back out further from the shore, to his allotted location. He now gave the order to lay his thirty-four mines – within just ten nautical miles of the western exit from Scapa Flow. It was a delicate operation and it was no longer dark. The crew struggled to get the mines safely into position. The weather was chilly but the men sweated heavily. They would lay some mines in a line, then turn north and lay some more, then north-east, then head back west.

It was a tense period – the time of maximum danger for the mission and the crew, as the destruction of *U-74* had already demonstrated. On the starboard side of the vessel, the first eleven of seventeen mines had been laid at the specified depth. Then, disaster. The cog mechanism that deployed the mines broke down. Beitzen fumed and questioned his officers. What could they do? He ordered his men to do everything they could to free the twelfth mine. Meanwhile, the remaining five were to be transported from the starboard side to the port side. The crew cursed. The day got lighter. The minutes ticked painfully by. Beitzen looked frequently at his watch: 'Will we never finish?'

Eventually, they got the twelfth mine out. The depth settings of the last seven mines were now changed. They would be set at 8 metres, instead of the 7 metres ordered. It was a long process and both Beitzen and his men looked nervously towards land to check there was no sign that they had been spotted. After two and a half hours of work, the task was finally complete. All thirty-four mines were laid. Relieved, at 8.35 a.m. Beitzen gave the order to dive. He turned to the north and then diverted to the west, finally heading back east towards the Norwegian coast.

U-75 remained underwater now for over five hours, finally surfacing at around 2 p.m. By the morning of 31 May, she was just off the Norwegian coast. She did not know it, but she was inadvertently heading towards the waters in which, in just a few hours' time, the Battle of Jutland – the biggest naval conflict of the war – was to be fought.

*   *   *

5 p.m., Tuesday 30 May. Scapa Flow – the natural harbour on the southern tip of the Orkney Islands, which is the home of Admiral Jellicoe's Grand Fleet. The name 'Scapa Flow' comes from the Old Norse word *Skalpafloi*, meaning 'bay of the long isthmus'. The sheltered waters have been used by ships for as long as there has been human habitation in this part of the world. It is a wonderful natural harbour, taking in 125 square miles of ocean and 1 billion cubic metres of water. There is space for a whole fleet, and the entrances can be protected by underwater nets to stop enemy submarines from penetrating the harbour and causing chaos. Sixty blockships have also been sunk in the many entrance channels to the harbour, to facilitate the protective nets and booms. Minefields, artillery and concrete barriers offer additional protection.

Most of the ships of the Grand Fleet are in their designated places, spread out across Scapa Flow. HMS *Hampshire* is in her usual location, her crew going about their regular daily duties. Stoker 1st Class Jack Beechey, aged twenty-one, is in the boiler room. He has just returned from home leave. He has given his sister, Doris, a pendant cross to remember him by when he is away.

Stoker 1st Class Thomas Harwood, aged thirty-two, is also aboard *Hampshire*; he joined the ship for the first time just five days ago and is beginning to make new friends.

So far, those on board have experienced a relatively quiet war – certainly compared with many soldiers in the trenches on the Western Front. But there is a sense of excitement in the air, of anticipation. Could it be that they are finally to get a chance to engage the German fleet and demonstrate the superiority of British dreadnoughts and British seamanship? The extra preparations on board ship, and the sense of added urgency amongst the officers, suggests that something is going on.

Of course, no one in Scapa Flow, and certainly no one aboard *Hampshire*, can know that Admiral Scheer has finally decided to risk taking on the British fleet. If successful, his action could tilt the balance of advantage in the war towards Germany. For the Allies, it is a dangerous moment. Churchill would later write that Admiral Jellicoe was 'the only man on either side who could lose the war in an afternoon'.

But if the British Navy is still unaware of German plans, then Admiral Scheer is notably in the dark too. He does not know that since the very earliest days of the war, the British Admiralty has developed, in its top-secret Room 40, a sophisticated naval intelligence-gathering operation which has broken German naval codes. In October 1914, a German cruiser was destroyed by Russian ships in the Gulf of Finland. While the German ship, *Magdeburg*, was on fire, her signals officer tried to destroy the ship's secret cipher book. He failed, killed before he could do so. The Russians passed on the ciphers and codebook to the British Admiralty. Unbeknown to the Germans, the British intelligence officers in Room 40 could now decipher every German wireless transmission and plot German ship movements. It was an incredible coup.

Already over the past two weeks, the despatch of a large number of German U-boats into the North Sea has been carefully noted in Room 40. The information has, of course, been relayed to Admiral Jellicoe at Scapa Flow, which is why advanced preparations for action are being put in place on all ships.

At noon on 30 May, Room 40 sent a message to Jellicoe warning him that intercepted messages showed that the High Seas Fleet would put to sea the very next day. Now, at 5.40 p.m., the Admiralty decides to pounce: it orders Jellicoe out from Scapa Flow and tells his subordinate, Vice-Admiral Beatty, in the Firth of Forth, to put to sea as well. Jellicoe, on *Iron Duke*, immediately orders the momentous signal to be sent to all his ships: 'Raise steam for Fleet speed, and report when ready to proceed.'

All across Scapa Flow there is suddenly an electric atmosphere as on ship after ship urgent preparations are made to depart. This time, there is a real feeling that it will be different – the Germans will be caught and brought to battle. Men scurry across the decks making last-minute adjustments. Firing gear is checked and weapons brought to battle readiness.

Almost simultaneously, at around 8 p.m., the ships of the fleet – battleships, cruisers and destroyers – send clouds of dense smoke up into the air as their engines start up and the stokers begin their back-breaking work down below. The ships now form up ready to go out to sea. In succession, they wheel into line, deploying perfectly on the basis of years of training. It is a display of strength, professionalism and precision. For those who witness it, it is a breathtaking sight, never to be forgotten, as the Grand Fleet now leaves harbour as one. Ahead, minesweepers ensure a safe passage.

As they pass from the safety of the huge natural harbour, the crews on the boom defence ships, guarding the harbour entrances with anti-submarine nets, give successive loud cheers as each vessel goes by. They watch for the names of great ships, names which echo down the hundreds of proud years of Royal Navy service. There is *Royal Oak*, there is *Bellerophon*, now *Vanguard*; *Iron Duke* herself, with Jellicoe visible on the bridge. Then *Marlborough, Revenge, Agincourt, St Vincent, Colossus, Invincible, Inflexible, Indomitable, King George V, Ajax, Orion, Conqueror, Thunderer*. And still there are more. There are lumps in many throats. Can any nation on earth defeat such a collection of mighty ships?

Hampshire is there too, helping to provide the protective screen around the powerful and precious dreadnoughts. Only for one vessel is this not a glorious occasion – the seaplane carrier *Campania* is stationed some five miles away from the main fleet anchorage and somehow manages to miss the general signal to leave. Her crew appear not to notice the departure from Scapa Flow of the largest fleet in the world. By the time they do realise, it is almost midnight and Jellicoe is long gone. They set sail, only to be ordered back by an irritated admiral, who does not want a lone vessel being picked off by waiting German submarines.

By 11 p.m., Jellicoe's fleet is at sea, along with Beatty's. Scheer's fleet will not leave harbour until 2.30 a.m. on 31 May; intelligence from Room 40 has now given the British a head start. Jellicoe and Beatty are leading the most powerful fleet ever assembled: twenty-eight dreadnoughts, nine battlecruisers, eight cruisers, twenty-six light cruisers and seventy-eight destroyers. The combined German forces amount to sixteen dreadnoughts, six pre-dreadnoughts, five battlecruisers, eleven light cruisers and sixty-one destroyers. If they meet, it is going to be a mighty clash. And if Jellicoe can bring all his ships to bear against the German fleet, victory should be his.

*　　*　　*

It is now noon the following day, Wednesday 31 May. *Hampshire*, along with the rest of Jellicoe's fleet, is in the middle of the North Sea, sailing at just over 14 knots towards where the German fleet is expected to be found. *Hampshire* has a special duty: to act as a linking ship between the armoured cruiser HMS *Minotaur* and the scout cruiser HMS *Active*. *Hampshire*'s squadron is tasked with reconnaissance, to prevent enemy light forces from identifying the location of Jellicoe's big battleships.

At 12.30 p.m., Jellicoe receives a message from the Admiralty. They have no definite news about the enemy fleet. It is assumed not to have left its harbour yet. Jellicoe can relax somewhat. What he does not know is that someone has blundered. The director of naval operations in London has misinterpreted the continuing presence of Scheer's wireless call sign at the naval base of Wilhelmshaven as confirmation that Scheer's fleet has not left port. In fact, it has, but Scheer's practice has been to transfer his normal call sign to a shore establishment while at sea. The Room 40 staff understand this. The director of naval operations does not. Jellicoe now concludes that his mission has become potentially just another sweep of the seas, rather than the interception of the German fleet. He maintains a Grand Fleet cruising speed of just 15 knots.

Vice-Admiral Beatty, meanwhile, is making his own journey

Col Henderson Van Velden Major Watson H Fraser Major Maxwell H De Jager
De Wet. Genl Louis Botha Lord Kitchener Col Hamilton

Newly built HMS *Hampshire* leaves Hebburn Dock on the Tyne,
9 March 1905.

HMS *Hampshire* in service, 1916.

Curt Beitzen, captain of the German submarine *U-75*.

The broken-backed HMS *Invincible*, with its two ends sticking up almost vertically from the sea. This was the sight that met the crew of *U-75* as they returned home through the waters of the Battle of Jutland.
© FOTOSEARCH / ARCHIVE PHOTOS / GETTY IMAGES

Kitchener in the iconic First World War recruitment poster, of which there were many versions. Kitchener insisted on 'God Save the King' being added.
© IMPERIAL WAR MUSEUM (IWM PST 2734)

Facing the music: a nervous Kitchener leaves the War Office to face MPs on 2 June 1916.
© IMPERIAL WAR MUSEUM (Q 56658)

ABOVE Kitchener, wrapped up against the wind and rain, disembarks from HMS *Oak* to meet Admiral Jellicoe at Scapa Flow, 5 June 1916.
© IMPERIAL WAR MUSEUM (HU 66128)

LEFT On the deck of HMS *Iron Duke* at around 3.45 p.m. on 5 June 1916. From left to right: Lieutenant-Colonel Fitzgerald, Admiral Jellicoe, Lord Kitchener and Captain Dreyer.
© HILARY MORGAN / ALAMY STOCK PHOTO

BELOW Admiral Jellicoe bids farewell to Lord Kitchener and his party on board HMS *Iron Duke*, 4 p.m., 5 June 1916. The 6 foot 2 inch War Minister towers above the Admiral.
© PRINT COLLECTOR / HULTON ARCHIVE / GETTY IMAGES

First signal of disaster: 'Battle cruiser seems in distress between Marwick Head and the Brough Birsay.' The telegram from Birsay should have been clearer: its ambiguity delayed the rescue effort and cost lives. © THE NATIONAL ARCHIVES

The cliffs off Marwick Head, Orkney, looking north. The Kitchener Memorial, unveiled in July 1926, looks out over the scene of the tragedy. © ROFF SMITH / NATIONAL GEOGRAPHIC IMAGE COLLECTION / GETTY IMAGES

The rocky shoreline where the first float landed, at Rivna Geo. A geo is a deep cleft in the face of a cliff, caused by wave-driven erosion. PHOTO COURTESY OF ORKNEY LIBRARY & ARCHIVE

Birsay Bay, Orkney, looking south towards Marwick Head. © DAVID LAWS

Skaill Bay, looking south towards where the third raft landed. © DAVID LAWS

Eleven of the twelve survivors of the sinking. Back row, left to right: Wilfred Wesson, Walter 'Lofty' Farnden, Alfred Read, Fred Sims (bandaged), Jack Bowman, William Phillips. Front row, left to right: Horace Buerdsell, Charles Rogerson, Dick Simpson, Samuel Sweeney, William Cashman.

© JOHN FROST NEWSPAPERS / ALAMY STOCK PHOTO

Three survivors with Surgeon Pickup, photographed outside Pallast, the farmhouse in which they took refuge after reaching land. From left to right: Warrant Mechanician William Bennett, the only surviving officer; Surgeon Pickup; Leading Seaman Charles Rogerson (standing); Shipwright William Phillips.

ABOVE The war medals of William Bennett. © DAVID LAWS

LEFT Reward notice for Kitchener's lost despatch cases.
© THE NATIONAL ARCHIVES

REWARD.

LOST OVERBOARD AT SEA

4 Despatch Cases.

1. Brown leather DESPATCH CASE about 17" by 12" by 5" with 3
initials on the top also some smaller writing.

2. Black leather DESPATCH BAG with straps about 18' by 12" with
brass lock.

3. Brown leather DESPATCH CASE similar to No. 1 but about 10"
deep instead of 5".

4. Wooden DESPATCH CASE about same size as No. 3 marked H.Q.
in big black letters.

The above have been lost at sea in the vicinity of Orkney and contain
correspondence which is only of value to the owner, who has authorised me to
offer a REWARD of :—

    £25 for a complete unbroken case.

    £1 to £20 for a portion of the contents.

On delivery to the Senior Naval Officer, Thurso.

F. E. E. BROCK,
Vice-Admiral.

LONGHOPE,
6th June, 1916.

BELOW Kitchener's coffin, constructed after HMS *Hampshire*
was sunk in case his body was recovered from the sea.
PHOTO COURTESY OF ORKNEY LIBRARY & ARCHIVE

The funeral procession of Lieutenant-Colonel Fitzgerald, Kitchener's aide and close friend.
© PRIVATE COLLECTION / BRIDGEMAN IMAGES

LEFT Journalist, conspiracy theorist and hoaxer Frank Power. © ILLUSTRATED LONDON NEWS LTD / MARY EVANS

MIDDLE The Eastbourne grave of Lieutenant-Colonel Oswald Arthur Gerald Fitzgerald, Kitchener's forty-year-old aide and closest friend, bearing the inscription 'Faithful unto Death'. © DAVID LAWS

RIGHT *Hampshire*'s Yeoman of Signals George Reeve with his wife, Martha, and daughter Winnie. Reeve was one of the 737 men who died on *Hampshire*. © DAVID LAWS

'Quite alright, inform Mother, George'. George Reeve's message to his wife after the Battle of Jutland. When it arrived, she feared it was news of his death. © DAVID LAWS

The envelope of the letter George Reeve's wife sent him after Jutland. It was sent back to her stamped 'Return to sender. Admiralty instructions.' He had died around twelve hours before she wrote her letter, which expressed joy and relief at his safe return from the battle. © DAVID LAWS

Saved from the sea – George Reeve's HMS *Hampshire* Football League 1915 winners medal. It was found on his body, which was recovered six weeks after the sinking, in the leather pocket of his webbing belt. It was returned to his wife, Martha, just over a year after his death. © DAVID LAWS

from the Firth of Forth, with his much smaller force of battle-cruisers. He is heading straight for the bait – German Admiral Hipper's 1st and 2nd scouting groups. Beatty has also concluded that Scheer is still in port. But Scheer, with his German High Seas Fleet, is in fact at sea, heading north-west, and is not far behind Hipper. Beatty, approaching from the west, is heading straight into the trap.

At around 2.15 p.m., Beatty's ship HMS *Galatea*, the flagship of the 1st Light Cruiser Squadron, spots a vessel in the ocean ahead. It clearly isn't a battleship – in fact, it is a Danish tramp steamer. *Galatea* moves forward to investigate. And then, a shock. The tramp steamer is there, but so too are other vessels: two German destroy-ers. Beatty's ship has uncovered the vanguard of the entire German fleet, though she has yet to realise this.

At 2.18 p.m., *Galatea* hoists her signal flag with the message 'Enemy in sight'. The Battle of Jutland has now begun. At 2.28 p.m., *Galatea* opens fire with her 6-inch guns. At 2.32 p.m., the Germans fire back – and land the first hit of the battle on their target. The Royal Navy is off to a bad start.

Jellicoe now hears news of the engagement. He still thinks that Scheer is in harbour but knows now that something is up. At 3 p.m., the order is given to *Hampshire* and the rest of the Grand Fleet to increase speed to 17 knots. By 4.10 p.m., *Hampshire* is sailing at 21 knots, quite close to her maximum speed. *Minotaur* is around 8,000 metres away. *Hampshire*'s engineer commander, Arthur Cossey, visits the men in the engine rooms to thank them for their hard work. He finds his men 'working like Trojans' and 'cheerful as crick-ets'. The crew have waited a long time to fire in anger at an enemy ship and they are now convinced that the moment is not far off. Not long afterwards, Cossey sees a German Zeppelin hovering over the sea and clearly acting as a spotter for the German fleet. It is fired at, and leaves without dropping any bombs.

Ahead of them, Beatty's ships are now engaged in a full-scale battle with Hipper's force: huge shells are shooting through the air. Some drop harmlessly into the sea. Others crash onto British and German ships, smashing machinery, severing limbs and causing fires and explosions which burn, maim and kill. In these early exchanges, the British ships are coming off worst.

At 4 p.m., the battlecruiser HMS *Indefatigable* is engaged in a duel with the German ship *Von der Tann*. At 4.02 p.m., a salvo from *Von der Tann* crashes onto *Indefatigable*. Then, a few minutes later, another hits the mark. Suddenly, there is a massive explosion on *Indefatigable*, with flames 200 or 300 feet high, and billowing brown smoke. Then, within seconds, there is a colossal double explosion – the ship's magazines have been hit. *Indefatigable's* massive funnels and enormous gun turrets are sent flying, and a huge column of flame and smoke erupts 1,500 feet into the air.

When the smoke has cleared, stunned sailors on nearby British ships can see the remains of *Indefatigable* lying low in the water. Within thirty seconds, the great ship rolls over and sinks into the sea. Of the 1,019 men on board, there are only two survivors, including a lucky sailor, Signaller Farmer, who only lives because he had been ordered aloft to clear the entangled signal flags just minutes before his ship was hit.

The mighty battlecruiser HMS *Queen Mary* is now also being showered with shells. Eventually, she breaks her back amidships, her bows and stern sticking out of the water at an angle of 45°. And then there is an 800-foot-high mushroom of fire and smoke from the middle of the ship. The final explosions tear her to pieces and she disappears into the sea. The scene is so devastating that even on the German battleships there is a moment of complete silence, as the enemy sailors survey the gruesome scene. Of her crew of 1,286 men, only twenty will survive.

It is now 4.30 p.m. So far, the Royal Navy is losing the Battle of Jutland. Jellicoe is aware of the disaster that appears to be unfolding to the south-east of him. As Beatty turns his remaining battered ships away from the Germans, to lead them towards Jellicoe, Jellicoe redoubles his efforts to deliver assistance. Finally, at 4.38 p.m., the High Seas Fleet is spotted and Jellicoe is quickly informed.

At 5.33 p.m., Beatty's vessels finally make the first contacts with Jellicoe's. At 5.40 p.m., on *Hampshire*, firing is heard from the south – the first those on *Hampshire* have heard of the great battle. The crew is immediately sent to action stations. At 5.47 p.m., flashes of guns can clearly be made out to the south-south-west. And then, at last, real action: they can see HMS *Defence* firing at the enemy.

At 5.52 p.m., *Hampshire* sights a ship on her starboard bow. Captain Savill looks through his binoculars and confirms it is an enemy vessel. She has three funnels and looks like a cruiser of the Kolberg type, from the German 2nd scouting group. For a couple of minutes, Savill thinks he sees one or perhaps two more battlecruisers in the haze, ahead of his target. He challenges the vessel, which then gives the wrong call sign. At 5.56 p.m., Savill gives the order to fire. The enemy is 8,500 metres away – well within range.

In just three minutes, *Hampshire* fires four mighty salvoes at her enemy. The second appears to strike home, and light smoke and steam is visible at the base of the German ship's centre funnel. After the second salvo, the enemy vessel turns away and is soon out of sight in the haze. By now, *Hampshire* knows that she is involved in her first major battle. On board, all of the crew are alert, and those above are looking out for any signs of danger. They are watching not just for German warships but for the undersea presence of the German Navy – the U-boats. It is always difficult for the lookouts to spot these. But now it is even more tricky – the sea is churned up by the sheer number of warships, all moving at high speeds and in close proximity.

At 6.05 p.m., the submarine lookout on the port side shouts out a warning. Captain Savill immediately turns *Hampshire* towards the spot where the submarine is sighted – going on the attack, but also reducing the size of the target he is presenting. HMS *Midge* also turns to attack. Savill closes on the apparent U-boat and orders 'open fire'. But the 'submarine' turns out to be a false alarm, which can now be clearly identified from the fore bridge.

Meanwhile, the battle around *Hampshire* is a furious one. HMS *Defence*, an armoured cruiser, is blown to pieces by German shells. Not a single man of the 903 on board survives. HMS *Warrior* and *Black Prince* are destroyed, with no survivors either from the 857 men on *Black Prince*. Eight British destroyers are also sunk.

Then, at 6.15 p.m., the Germans engage the 3rd Battlecruiser Squadron, including *Invincible*, *Inflexible* and *Indomitable*. The heaviest of the German shelling is concentrated on *Invincible*. She has not been designed to take this much punishment; her high speed was supposed to keep her away from trouble. *Invincible* herself delivers some hits to the German ship *Derfflinger*. But both *Derfflinger* and *Lützow* are now targeting *Invincible*, and with greater success. The shells landing on her have caused the ship to burst into flames, with the metal superstructure glowing red.

Suddenly, at 6.34 p.m., there is another devastating explosion. *Invincible* has blown up – a shell has penetrated the midships turret and the flash has raced down into the magazines below. The upper bridge awning is blown high up into the sky above the dying vessel, and within a few seconds the ship has disappeared into the sea: the explosion has literally broken her in half. The column of smoke and debris soars hundreds of feet into the sky, metal and pieces of wood being showered over nearby vessels such as *Indomitable*.

On other ships, men simply cannot believe that *Invincible* is gone – destroyed in barely half a minute. All that is now left of her are the ends of her bow and stern, sticking separately out of the water in opposite directions, at almost vertical angles. Of the 1,032 men on board, there are only six survivors.

The watches on *Hampshire* are now even more on edge, with the U-boats believed to be waiting to take their chances too. At 6.54 p.m., a periscope is spotted on the port beam of *Hampshire*. Savill again orders *Hampshire* to pursue the submarine and to open fire on her. The submarine is identified by the officer of Y Group, fore turret and the control top. She dives and is not seen again.

By 7 p.m., the Cruiser Squadron is abreast of the rear of the battle fleet, with the 2nd Battle Squadron leading. At 8 p.m., heavy firing is again heard from the battle fleet. This continues for a prolonged period, but *Hampshire* is not engaged.

At 8.40 p.m., an unmistakable jar is suddenly felt on *Hampshire*, and a very large swirl as if from a submarine breaking surface is seen in her wake. This disturbance seems to pass only 20 metres from the starboard beam of HMS *Chester*. The shock on *Hampshire* is sufficient to knock down a shell in the fore turret and to cause the men in the fore shell room to ask if the ship has been torpedoed. Some men down below fall over as the ship lurches. It is a nervous moment. Two observers think they saw a periscope.

But the battle is now winding down in the growing darkness and rising mist. The Germans wish to make their escape to the east. Jellicoe is unwilling to jeopardise the safety of the British fleet by being too adventurous and risking attack by German destroyers armed with torpedoes.

At 11.35 p.m., the reflection of gun flashes is observed from *Hampshire*, but little more. It is a nervous but uneventful night. At 3.15 the next morning, with the sun starting to come up, a huge Zeppelin is seen flying over the battlecruiser fleet, bearing south-south-east. Most of the rest of the British fleet can see the airship too. Indeed, HMS *Revenge* cannot resist opening fire with her huge 15-inch guns at maximum elevation. HMS *Conqueror* joins in with her smaller, 13½-inch weaponry. Wisely, the Zeppelin moves slowly away, out of range.

The battle is now over. During the night, the Germans have slipped through the British fleet and headed off to the east, back to safety. A failure of communication, courage and initiative by the British has allowed their German foes to escape. The Royal Navy has undoubtedly come off worst, losing around 6,100 men killed to the German figure of 3,000. Counting ships, the British have lost six cruisers and eight destroyers, to the Germans' six cruisers and five destroyers – and only one of the German losses is of a battle-cruiser, while the Royal Navy has lost three.

* * *

Over the next few days, the British fleet returned to port. *Hampshire*'s final duty was to search for the damaged HMS *Warrior*; not finding her, she also set course for home. At Britain's naval bases, the men on shore prepared for the return of ships from battle. By the evening of 1 June, at Scapa Flow, they were making the first coffins. On the first night alone, they constructed around 200. The old battleship HMS *Victorious* had been converted for use as a floating dockyard. Now the first ships were returning, many bearing the physical scars of battle, and disbursing their wounded and their dead. By morning, the coffins were all laid out on the quarterdeck ready for use – a depressing sight.

For some vessels, badly damaged by German shells, the journey home was yet another grim battle. Some of these ships made it back, often after long and dangerous journeys. Others, such as *Tipperary* and *Sparrowhawk*, sank beneath the waves.

On the ships that had been hardest hit, there were too many dead bodies to take back home. Instead, while the vessels moved slowly forward, burial services were held on board. The dead bodies were wrapped in blankets and hammocks, which were then sewn up, with the sea boots sticking out. In some cases, too little of the body had been recovered to fill the sacking right up.

A row of mess tables or gratings were put on decks, with one end over the starboard side of the vessel. The bodies were laid on these, with a heavy shell tied to the sea boots to ensure the corpses sank. Two bodies were committed to the sea at once, with a Union Jack lying over them. The Church of England padre would deliver his blessing, and then the platforms would be tilted and the bodies would slide off into the sea below.

Those watching from HMS *Barham* noticed with horror that the bodies from their ship did not sink immediately. Instead, they floated for a while in a horizontal position, until the weights took effect and pulled the feet slowly down into the sea. At this point, the bodies gradually stood upright in the ocean, with about half the canvas showing from the water, as if the dead sailors were taking one last look at the ship and crewmates before disappearing under the waves. It was a gruesome and haunting sight.

The first ships sailed back into Rosyth on the morning of 2 June, and at 11.30 a.m. on the same morning the main body of the Grand Fleet arrived back at Scapa Flow, to a low-key welcome.

What public reception would the returning ships of both navies receive? Given they had a shorter journey to travel back, the German fleet got back to port first and reported their striking successes in sinking a number of major British ships. Scheer now claimed victory, announcing that his fleet had sunk three battlecruisers, one super-dreadnought, two armoured cruisers, two light cruisers and thirteen destroyers. The Germans admitted to losing only a couple of ships, covering up the loss of others. Before long, news of a great German naval victory was being beamed around the world. And by 5 June, the German Emperor himself was visiting his fleet to congratulate them.

This was not just good propaganda: the German Navy had inflicted greater losses of men and ships on the British, in spite of the overwhelming superiority of the British fleet. Meanwhile, the British response was delayed not just by the longer journey in getting back to port but by the sense of loss and disappointment amongst those at Scapa Flow and at the Admiralty. Expectations of an overwhelming Royal Navy triumph had been high, so the actual outcome seemed initially like a disastrous defeat.

As the British ships arrived back, the surviving sailors were keen to let loved ones know that they were safe. *Hampshire* was back in the relative safety of Scapa Flow on the morning of Saturday 3 June. The ship's chaplain offered to send telegram messages on behalf of the crew to loved ones who might be worried about whether they had survived the now well-publicised battle. On board, many now wrote their own detailed letters home to wives and parents. While Captain Savill wrote his official report, Private William Bridges penned a letter to his parents, as did nineteen-year-old

Midshipman Edmund Fellowes and eighteen-year-old Midshipman Charles Tucker. They all wanted to reassure worried parents and loved ones that they had survived the battle and were safely back in port.

George Reeve, the Yeoman of Signals, now sent a brief post office telegram to his wife, Martha: 'Quite alright, inform Mother, George.' He then sat down on the afternoon of 3 June and wrote her a longer letter. It is clear that he was deeply affected by the news of British losses:

> *I suppose you will have read the papers about the fight and are very anxious about me. We were in it of course, but had the good fortune to come off scot free. I am not going to attempt to give you details of the fight, you will probably learn much more from the newspapers than I can tell you dear. Then again, I haven't the heart to say very much at present, I have lost too many friends. The Queen Mary, Invincible and Black Prince are all Portsmouth ships and a good number of the signalmen are friends of mine. You will observe the enemy's losses cannot be definitively stated but there is no doubt they are as large if not larger than ours. The only thing that stopped us from bagging the whole crowd of them was the mist. I must say the weather has always been in favour of the Germans up to the present. We got in a few hits with the opportunities that did offer. I will now conclude dear hoping you are both alright … I remain with fondest love to both, your ever loving husband, XXXXXX George XXXXXXXXX.*

The Admiralty knew that in the face of German triumphalism and with the personal communications from individual officers and men, saying nothing was not an option. Jellicoe sent the Admiralty a brief summary of his losses and the imagined fate of the German fleet. It took the Admiralty until 7 p.m. on 2 June to release a brief communiqué, put together by a committee of Arthur Balfour, First Lord of the Admiralty; Admiral Sir Henry Jackson, First Sea Lord; and Vice-Admiral Sir Henry Oliver, Chief of Staff.

The communiqué was strikingly frank and started by acknowledging the 'heavy losses' faced by the British battlecruiser fleet. It then proceeded to list the British vessels sunk, while describing the German losses as 'serious' – but naming only two German ships as definitively destroyed. The government might just as well have described the outcome as a British defeat, for that conclusion could certainly be quickly reached by the depressing tone of the announcement. There was not even a reference to the fact that the Grand Fleet had been left in command of the seas and that the Germans had fled back to port. It was an extraordinary piece of wartime news mismanagement, prioritising candour over any attempt to communicate Royal Navy achievements.

The press unsurprisingly took their lead from this gloomy pronouncement. Some returning sailors – even the wounded – were now jeered publicly by civilians who had read newspaper accounts of the 'German victory'. The Royal Navy was furious at the Admiralty's naivety and its failure to highlight British successes. Letters of protest quickly poured in. After this furious response, and supplied by Jellicoe with further reports, the Admiralty tried to correct the defeatist tone it had struck by issuing a second communiqué the next day, 3 June. This was followed by a third communiqué on 4 June which grossly exaggerated German losses.

In time, the Battle of Jutland would be seen, on balance, as a British success, though not because Jellicoe had sunk more German ships or killed more Germans. He hadn't. Instead, Jutland is now seen as a British success because the Germans had failed to land a decisive punch. Indeed, for the rest of the war, their fleet dared not venture out again. Jellicoe was the man who might have 'lost the war in an afternoon'. At Jutland, he did not. That turned out to be enough.

But that is not how it must have felt at Scapa Flow on 2, 3 and 4 June, as the ships were being repaired and the bodies buried, with the empty berths providing vivid proof of British losses. Some 6,094 British sailors had lost their lives in a matter of hours. That might seem small by the standards of France and Flanders, but it was a lot by usual measures – more than the 5,774 British soldiers killed directly by enemy action in the whole three years of the Boer War. And out there in the North Sea six great ships – *Indefatigable*, *Invincible*, *Queen Mary*, *Black Prince*, *Defence* and *Warrior* – and eight destroyers – *Ardent, Fortune, Nestor, Nomad, Shark, Sparrow-hawk, Tipperary* and *Turbulent* – lay smashed and broken under the waves.

Admiral Jellicoe was a proud man and – up until now – a renowned naval leader. But by 4 June his morale and confidence must have been battered as he prepared for the arrival the following day at Scapa Flow of Britain's greatest Field Marshal and Secretary of State for War, Lord Kitchener. At least, he must have felt, Kitchener's mission to Russia seemed routine and low-risk by the standards of Jutland. Jellicoe had a plan for Kitchener's voyage. He had allocated *Hampshire* for the task and had identified two destroyers to provide escort for her precious cargo.

But as Jellicoe went to bed on the night of 4 June, a slow-moving area of low pressure was making its way across northern Scotland. In Scapa Flow, the winds were rising and forecast to go on rising. Jellicoe's best-laid plans were about to be blown away.

* * *

As *Hampshire* was heading back west to Scapa Flow, another vessel was heading eastwards, towards a different port: *U-75*, on the way home after laying her mines off Orkney.

The journey home had seemed to the crew of *U-75* to be quite routine. At least, that's how it was until 1 June, when the U-boat was close to the Jutland Peninsula. That was when the crew noticed that all was not normal. They were cruising on the ocean surface to make better speed, carefully scanning the horizon to protect against the danger of British ships.

First, they came upon a large oil spill. Then the crew realised that they were sailing over an ocean covered with debris – parts of ships, boxes, pieces of furniture, dead fish and seagulls, and all sorts of flotsam. Soon, and more shockingly, they realised that the dark shapes they could see in the water were dead bodies; some were German sailors, others British. They saw no survivors. Those who witnessed these sights were silenced by the enormity and horror of it. Suddenly, the real consequences of conflict were brought into vivid shape.

At 2 p.m., 6 miles in the distance, Captain Beitzen suddenly saw the most dramatic sight of all. Sticking 20 metres straight up out of the water were the bow and stern of an enormous broken-backed vessel. But was it a German or a Royal Navy ship? It did not take long to identify the wreck as the 20,000-ton British battlecruiser HMS *Invincible*, attacked the previous evening by German battlecruisers. *Lützow* and *Derfflinger* had fired three salvoes each at the massive British vessel; one of these had hit *Invincible*, penetrated the ship's magazines and caused a catastrophic explosion. In thirty seconds, *Invincible* was gone – literally blown in half in 50 metres of water. But the broken-backed ship still refused to sink. Her bow and stern stood in the water, a dreadful monument to the carnage of war.

Who knows what emotions of pride or shock were felt by the crew of *U-75* when they sailed past this tragic sight? But they had to remain focused: they had spotted a British destroyer close by. As they headed away from the location of the sea battle, Beitzen and his crew must have felt a sense of relief that their mission was almost over and that they were returning apparently unscathed.

But the next day, 2 June, *U-75* faced the third challenge of her mission – and the most dangerous. The weather took a turn for the worse, with pouring rain and high winds, which whipped up the seas around the submarine. Beitzen ordered the closing of the diesel air intake to avoid taking in water. But the hatch at the top of the conning tower had to be kept open to safely secure air for the crew and her engines. Suddenly, a huge wave crashed against the submarine, flipping the heavy metal hatch over and sealing it shut. Inside, the engines were using the air and sucking it out of the submarine.

Beitzen and other crew who had been on watch on the conning tower frantically struggled to reopen the hatch. They could not understand why this was proving impossible, but they soon realised that there was now an air pressure difference inside and outside the hatch, locking it firmly in place. If they did not act quickly, the crew inside would slowly suffocate. Beitzen banged furiously on the hatch to alert those inside. But there was no response. He and the crew struggled again to get the hatch open, but without success. They were just beginning to fear for the safety of the crew when the U-boat's chief engineer, who had been working on repairing the gyrocompass, suddenly realised the danger they were in and ordered that the air intake should be speedily reopened. It was a close shave, preventing an ugly end for the crew.

It would also have been a potentially huge embarrassment for Beitzen. He might have been found by Allied ships, a U-boat commander locked out of his own ship. The Allies might have been able to access *U-75* and capture her secret sailing orders. The Orkney minefield might have been identified in time to save Kitchener. But it was not to be.

Surely this was the last danger that *U-75* faced, Beitzen must now have thought. The crew assumed so too, but on the very same day, 2 June, near the Horns Riff off the German coast, *U-75* was spotted by British submarines. Three times the vessel had to evade possible destruction.

Finally, on 3 June, *U-75* reached the safety of her home base at Heligoland. It had been an eventful first mission, although it had lasted less than two weeks. Beitzen was pleased that his task was successfully completed. He had laid thirty-four mines as instructed. What would they ensnare? A merchant vessel? A destroyer? Something even larger? Or, perhaps, nothing at all?

In his wildest dreams, Beitzen could not know what mighty prize his mission would deliver. As he relaxed back on land that afternoon of 3 June, a secret telegram was delivered to a house in Kent, England: Broome, the country residence of Field Marshal Lord Kitchener. It was from the Chief of the British Military Mission in Russia. It reported a conversation earlier that day with the Emperor of Russia, confirming that he wished Kitchener's planned mission to his country to go ahead.

Kitchener was delighted. He had long believed that Russia's successful continuation in the war was essential to Allied victory. He was looking forward to the trip as something of a break from the normal pressures of his job. That evening, he packed his bags.

Meanwhile, just below the water surface, and not far from Marwick Head, thirty-four red mines, with protruding black spikes, bobbed up and down in the swelling seas of the Atlantic.

THE MISSION

'Every precaution is to be taken against enemy submarines.'
SAILING ORDERS, HMS *HAMPSHIRE*, 4 JUNE 1916

Sunday 4 June. 4.30 p.m. London Bridge Railway Station.
The cipher clerk allocated to Mr O'Beirne of the Foreign
Office, Leonard Rix, is due to accompany his boss on Kitchener's
mission to Russia. He is looking confused, stressed and worried.
The train for Scotland, with Lord Kitchener and all his accompanying party on board, is due to leave at 4.40 p.m. But nowhere is a
train with such a destination to be found.

Eventually, a ticket officer is able to assist: 'The Edinburgh train
doesn't go from London Bridge. You should be at King's Cross –
and you'd better hurry!' A flustered and red-faced Rix dashes off
down the concourse, heavy cases in hand. He is now in a complete
panic, imagining both his boss and Britain's War Minister waiting
on the platform at King's Cross, cursing him, glancing furiously at
their watches.

Lord Kitchener has spent most of the afternoon at the War
Office. He then has tea with a friend, who accompanies him to
King's Cross. The rest of his party is awaiting him on the platform.

A carriage has been reserved for them on the overnight express to Edinburgh. From there, they will carry on to Thurso and then make the short sea journey over the Pentland Firth to the British naval base at Scapa Flow.

'There's a problem, my Lord,' Kitchener is now informed. 'It seems that Mr O'Beirne's cipher clerk may have gone to the wrong railway station. Shall we wait for him?' Kitchener shakes his head. He does not want to be the cause of delaying the train. He gives orders that the stray clerk should be tracked down and sent on north with O'Beirne by special train.

Kitchener then turns away sharply and boards the carriage reserved for him and his delegation. He doesn't want to stay on the platform and attract attention. His friend and private secretary Sir George Arthur remains on the platform to see the train off. Sir George is already a little concerned about the apparent lack of secrecy around the visit: a week before, he received a telegram from a Russian contact asking him if he was to join the supposedly confidential mission. He knows that the Russian military and its government are notoriously leaky. He has also heard a Royal Navy officer question whether HMS *Hampshire* is an appropriate choice to carry a cargo as important as Lord Kitchener. Kitchener himself seemed unworried, remarking that it was a matter for the Admiralty and he 'supposed it would be all right'. But these worries are still in the forefront of Sir George's mind.

The train is now about to leave. The guard is slamming shut the few remaining open doors. People on the platform are waving off friends and loved ones. Unusually, something then makes Britain's War Minister think again. He rises from his seat, opens the carriage door and descends again to the platform. Quietly and a little sadly, he says to Sir George, 'Look after things while I am away.' Then, as if unable to explain the reason for his last words, he swiftly re-boards the train and returns to his seat, looking away, out of the far window.

A few minutes later, the train whistle sounds. 'Stand away,' cries the guard. Slowly at first, and then with gathering speed, the train pulls out of King's Cross Station. The small group on the platform watch the train depart, then turn and head back to their waiting cars. The mission to Russia has begun.

*   *   *

Why Russia? And why now? Why travel on a dangerous sea jour-ney across thousands of miles?

Much though Kitchener loved France and understood that the Western Front was for Britain the decisive theatre of operations, he had always appreciated more clearly than many the vital importance of Russia. While Germany was pinned down in a two-front war, the division of its resources would assuredly guarantee that it could not triumph. So, Kitchener appreciated the crucial importance of Russia. He appreciated the size of the country and the huge number of men the Russian Army had deployed in the field. He also un-derstood Russia's great vulnerability: the weakness of its economy, and its relative backwardness compared with the modern economic powerhouse of Germany. If Britain was short of ammunition and equipment to meet its needs, Russia was shorter. If Britain's robust finances were being stretched, Russia's were almost broken.

In May 1916, a large number of ships in England, France and across the Atlantic were awaiting the spring reopening of the great ice gate to the north of Russia. This sea route was closed by ice for almost half the year, with the thaw often not occurring until the second half of May, and with the route speedily icing up again by mid-October. The Allies had hoped that using ice-breaking Russian ships could prolong the period of open seas, but the Russian efforts were often badly planned and ineffective.

Russia was now desperate for new equipment and resources to prop up her struggling armies, and the British government was keen both to discuss Russian needs and to talk about how the supplies would be paid for. Their first objective was to keep Russia in the war: without her armies, millions strong, Germany could switch all her forces to the Western Front, crushing France before Britain was able to fully deploy her New Armies and well before America might join the war.

To get to Archangel, British ships had to make a journey of some 1,650 miles from Scapa Flow. Not only were they constrained by the ice but by the risk of U-boat attack and by the outside possibility of encountering a German surface ship. The Germans had also sown a large number of mines across the 90-mile Gorlo, the long, narrow channel into the White Sea.

Throughout the war, Kitchener had remained closely in touch with the Russian government and with Grand Duke Nicholas – the Tsar's cousin and the Supreme Commander of Russian forces. He had committed himself to helping secure arms and ammunition for the Russians from the USA and Japan, appointing General Ellershaw to carry out his policy of doing everything possible to support the Russian war effort.

As early as December 1914, Kitchener established a Russian Supply Committee in the War Office, under the chairmanship of U. F. Wintour. The Russians, in turn, trusted Kitchener and respected his sometimes blunt advice. They admired him as a distinguished soldier and as a war leader, and they knew he was more sensitive to

Russian needs than many in the British military, with their obses-
sive and narrow focus on the Western Front.

In spite of some assistance from the Allied nations, in early 1916
the Russian armies were still badly short of equipment, including
both heavy guns and rifles. They wanted much more help. At the
same time, the Treasury in London was becoming concerned as to
how and if the Russians were ever going to pay for all this support.
With enormous British spending on the war, Treasury ministers
and officials were nervous about offering blank cheques to other
nations. The cost of the conflict was astonishingly large, and the
formerly strong British national finances were now diving deep
into the red as its Treasury essentially presented a blank cheque for
its own war leaders to fill in.

Kitchener understood the need to talk finances with the Russians. But he could see a bigger threat to Britain and France if
Russia collapsed or if discontent in Russia led to revolution or a
separate peace with Germany. So it was agreed in London at the
end of April 1916 that a high-level mission should be despatched.
It was to have two main purposes: to encourage and support Russia
to stay in the war, and to consider the delicate issue of payment for
the equipment being shipped.

Asquith's original plan was to send Lloyd George, the Minister of
Munitions, to lead on munition supply and Reginald McKenna, the
Chancellor, to deal with financial matters. But at the Cabinet meeting on 28 April, Kitchener announced that he would like to lead
the mission. With his close connections to the Russian leadership,
including Grand Duke Nicholas, he was an obvious choice. Asquith
liked the idea. He knew that Kitchener was respected by the Russians and he was clearly senior enough to lead the delegation. And a
further period with Kitchener out of the country might ease some of

the ongoing tensions over his leadership of the War Office. Asquith decided that Kitchener and Lloyd George would go together.

The urgency around the mission appeared to dissipate in late April with the Easter Rising in Dublin. Securing peace and order in Britain's own backyard now took priority. But news of the impending mission had already been passed onto the Russian Ambassador in London. And on 12 May, Major-General Sir John Hanbury-Williams, the head of the British Military Mission in Petrograd, reported rumours in Russia of the planned Kitchener visit. He also confirmed that he had discussed the idea with the Tsar, who was very enthusiastic.

The very next day, the Russian Emperor let it be known that a visit by Kitchener would be warmly welcomed, and an official invitation from the Tsar was issued. By mid-May, it seemed to be common knowledge in senior military and diplomatic circles in both London and Petrograd that Kitchener would be visiting.

On 14 May, the Tsar sent a telegram to London stating, 'Lord Kitchener's visit to Russia would be most useful and important.' This was the first that Britain's monarch, King George V, had heard of the matter. When he asked whether it was true, Kitchener admitted that the matter was under discussion. The next day, Kitchener sent a short reply confirming that 'nothing would give me greater pleasure than to visit Russia' but noting that the details of the trip were not yet confirmed and would require the permission of both Asquith and the King.

It was now a busy time in Whitehall, with the government dealing with the fallout from the Easter Rising, and preparations taking place for a massive British assault on the Somme in late June or early July. Kitchener was still keen to go to Russia, but he was determined to be back before the Somme battle, in which many of his New Armies would be deployed.

And then, suddenly, there was a change of plan. On 22 May, twenty-four hours after *U-75* received the sailing orders for her Orkney mission, Lloyd George opened a short letter in the scrawled but distinct handwriting of the Prime Minister:

Secret. My dear Lloyd George, I hope you may see your way to take up Ireland; at any rate for a short time. It is a unique opportunity and there is no one else who could do so much to bring about a permanent solution. Yours very sincerely, H. H. Asquith.

Asquith now regarded the problem of Ireland as more pressing than the Russia mission. He valued Lloyd George's powers of persuasion and felt he could be instrumental in delivering a settlement in the delicate talks underway. It must have seemed a relatively minor decision at the time. But small decisions can have large consequences. Asquith's letter saved Lloyd George's life, helped end Asquith's career, changed the course of the war and the peace, and would in time serve to shatter the unity of the Liberal Party.

On 26 May, it was decided by the British Cabinet that the Russia mission should still go ahead and that the only senior representative of the British government would be Kitchener. The King approved the visit on the same day and on 27 May a message was sent to Hanbury-Williams, confirming that Lord Kitchener would accept 'the gracious invitation of the Emperor'.

The message stated that Lord Kitchener would be accompanied by a party of twelve, including Brigadier-General Ellershaw, Mr O'Beirne of the Foreign Office and Kitchener's aide and close friend Lieutenant-Colonel Fitzgerald. The party was expected to arrive at the north Russian port of Archangel on 9 June. Ellershaw had been Britain's representative in the arms talks with Russia for the past year. O'Beirne had worked in the British Embassy in Petrograd and had a masterful knowledge of all things Russian.

The Admiralty was left to make the practical arrangements for the voyage, and to consult with Admiral Jellicoe, who was to plan for a visit starting from London on 5 June. The date was later to be moved forward by one day. It must have seemed another minor decision. But it was to have momentous consequences.

On 1 June, perhaps prompted by news of the great naval battle at Jutland, Kitchener took the opportunity of attending a meeting of the Cabinet's War Committee to ask Arthur Balfour, First Lord of the Admiralty, whether he might stop off to have a look at the British fleet at Scapa Flow and meet Lord Jellicoe on his way to Russia. But he made clear that he did not want to lose too much time – 'I should not have more than an hour or so.' Balfour agreed. This altered the details of the planned sea voyage. Kitchener had initially envisaged boarding *Hampshire* at Thurso Bay, on the northern tip of the mainland, and then heading straight off towards Archangel. Now, Kitchener would go first to Scapa Flow, in the Orkney Islands.

On 2 June, the Admiralty sent a message to Jellicoe indicating that Kitchener wanted to be met at Thurso by HMS *Hampshire*. He would then proceed to Scapa Flow to call on Jellicoe before embarking on his mission. For Jellicoe, these details of the Kitchener visit would have seemed very small matters after the enormity of the Battle of Jutland. He was preoccupied with sending reports to the Admiralty and trying to correct the growing perception that the Royal Navy had suffered a significant defeat. All across Scapa Flow, the warships were carrying out repairs, resupplying their stores and filing their reports.

On 3 June, the captain of HMS *Hampshire*, Herbert Savill, was on board his ship writing his own report on his vessel's contribution at Jutland. Once finished, he sent the short draft to his immediate boss, the Rear-Admiral commanding the 2nd Cruiser Squadron. He was pleased to have the paperwork out of the way. He now knew that his ship was being lined up for another mission.

However, Jellicoe was less than keen on the idea of *Hampshire* collecting Kitchener from the mainland to take him to Scapa Flow. On 4 June at 3.30 p.m., he cabled the Admiralty: 'I do not think it desirable for "Hampshire" to embark party at Thurso, owing to danger of submarine attack and suggest they come over in a TBD [torpedo boat destroyer]. Is this approved?' The Admiralty signalled its agreement.

And then, it was almost all off. By 3 June, Kitchener had become concerned that he wouldn't be able to achieve enough in the time available – after all, it would take him six days to travel from Scapa Flow to Petrograd, and the return journey was scheduled for 21 June. Was it worth it?

Kitchener remembered his last overseas visit to the Dardanelles. Had his enemies not tried to remove him in his absence? He feared to be away too long. The Russian Finance Minister apparently also pressed for the mission to be delayed.

But it was the Tsar who finally settled it, making clear through Hanbury-Williams that he considered the trip to be a priority. Kitchener received this final confirmation on the afternoon of Saturday 3 June. He was, in truth, delighted at the idea of getting away from the stresses and strains of London – after all, just days before, he had survived the rare censure vote in Parliament. A friend, visiting him in the War Office in late May, observed that 'the Field Marshal was in rare spirits, looking forward eagerly to his time in Russia, merry as a schoolboy starting for his holidays'.

So it was that at 4.40 p.m., on Sunday 4 June, Kitchener's train set off north from King's Cross. As the train left the station, a secret message in cipher was sent from the Admiralty to naval headquarters at Scapa Flow informing them of Kitchener's departure from London and of his expected arrival in Thurso 'tomorrow morning Monday 5 June'. A destroyer, HMS *Oak*, was to be made ready to take the party from the harbour at Thurso across the sea to Orkney. At Scapa Flow, Kitchener would meet and dine with Admiral Jellicoe. Then, wasting no time, it was to be onwards to Russia.

After receiving the Admiralty's 4.40 p.m. message, Jellicoe sent the secret sailing orders, marked 'To be destroyed when complied with', from his HQ on HMS *Iron Duke* to Captain Savill on HMS *Hampshire*. The orders were copied to the Rear-Admiral commanding the 2nd Cruiser Squadron.

On *Hampshire*, Captain Savill carefully read his orders. After the Battle of Jutland, he had assumed that for now the brief drama of war was over, and that his ship might be in for a quiet period of patrolling. But it was clear that this was a special mission, with real risks and dangers. In eight numbered sections, over one and a half pages, Jellicoe set out clearly his instructions. *Hampshire* was to be ready to leave Scapa Flow on the evening of the following day, Monday 5 June. The exact sailing time was to be as convenient to Lord Kitchener. The destination was the north Russian port of Archangel. The members of the mission were going to arrive at Scapa at about 1 p.m. There were expected to be seven officers and senior delegation members, including Kitchener, and six servants. The protection officer had, perhaps, been forgotten, as in the event the mission contained not twelve but thirteen men, as well as Kitchener himself.

Hampshire was to proceed at 18 knots up the east coast of Orkney until she reached a latitude of 62°, after which she was to make 16 knots. Jellicoe warned that the German commerce raider *Möwe* and one other similar raider might be encountered on the route. This was not reason to delay the journey, but a 'sharp lookout' must be kept for this threat.

Hampshire was to keep to the secret route for merchant vessels leaving east coast ports for Russia. She would communicate by wireless with the senior naval officer in the White Sea to obtain information about any threats from mines or other risks in that area. After delivering Kitchener to Archangel, *Hampshire* would recoal at Yukanski (now known as Ostrovnoi), drawing on a stock from a vessel which would be specially sent for this purpose. If the vessel did not arrive, they were to use local coal stocks – but sparingly.

After coaling, *Hampshire* would return to Scapa Flow at 17 knots, taking broad zigzags across the route laid down from Archangel to the north Irish Channel. Weather permitting, two destroyers would screen *Hampshire* for the first part of her journey from Scapa, before returning to base. On the way back, *Hampshire* would report her position to Scapa in sufficient time that a destroyer screen could be sent out again to bring her safely into harbour.

The final paragraph contained a strong warning: 'Every precaution is to be taken against enemy submarines. They have recently been reported to be off Stadlandet in latitude 62° north: no information has been received that they are operating further north.'

Meanwhile, at around 6 p.m. on the evening of Sunday 4 June, Mr O'Beirne of the Foreign Office, now reunited with his geographically challenged cipher clerk, were on the way by special train to Thurso, following shortly behind Kitchener and his party. They were determined not to miss the boat for the crucial mission to Russia, and were hugely relieved when they discovered that they were back on track to link up with the rest of the mission. Thank God, they reflected, as they lay back in their seats and rested on the way to Scotland. Thank God they would not suffer the humiliation of missing this crucial visit to Britain's key wartime ally. They were going to catch up with Kitchener. It was not long before they would bitterly regret it.

THE FATEFUL VOYAGE

'Battle cruiser seems in distress between Marwick Head
and the Brough Birsay – Corporal Drever.'

7.45 P.M., 5 JUNE 1916

Monday 5 June 1916, 6.50 a.m., Scapa Flow naval base, Orkney Islands.

The destroyer HMS *Oak* slips anchor and, passing the big battleships of Jellicoe's fleet, sets course across the Pentland Firth for Scrabster, the small harbour sitting under steeply sloping grass banks a mile and a half from Thurso, on the northernmost coast of Scotland.

HMS *Oak* is a small vessel, weighing in at just 990 tons, with a crew of seventy and a length of just 75 metres. She was built in Glasgow in 1912, and she is tender to the flagship of the Grand Fleet, HMS *Iron Duke*. *Oak*'s hull is painted white to distinguish her from other ships. In the course of her duties, she has carried some of the most famous people in the kingdom, including – in 1915 – King George V, when he travelled to Scapa Flow to inspect the Grand Fleet.

It is now 11 a.m., Monday 5 June, at Thurso Railway Station – the northernmost railway station in Britain, which opened just forty-two years earlier. Kitchener's train pulls into the station. He has completed the first 700 miles of his journey to Russia – the last 150 miles of it on the single-track line from Inverness. Now Kitchener and his entourage are taken by car to Scrabster.

Before boarding HMS *Oak*, Kitchener and his party stretch their legs and walk around the harbour. To their north, across the waters of the Pentland Firth, lie the Orkney Islands, just an hour or so away by sea. And between the islands of Orkney, Hoy and South Ronaldsay is the massive natural harbour of Scapa Flow. Home of the British fleet, its entrances are carefully protected from U-boat attack.

As Kitchener's party look out towards the Orkney Islands, they can see the choppy waters being whipped up by a gale blowing down from the north-east, and they screw up their eyes against the wind gusting strongly into their faces.

Kitchener is accompanied by a thirteen-man party – a mixture of senior government members and officials, a personal protection officer and five valets. Kitchener's own valet of many years' standing is 35-year-old Henry Surguy. His police protection officer is Detective Sergeant Matthew McLoughlin, a 37-year-old Irishman who has previously undertaken close protection duties for both Edward VII and George V. The job might seem a dangerous one, but those in the know are aware that it's actually rather a 'cushy number'. No officer attached to such senior protection duties has ever died in the course of his service.

Kitchener's personal military secretary is Brevet Lieutenant-Colonel Oswald Fitzgerald, his long-standing friend and confidant who has served the Field Marshal for the past twelve years. There are rumours that Kitchener and Fitzgerald are partners or even lovers.

But there is no evidence – it is all speculation and guesswork. Aged forty, Fitzgerald is another Irish national who was born in India. He is accompanied by his own valet: William Shields. Shields is a former lance corporal who has been unable to serve at the front, after suffering a wound on active service in 1914.

Who are the other members of the party? Hugh James O'Beirne is a 49-year-old Foreign Office minister who was also born in Ireland. O'Beirne is an expert in Anglo-Russian relations whose first posting as a diplomat was in Petrograd. He is accompanied by a valet – James Gurney – and his wayward shorthand clerk, Leonard Rix, aged thirty-one.

Two senior civil servants from the Ministry of Munitions are also on the visit: 59-year-old Sir Hay Donaldson and 52-year-old Leslie Robertson. Donaldson is chief technical adviser in the Munitions Ministry and he has been given the temporary military rank of brigadier-general. Robertson is deputy to Donaldson; his temporary rank is lieutenant-colonel. Another valet, thirty-year-old Francis West, is accompanying Donaldson.

The final members of the mission are two military officers: 44-year-old Brigadier-General Wilfrid Ellershaw, an artillery officer and instructor at Sandhurst, and Second Lieutenant R. D. Macpherson of the Cameron Highlanders, born in Russia and, at nineteen years of age, the youngest member of the group. Macpherson is fluent in Russian and will help translate for the mission. Macpherson's tartan trousers and youth make him instantly stand out from the rest of the group. Needless to say, Ellershaw is accompanied by a final valet: Driver David Brown, aged thirty-two, of the Royal Horse Artillery.

At 11.20 a.m., Kitchener and his most senior staff and colleagues board HMS *Oak*, which sets sail immediately for Scapa Flow. The servants and baggage are put on board a separate vessel, the fleet messenger *Alouette*, and sent straight to *Hampshire*. The *Alouette* party of seven includes four men dressed in khaki uniform and three in civilian clothes. The four in khaki include Detective Sergeant McLoughlin, along with Driver Brown, Henry Surguy and William Shields. Amongst those not in uniform is the shorthand clerk, Rix, still hugely relieved to have caught up with the rest of the mission.

Meanwhile, on HMS *Hampshire*, the crew finally guess that something is up. The ship has been fully coaled and the padre has said he understands that they are taking a party of diplomats to Bergen in Norway. Just before noon, *Hampshire* is ordered to take up a new anchorage, just a short distance from HMS *Iron Duke* – and now the crew are in no doubt that something out of the ordinary is going on. Just after midday, the blacksmith on *Hampshire* is outside on the deck, connecting the ship's cable to the buoy in the vessel's new position. The wind is blasting across the ship and the rain is pouring down. Suddenly, the blacksmith loses his footing on the slippery deck and his leg is jammed by the ring of the cable. He screams in pain as the blood pours from his wound. Men run to his assistance and he is quickly transferred to the hospital ship *Soudan*.

At just after noon, HMS *Oak* arrives in Scapa Flow and ties up alongside the enormous battleship *Iron Duke*, Jellicoe's flagship – a recently built, 25,000-ton dreadnought, of almost 200 metres in length. The vessel towers over little HMS *Oak*. Kitchener will be accompanied on board *Iron Duke* by Fitzgerald, Ellershaw, Donaldson, Macpherson, O'Beirne and Robertson.

Kitchener and his party board *Iron Duke* at 12.14 p.m., according to the ship's log. He and his team are dressed in long military overcoats, fluttering in the wind. It is already a distinctly unpleasant day, even by the standards of weather this far north. It is cold – just

45° Fahrenheit. Indeed, it is the coldest June in these chilly islands for forty years. It is also raining hard. The sea is rough and a strong wind of over 30 mph blows in from the north-east; it is already a force 7 gale. The passage from Thurso itself has not been too bad, being protected to some degree from the worst of the winds by the islands themselves.

Kitchener, carrying a long stick in his left hand, now proceeds cautiously along the gangway between *Oak* and *Iron Duke*, carefully picking his way across the slippery wooden slats that criss-cross the wooden plank. Behind him, the captain of HMS *Oak* salutes smartly and the rest of Kitchener's party prepare to follow on behind. The wind is now strong enough that they have to be careful not to be blown over. Two sailors on *Iron Duke* hold onto the gangway ropes to try to stabilise the walkway.

Kitchener is given a quick tour of the flagship, this time without his overcoat, looking inside the gun turrets and inspecting some ratings on the mess decks – to general delight and spontaneous applause from the crew, who all recognise the distinct height and features of the Field Marshal, made famous in newspapers and in the renowned recruiting posters.

After the tour, Admiral Jellicoe invites Kitchener and his team to lunch, along with other senior naval staff. Over hot food, Kitchener discusses his mission to Russia. He does not seem overly optimistic about his prospects for success, but he is looking forward to the trip, almost as a respite from the enormous pressures of his work. Inevitably, he wants to hear about the historic naval battle at Jutland. This is still being interpreted by the world's media as a German victory, but Kitchener is interested to hear the full facts and Jellicoe's own appraisal of the result. 'Could the battle be considered a British victory?' the relaxed Kitchener asks.

After lunch, Kitchener joins Jellicoe and his Fleet Paymaster, Victor Weekes, and a couple of other senior officers in the fore cabin of *Iron Duke*. Kitchener makes clear to his host that while he is rather looking forward to the break from his usual duties in London, his trip needs to be a swift one: he wants to be back after just three weeks, preferably by 21 June. If he is to stick to this incredibly ambitious timetable, then he hasn't any moments to spare. Of course, Kitchener could not mention the forthcoming British attack on the Somme, but this must have been to the forefront of his mind. He asks a couple of times how long the sea journey will take, seeming concerned to hear the replies. He emphasises that he wants to be away as soon as possible, as there will be much to do on his return – he has, in short, not a day to lose.

Ten years later, Victor Weekes was to claim that Jellicoe suggested delaying the journey by a day or two because of the ongoing storm. That would have meant leaving on the previously planned date of 6 June. Weekes suggested that this delay was explicitly rejected by Kitchener. Jellicoe himself was later to recall only that it was obvious that Kitchener would contemplate no postponement. Whatever was said, the result was to be the same. There would be no delay to await better weather.

Now was also the time for Jellicoe to share with Kitchener a change in the routing arrangements, though it must have seemed to Britain's War Minister to be a minor matter at the time. In contrast to the earlier plan, Jellicoe had now decided to send Kitchener on a westerly, rather than easterly, passage around Orkney. Jellicoe explained that this would offer better protection against the northeast winds from the storm. He and his senior officers were intent on making one further change to the original sailing orders for *Hampshire*. They were concerned by the short length of the visit to Russia and realised that it would be neither sensible nor possible for Savill to make two return journeys in just three weeks. Jellicoe therefore now cabled the Admiralty, asking their permission for *Hampshire* to stay in Archangel during Kitchener's visit and then bring him and his mission back by his target date of 21 June.

At around 4.15 p.m., Kitchener and his team of six left *Iron Duke*. A photographer was on hand to record Admiral Jellicoe's farewell, with Kitchener towering above him and the others present. The same photographer also captured Kitchener and his party descending into the drifter *Mayberry* for the short journey to HMS *Hampshire*. It was the last photograph ever to be taken of Britain's War Minister. In the background, the choppy seas are visible. By now, the force 7 gale of noontime had become a force 8 gale and the wind was no longer from the north-east but blasting down from due north.

Jellicoe's original sailing orders, issued on the previous day, had directed HMS *Hampshire* to the east of Orkney. She was to proceed at 18 knots along the east coast of South Ronaldsay, then steer to latitude 62° north of Stadlandet, where her escort of two destroyers would leave her. After that, she had strict instructions to reduce speed to 16 knots and zigzag.

This easterly route was the usual route taken by warships, and it was routinely swept for mines. *Hampshire* was to proceed midway between Shetland and Norway, keeping not less than 200 miles from the Norwegian coast. But on the morning of 5 June, Jellicoe and his staff reviewed the plans. That morning, a strong gale was blowing down from the north-east. Jellicoe was concerned that the strong north-easterly winds might prevent the destroyer escort from keeping up with *Hampshire*. U-boats had recently been sighted off the eastern exits from Scapa, often used by the fleet. Jellicoe decided that the western course around the island would be safer. At least that side of Orkney would be protected from the north-east gale, he thought, allowing the destroyer escort to keep up. And the gale was building in strength. At 4 a.m. it was a force 5 gale. At 8 a.m., it was measured at force 6. By noon it was force 7 and strengthening further.

As this prevailing wind from the north-east rose in severity, Admiral Jellicoe changed his orders. Surprisingly, these revised orders have not survived and their exact timing is unknown, but it is thought that they were issued some time before 3 p.m.

It probably seemed a small decision at the time, amongst all else that was occurring. But it was to have major consequences.

The westerly route around Orkney was in frequent use by other shipping traffic: in the eight days up to midnight on 5 June, two cruisers, four destroyers, two minelayers, four yachts, six freighters and thirty-seven trawlers were sighted by the lookout in Birsay. The route – close to the shoreline and under constant observation – had come more into favour after the battleship *King Edward VII* had been sunk by a mine off Cape Wrath on 6 January 1916 – fortunately, with the loss of only one of her 777 crew members. The rest of the crew were rescued by four destroyers. She took around nine hours to sink.

It was unlikely, considered Jellicoe, that a submarine could easily operate against ships in the prevailing stormy conditions. Jellicoe also thought that it was 'practically impossible' for his favoured westerly route to have been mined, because it was so close to shore that in his view any attempt would have been spotted by the land-based lookouts, particularly at a time of the year when it was light for around twenty hours a day.

Jellicoe's memoirs record that 'minesweeping on either side of the Orkneys had not been practicable for three or four days owing to the weather conditions'. This was, in fact, untrue. However, these particular waters, to the west of Orkney, had not been swept for mines, and there had been several recent reports of German submarines having been sighted both east and west of Orkney.

Jellicoe had one other westerly option for rerouting: he could send *Hampshire* further west to Cape Wrath and then bring her due north to join the main shipping route to Murmansk and Archangel. But this option was rejected when the news was reported that the bad weather had prevented minesweepers from reliably clearing the route. The area was actually being swept by Captain Lionel Preston that forenoon with his eight fleet sweepers, which were off Cape Wrath at noon when a signal from Jellicoe warned them that a submarine had been spotted by a British patrol vessel at around 9.15 a.m., north-east of Cape Wrath and steering west. The concern was that the submarine might have laid mines. Captain Preston continued sweeping until 6.30 p.m., but his sweeps were parting in the heavy seas and at 7 p.m. he stated that the weather was too bad for reliable work.

So, Jellicoe preferred the option that would direct *Hampshire* up the west side of Orkney, just a few miles from the land. He thought this would shield the ships from the north-east wind, allowing the destroyer screen to keep up, and he was unworried about the risk of mines. No vessel had been attacked or damaged in this area, and it was assumed that German surface minelayers could not operate so close to the well-guarded British shoreline.

In fact, by the time Jellicoe and Kitchener had sat down for lunch on *Iron Duke*, the winds were no longer blowing from the north-east. In his memoirs, Jellicoe claimed that 'by the afternoon it was blowing a gale from the north-eastwards'. This is simply not true. In fact, the last reported north north-east winds were at noon. By 1 p.m., the winds were blowing from due north and were approaching force 8. By 5 p.m., exactly as Kitchener was leaving Scapa Flow, they were blowing from the north-north-west.

Even fiercer than that morning's north-east gale were the north-westerly gusts that were now about to sweep the waves down towards the Orkney Islands and blast the land with storm-force winds so severe that a man would struggle to stand up in them.

A wise course would now have been to delay the departure until conditions were clearer. But there were to be no delays. And at around 4.25 p.m., Kitchener and his party arrived on *Hampshire*, having been brought over from *Iron Duke* in the fleet drifter *Mayberry*, bouncing around in the rough seas. She tied up next to *Hampshire*, and Kitchener and his staff proceeded carefully on board as *Mayberry* rose and fell on the heavy swell, with the rain pouring down around them.

The two small Acasta-class escort destroyers, *Unity* and *Victor*, weighing in at less than 1,000 tons each and with crews of just eighty men, had by now slipped their anchorages and were already heading off for their meeting point off Tor Ness on the south-west tip of Orkney.

Hampshire's important guest was until now a closely guarded secret. But as soon as Kitchener boarded, news of his presence spread fast amongst the crew. His was an instantly recognisable face. Stoker Sims, who was working on deck making ready the pinnace boat, spotted Kitchener and his staff as they made their way up to the main deck. William Bennett, the Warrant Mechanician, didn't see Kitchener, but he did see his closest aide, Colonel Fitzgerald. Rumours now spread fast that the ship's destination was not Norway but Archangel. The vessel was suddenly alive with excitement, gossip and speculation.

As *Hampshire* was being prepared for departure, on the hospital ship *Soudan* the unfortunate blacksmith, injured on *Hampshire* a few hours beforehand, was having an operation to amputate his leg. He was crippled for life, and he was now stuck in Scapa Flow as his friends embarked on what was clearly an important and exciting mission. He cursed his luck. Fate had conspired to ensure he missed this crucial opportunity. It had also intervened to save his life.

Hampshire slipped her buoy at around 4.45 p.m. and headed south-west into the storm-lashed seas of the Pentland Firth. It was still light, and at this time of year, so far north, it was due to remain so for almost six more hours. Sunset was due at 9.20 p.m. and twilight was at around 10.30 p.m.

At 4.55 p.m., Jellicoe sent a further telegram to the Admiralty to finalise the details of *Hampshire*'s journey. Given Kitchener's determination to get back to England by 21 June, Jellicoe wanted *Hampshire* to stay at Archangel, recoal there and bring Kitchener back. Jellicoe was seeking to save time, and avoid *Hampshire* having to twice cross the German minefields to the north of Russia. Just over an hour later, the Admiralty approved the request.

Hampshire soon passed through the torpedo nets guarding the harbour at Scapa Flow. Captain Savill now ordered 18 knots. But the wind, which at noon had been 33 mph at force 7, had now increased to 36 mph, force 8. And that wind, which at noon had been coming down from the north-east, had now shifted, at 5 p.m., to come from the north-west. The three ships and their crucial charge were now heading straight into the oncoming gale.

Everything on *Hampshire*'s deck was battened down. The hatches were sealed to make them watertight. Only the hatch to 14 Mess was left open, so that there was an access for men still on deck, including Stoker Sims, who would shortly go below after completing his two-hour clean of the pinnace engines.

Hampshire reached the destroyer rendezvous point, off Tor Ness, on time at 5.45 p.m. *Unity* and *Victor* were waiting. The three ships now all turned north, past the landmark of the Old Man of Hoy, a 140-metre sea stack set in front of enormous cliffs. The sea was already rough. It was about to get rougher. The three ships advanced, unprotected by land and by the natural harbour of Scapa Flow, into the turbulent seas off western Orkney. Huge waves swept over *Hampshire*'s decks in great frothing sheets. At this point, Captain Savill must have realised that the storm conditions and wind direction were very different from those he was expecting. The islands to his right were no longer protecting him from the gale: instead, the wind was full on. He kept close to shore, hoping this might provide calmer water.

Unity and *Victor* were much smaller ships than *Hampshire*. From this moment, the captains of both knew that they would struggle to keep up. Savill had decided that the risk of a U-boat attack in this weather was low, and he would not sacrifice speed to keep his escorts. It was to be a fatal error. So, *Hampshire* sailed on, alone, into the gale.

By 7.30 p.m., the storm was at its height, the winds sweeping down from the north-west at speeds of around 40 mph. Enormous waves crashed over the ship. Ahead, unknown to the 749 men on *Hampshire*, were the string of mines laid by *U-75* just one week before. They were directly across the path of the ship. They were fixed at 7 or 8 metres below high water to allow smaller vessels to pass over them. But *Hampshire*'s draught was 8 metres. And at this time, it was still a few hours before high water.

Hampshire was around one and a half miles out to sea, between Marwick Head and the Brough of Birsay, steering north 30 east with engines at half ahead. She should have been managing at least 15 knots, but with the turbulent seas she was down to just 13½. She was slightly closer in to shore than was normal on this route, but below her were 30 fathoms of water – over 50 metres – assuring her captain that she had no risk of hitting rocks.

On shore, in the light of a June evening, the ship's slow progress could be seen by anyone unwise enough to be outside on such a night. John Fraser, a twelve-year-old from Feaval, was indoors when his father arrived and shouted for him to come outside to see the huge ship battling northwards through the storm. It was 7.35 p.m. As they stared out across the windswept fields and surging seas, squinting to protect their eyes against the rain and the gale-force winds, there was suddenly an outpouring of smoke from the ship, and a large explosion could be seen. A huge tongue of flame shot out around the forward gun turrets, in front of the foremast. They watched open-mouthed.

A cloud of yellowish smoke, blown by the north-west wind, now drifted towards Marwick Head. John Fraser looked in horror at his father. He could see that the ship was turning towards the land. 'He's going to beach her,' his father shouted. But then the cruiser seemed to turn again and headed back out to sea.

Further on down the cliffs, thirteen-year-old Peter Brass was also out that night tending sheep. He saw *Hampshire* sailing near the shoreline and then witnessed a huge volume of smoke coming from the vessel, which was suddenly obscured by a downpour of rain. Peter rushed off to get his father from their nearby farmhouse, Pallast. It was 7.40 p.m.

Up towards Birsay, a few miles away on the north-west tip of Orkney, Territorial soldiers from the Orkney Royal Garrison Artillery were continuously on watch both from Marwick Head and from the nearby ruins of the sixteenth-century Earl's Palace at Birsay. On duty that evening were Gunners Norn and Angus, under the command of Corporal James Drever.

In Birsay, at 7.40 p.m., Gunner Joe Angus was on watch in the middle of the village. He had not been on duty for long when he was surprised to see *Hampshire* make her way around Marwick Head, battling the storm. Cruisers were not a common sight on this route, and certainly not so close to shore. Angus was watching *Hampshire* for a few minutes, grateful that he was on land and not being bounced around in the ocean by the furious gale. Other than the weather, it all seemed routine. And then it happened, clearly visible in the evening light. There was a huge explosion on the front part of the ship: a flash, followed by flames, and smoke pouring out from behind the bridge. The smoke had barely cleared when there was a second explosion from the same part of the ship. As Angus watched, he could see that the ship seemed almost immediately to dip down by the head. Her bow and forward turret were starting to submerge below the enormous waves.

Angus, stunned, and instantly realising the seriousness of the situation, immediately left his station and ran down to the Territorials' billet in Birsay to report to his superior, Corporal James Drever. The wind and rain were sweeping across the street, but Angus was determined to deliver his message. He arrived at the billet soaking wet, and breathlessly reported what he had seen to the corporal, who ran outside at once to assess the situation.

Angus wasn't the only man in Birsay who had seen what was happening. At home that evening in his small house just above the beach was a Royal Naval Reserve sub-lieutenant, John Spence, who was recovering from an injury. His house was on the seafront, overlooking the bay. At 7.45 p.m., his sister-in-law, 53-year-old Miss Cumloquoy, the local sub-postmistress, came rushing into the house in a great state of excitement: 'Come at once. There's a warship off the coast, and I think it's in real trouble.'

Spence dashed out of his front door and quickly made the distance of 50 metres down to the beach. The wind was blowing fiercely and Spence noted the choppy seas and the surf crashing in from the Atlantic. Out to sea, he immediately sighted *Hampshire* and could identify her as a cruiser. 'I think it may be HMS *Minotaur* – I've seen her before,' he shouted. He knew instantly that the vessel was in serious trouble: the ship's forecastle was almost flush with the water, and at the back of the cruiser her propellers were visible above the waves. She was clearly sinking, head first, into the ocean.

Each time the ship rose and fell in the massive swell, Spence could see her going further down into the water. He watched in shock and horror, and was now joined by Corporal Drever, who had run the short distance from his billet. Together, they viewed the bleak scene, 'That ship is going down by the head,' said Spence.

A stunned Drever realised that he needed to act fast. There was no telephone in Birsay, so Drever rushed off to the post office, some 200 metres from the lookout and 100 metres from the beach. He banged loudly on the door. The sub-postmistress, Miss Jessie Anne Cumloquoy, opened it. After alerting John Spence, she had rushed immediately there, guessing that she would have to send an urgent telegraph. She was ready, but in a highly emotional state.

Corporal Drever grabbed the signal pad and wrote out his message: 'Battle cruiser seems in distress between Marwick Head and the Brough Birsay – Corporal Drever.'

'Seems in distress'? That was something of an understatement. At least one and perhaps two explosions had been seen on *Hampshire*. Smoke was billowing from the middle of the ship, and the vessel was already sinking head first into the waves. Nevertheless, that was his message.

Drever would later claim that Gunner Angus had said nothing

about an explosion. Could this possibly be true? Even if true, would Drever not have asked? Did he not see the smoke billowing from the ship? Whatever really happened, it was an extraordinary omission. Drever was responsible for sending a clear and detailed appraisal of the situation to the military authorities. He utterly failed to do this.

Drever now wrote in the time – 8.45 p.m. British Summer Time (7.45 p.m. GMT) – and handed the postmistress the message to send to 'Artillery', the telegraphic address of the commanding officer of the Royal Garrison Artillery Station at Kirkwall. The message was also addressed in duplicate to the commander of the Western Patrol, Stromness, and the vice-admiral commanding Orkney and Shetland, Sir Frederick Brock.

Miss Cumloquoy had never seen anything like the disaster that was now unfolding. She was in a nervous state as she sent the message off just four minutes later, at 7.49 p.m. At 7.50 p.m., the message was received at Stromness Post Office, and at 7.54 p.m. it was handed to the first person who could take some decisive action to save those on *Hampshire*: Captain F. M. Walker, the commander, Western Patrol, Stromness.

The message may have lacked clarity, but Captain Walker was taking no chances. He immediately ordered the yacht *Jason II* and the trawler *Cambodia* to be put to sea. He then telephoned Vice-Admiral Sir F. E. Brock at Longhope. It was 8 p.m. On *Hampshire*, men were throwing themselves into the icy seas. The ship had only minutes to go before she would disappear under the waves. Time was now of the essence.

Brock, an experienced officer who had served in the Royal Navy since 1879 and who was now aged almost sixty-two, was in his office at Longhope with senior members of his staff. Walker swiftly described the message he had received and indicated that he was sending out his two ships. The vice-admiral had been one of the senior officers who had been on *Iron Duke* taking lunch with Kitchener earlier that day. But what was this ship now being described? Surely it could not be Kitchener's? *Hampshire* was not a 'Battle cruiser', as described in the telegram. She was an armoured cruiser – a fine distinction. Brock also understood that *Hampshire* had been due to sail eastwards, not westwards, around the islands. But if not *Hampshire*, what other vessel could it be?

Brock guessed that it must be *Hampshire*, but how serious was her predicament? What did 'in distress' mean? Perhaps the ship was struggling as she entered heavy seas away from the protection of land? Could she be easing up her speed in the choppy waters, to secure some fittings? To Brock, the message was far from clear. He dithered. 'Don't send the ships for now,' he concluded. 'But keep them in readiness and let's get a further report as to the latest position of the vessel.' He was a vice-admiral; Walker a mere captain. Walker had to obey his orders.

But it was a disastrous error. In the seas off Orkney, hundreds of men were now fighting for their lives in bitterly cold waters. And in just an hour and twenty minutes it would be sunset. Searching for survivors in the darkness would be nightmarishly difficult.

Back in Birsay, Sub-Lieutenant Spence had now walked 20 metres further along the beach to meet his brother-in-law, a farmer, who had just arrived to sound the alarm. He had seen the disaster from the cliffs above Birsay. Breathlessly, he described what he witnessed:

I saw the ship coming around the headland. While I was watching her, I saw a red flash accompanied by black smoke, and I saw water shoot up from her. The smoke had just cleared away when there was another explosion of a similar nature, from the same part of the ship – right at the foremast. The ship then seemed to change direction and head towards the shore, before heading back in the old direction, head on to the wind.

'Look!' interrupted Spence. While they were talking, the forward turret of *Hampshire* had disappeared into the water and the ship seemed to be sinking more rapidly. The dark smoke was continuing to belch from the remaining three funnels into the sky, before being blown towards the land. The still-rotating propellers at the back were now completely clear of the waters as the ship gradually sank into the sea.

As they watched, they saw with horror that funnel after funnel was disappearing beneath the waves, enveloping the vessel in smoke. The ship's plunge forward was at an increasingly sharp angle. When the last funnel had disappeared, the ship was at almost 45°. Men were leaping into the huge waves. The propellers now appeared to be slowing almost to a halt. It was around 8 p.m.

When the after turret had also submerged, the front of the ship appeared to hit the bottom of the ocean, 60 metres down. It hung in this position for a minute or two. Would it remain there, and give time for men still on board to be rescued? The stern was now moving up and down with the swell of the ocean. The muzzles of the after gun turrets were just about visible above the waves and water.

As they watched from the land, the back of the ship then gradually sank, too, so that the angle of the vessel in the water became less acute. From the shore, a small crowd of local residents were now observing. One or two of the women were in tears. Corporal Drever, having sent his message, had rushed back from the post office to the lookout station, a distance of around 200 metres. From there, he stared out to sea. Just as he arrived, there was the most shocking scene yet. HMS *Hampshire*, with all her 11,000 tons of metal and machinery, suddenly somersaulted over towards the shore and plunged below the waves. On the narrow beach in Birsay, there were gasps amongst the small assembled group, and tears for those who were clearly not going to survive. It was 8.05 p.m. – barely twenty minutes after the explosion was first seen. Not a single rescue craft had yet been sent out. At Longhope, the vice-admiral was still trying to establish the route *Hampshire* had taken.

Stunned, Drever now ran back to the post office. His first message had already been sent. He asked the agitated and upset postmistress, still standing at her telegram machine, 'Can you add to the message that the ship has now sunk?' The distressed and emotional Miss Cumloquoy gasped, 'Oh my gosh. OK. OK.' She later recalled signalling to Kirkwall, 'Oh, the ship has sunk. Can that be added?' She said that she understood Kirkwall to reply that 'it was all right'. So, she now told Corporal Drever that his amended message had been transmitted.

But the telegram form itself was left unamended, and in Kirkwall the telegram operator did not realise that words needed adding to the message. Indeed, he was later insistent that he was not asked to add anything. Instead, with a striking lack of initiative and imagination, he noted the original message and pressed the key confirming this had been sent. A second clerk then signalled the message on to Stromness.

At 8.15 p.m., Vice-Admiral Brock was still in his office with senior members of his staff, trying to decide how to respond to the 'Battle cruiser in distress' message. Brock phoned the Brims Ness Signal Station at the far south-west of Orkney. 'What ships have passed westwards tonight, and at what time?' The answer was given immediately: 'HMS *Hampshire*, accompanied by two destroyers.' *Hampshire* had passed by at around 5.45 p.m. The jigsaw pieces were now fitting together.

But time was still being wasted. The crew of *Hampshire* – those not already dead – were fighting for their lives in the icy Atlantic waters. On the seafront at Birsay, men now set off south along the coast. They could tell immediately that any survivors would be blown in a south-easterly direction. Could any be saved? Sub-Lieutenant Spence decided to stay on the seafront, as his injured foot would make him ineffective in any rescue efforts. He looked out to sea, hoping that rescue boats would soon arrive.

At 8.20 p.m., fifteen minutes after *Hampshire* had disappeared under the waves, a second message was sent from Birsay by Corporal Drever. Had he doubts that his first message had been received? This time there could be no ambiguity. The telegram was short and clear: 'Vessel down.' The message was sent to the commander of the Western Patrol, Stromness. It was received at 8.31 p.m.

As this message was being sent from Birsay, it crossed with a new transmission from Vice-Admiral Brock, timed at 8.30 p.m. Unbelievably, Brock was still dithering, asking for more information about the position of *Hampshire*: 'Reference wire battlecruiser in distress reply instantly if guns are visible. How many funnels and masts, what led you to consider her in distress also state what her present conditions are.'

The captain of *Jason II* and the skipper of *Cambodia* were waiting in Captain Walker's office at Stromness, when the 'Vessel down' message came through from Birsay. They left immediately to put to sea. They did not know the name of the ship that had sunk, nor about her precious cargo. But, at last, help was on the way.

As the two captains departed, Captain Walker immediately picked up the phone and asked to be put through to Vice-Admiral Brock. It was 8.35 p.m. 'We've just heard she's sunk.' Brock's response was at last decisive: 'Send out every available ship. And send out shore rescue parties by car.'

But it was already almost an hour since the original explosion had struck *Hampshire* – seen clearly by lookouts and just 1½ miles from the shore. Valuable time had been wasted. And the sun was gradually setting, threatening to cover the scene of the disaster with a blanket of darkness that could cripple the rescue efforts.

Having at last taken a decision, Brock then immediately asked to be put through by phone to the Commander in Chief, Admiral Jellicoe, on *Iron Duke*. Jellicoe received the news of *Hampshire*'s sinking in stunned silence. It was being widely reported that he had just lost the most important naval battle of the war. Was he now responsible, too, for losing Britain's Secretary of State for War, the symbol of British resolve in this crucial hour of the nation's history?

A shocked Jellicoe asked that all available and suitable warships be put to sea, including the four destroyers of the Grand Fleet which were always available at short notice for emergencies. HMS *Unity* and *Victor* had only just returned from their unsuccessful escort mission around an hour before when they received a message from the captain of the Fourth Flotilla to 'raise steam for full speed with all despatch'. At 9 p.m., another signal ordered them to proceed as fast as possible to assist *Hampshire* off Birsay.

Back at Birsay, the Territorial watch sent its clearest and most dramatic message yet, timed at 8.35 p.m. and reaching Vice-Admiral Brock's HQ at 8.50 p.m. This time it was from Gunner Norn at Earl's Palace, Birsay, and it was sent to Kirkwall, Stromness and to Longhope: 'Four-funnel cruiser sank twenty minutes ago.

No assistance arrived yet. Send ships to pick up bodies.' Now, there could be no doubt that it was *Hampshire*, and no doubt of the seriousness of the situation. A further telegram from Corporal Drever was sent at 8.50 p.m.: 'Four boats load of men off Marwick Head reported by Robertson Quockquoy Birsay.'

At 9.20 p.m., Gunner Norn handed in a fifth telegram, which was received at 9.25 p.m.: 'Ship 1½ miles from shore. Two explosions observed.'

At last, some efforts were being made to save the survivors. And help was finally on the way. At just after 9 p.m., Captain Walker was himself heading out into the stormy seas in the water tug *Flying Kestrel*. But a north-west gale was still blowing, with 15–20-foot waves and an eastward tide. *Flying Kestrel* was confronting solid seas over her decks, with sea spray sweeping over her funnel. Her normal speed was 11 knots, but in these conditions she was making just 6. Behind Walker were two more trawlers, *Northward* and *Renzo*. It was now only half an hour until sunset. They had already lost some forty-five minutes of daylight search time. By 10.30 p.m., the last glow of twilight would be gone, and on this cloudy night, all would be darkness. Searching at night, in rough seas, would be almost impossible.

Could they save anyone? Like *Hampshire* before them, they would now need to sail head first into a force 8–9 gale, with winds at the strongest of the day. Stromness was over 10 nautical miles by sea from the scene of disaster. Captain Walker knew that it would take anything up to two hours to get the first vessels to the men in the water. Would that be soon enough?

But what about the Stromness lifeboat, *John A. Hay*? This was a 40-foot, self-righting motor-boat which could travel at 7½ knots in good weather and carry up to sixty survivors. She could have made the 10-nautical-mile journey to the coastline near the wreck in a couple of hours, and she was manned by an experienced Orkney crew. Surely that had now also been despatched? But this local vessel remained on dry land. Had Captain Walker decided that the lifeboat, with her hugely experienced local crew, would take too long to get to the scene of the disaster? Or was it simply that no one had thought to call her out? Stromness was the nearest lifeboat station, and the scene of the disaster was well within her radius of operations. Moreover, the wind was now blowing survivors to the south-east, making the distance from lifeboat to survivors much shorter than the distance from the lifeboat to the more northerly wreck site. The lifeboat should have been called out. She did not need to reach the point where *Hampshire* sank. She could more usefully have searched closer in shore, around the Bay of Skaill and northwards, where the survivors were being blown.

But no one thought to call out *John A. Hay*: this was a military operation, in a naval-controlled area. Nor did anyone think to call out the Stromness Board of Trade Rocket Apparatus Brigade, with their cliff ladders. These specially trained men could have reached the rocky shores where survivors were likely to land, taking their rescue equipment with them, by around 9.30 or 10 p.m. – comfortably in time to give assistance. But nobody called on their services.

From Scapa Flow, now, the four destroyers Jellicoe had ordered out weren't far behind the vessels sent from Stromness. HMS *Unity*, HMS *Victor* and HMS *Midge* all left harbour between 9 p.m. and 9.10 p.m. HMS *Owl* followed at 9.20 p.m., just as the sun, hidden by the clouds, was setting. They could only make 12 to 15 knots, but this was still considerably better than *Flying Kestrel*. They passed her, one by one, by the Kirk Rocks in Hoy Sound, not far from Stromness.

Realising the scale of the disaster, Jellicoe sent a further five destroyers later – HMS *Menace*, *Munster*, *Napier*, *Oak* and *Opal*. But
these vessels did not set off until after 1 a.m. They were joined by
the trawler *Mafeking*.

The conditions facing the rescuers were dreadful: the winds had
reached their height almost exactly when *Hampshire* had sunk, and
by 9 p.m. they were still blowing at force 8 to force 9. It was only a
short distance to *Hampshire*, but it took two and a half hours after
the sinking for the first ships to reach the scene of the disaster, at
around 10.30 p.m. At this time, HMS *Unity* sighted wreckage in the
water. She and the other three destroyers now began their search.

Flying Kestrel reached Marwick Head shortly afterwards. It was
precisely at this moment that the last rays of twilight departed. The
rescue mission had arrived exactly as darkness fell. On the ships and
on the coastline, eyes squinted to make out signs of life in the waters.

What nobody could judge, at 10.30 p.m. on 5 June 1916, was whether a single man from *Hampshire* could yet be saved. And what no one
in the land or sea searches knew was that amongst those either dead
or dying was one of Britain's most famous ever war leaders.

THE FIGHT TO SURVIVE

'They were clustered around – dying as you looked at them.'
WARRANT MECHANICIAN WILLIAM BENNETT, RAFT 1

At around 8.05 p.m., HMS *Hampshire* rolled forward and sank beneath the waves, bows first, keeling over to starboard. The storm was at its height, with powerful winds and massive waves.

Many of the crew were already dead. Some had been blown up in the massive explosion or had drowned as the icy waters flooded into the ship. Others jumped overboard but died instantly when their necks were broken by life-support belts which snapped up under their chins.

Now, large numbers drowned as *Hampshire*'s plunge into the ocean dragged down those huddling in the unlaunched boats, as well as others too close to the ship to swim away. Those of the 749 men and boys on board who had managed to escape were now swimming for their lives in the icy water, with huge waves crashing over them, or clinging to the three Carley floats which had safely got away from the ship. Hundreds were in the water. But how many could reach land – land they could see clearly just over a mile and a half away, in the evening light of a long Orkney June day?

Some who could not make it to the rafts drowned relatively quickly in the bleak conditions, but even those who reached the Carley floats weren't safe: many were only half clothed, and the bitterly cold sea swept over and swamped the rafts, frequently casting the exhausted survivors off and back into the water.

The floats were now seriously overcrowded. The large ones were designed for just forty-five men inside, sitting or standing on the platform in the water, with another twenty-two men on the outside, submerged in the sea but holding onto the ropes that ran around the sides. In reality, each large float now provided for some seventy to ninety men. The smaller float was designed to carry just eighteen men. It was also full.

The Carley rafts weren't designed to protect men for long in the water. They were mere floats, to help men to survive until rescue craft reached them. But there were at present no rescue craft – none from the ship, and none from the land either.

The survivors were mostly men used to the sea and its challenges. They knew that in these conditions, exposure could kill in just an hour or two. With the mountainous seas, drowning was the major immediate risk. But closely after this was hypothermia: in waters this cold, death could be expected within an hour or two at most. Those exposed to the high winds might be expected to survive only half an hour. The sea temperature was around 9° centigrade. With the wind chill, it felt like freezing. And heat is lost by human beings significantly more quickly in water than in the air.

Many of those in the water died relatively quickly, swamped by wave after wave, and eventually – exhausted – succumbing to the cold, giving up hope and drowning. As time in the water increased, the men's body temperatures started to fall rapidly. Even those in the rafts started to shiver and shake uncontrollably. Their limbs

became numb. After some time, the shivering would stop and confusion took over. In severe cases, cardiac arrest followed. Those of
older age would have died quickly, but the young were struggling
too. There were seventy-four sailors below the age of eighteen on
Hampshire when she sank. Only one would survive.

Many of those hanging onto the sides of the floats began to lose
their grip as their bodies closed down the peripheral muscles of the
limbs to protect core body warmth: adrift on the furious seas, they
soon drowned. Nor was it possible in these conditions to guide the
rafts, which were pounded by the enormous waves and driven by
the strong tide and the north-west winds.

But the experienced sailors who could still think clearly, amongst
them Warrant Mechanician William Bennett on Float 1, Petty
Officer Wesson on Float 2 and Petty Officer Sweeney on Float 3,
soon began to realise that they did have one thing – just one – in
their favour. The furious sea and tremendous gale were blowing the
rafts back towards shore. They were not, it has to be said, being
blown back on the shortest route: for that, they would have needed
westerly winds to send them due east. But they could see that the
north-west wind was blowing them in a south-easterly direction.
If they could only survive long enough, they would eventually and
inevitably strike land.

But while the direct route to land was just a mile and a half away,
the longer and more angled route dictated by the wind and the tide
turned a tough 1½-mile journey into a tortuous 5-mile ordeal.

Forty-five minutes after the ship went down, some men on the
rafts had already died of cold and exhaustion. Those who were
clearly dead were now pushed off into the sea, to make more space
for others. If their bodies were held up by life-support belts, they
floated away, driven to shore by the same relentless waves and winds

that were powering the rafts. Those without lifebelts soon disappeared under the waves. Their bodies would never be recovered.

Float 1 was now at least nominally under the command of Warrant Mechanician William Bennett. Bennett had been in the engine room when the first explosion went off. He had later fallen into the water, but with a life-saving 'waistcoat' on. He swam urgently away from the ship, but when *Hampshire* plunged below the surface he was sucked down. When he resurfaced, the ship was gone. Bennett concluded that unless he could board a float or a boat, his fate was sealed. In the near distance, he could now see rafts in the water – the Carley floats. He swam towards them and eventually reached a raft after about a quarter of an hour. But it was full. It was designed for forty-five men. There were at least fifty inside – maybe more. Many others were clinging on for dear life in the water. He joined them, grabbing at the surrounding ropes with his numb fingers. His whole body felt bitterly cold. He drifted along outside the raft for about fifteen minutes, desperately trying to avoid being drowned.

And then, just when he was resigning himself to death, a voice could be heard, using his name and urging him inside the float. He wasn't certain if it was seventeen-year-old Able Seaman Dick Simpson or Able Seaman Jack Bowman, but he could hear the words 'Jump in, Mr Bennett. These blighters won't pull.' However, there was still no room inside the float, and pretty soon other survivors had reached the raft and were competing to cling onto the outside.

There were now simply too many men in and around the raft. Most of it was under the water and in danger of sinking. The word was passed round that all men with lifebelts should leave, to give the others a chance. Twelve brave men with lifebelts on volunteered to go. They half-joked that they would make it to land sooner than the others, before disappearing into the dark and surging seas. Perhaps some thought that swimming would keep them warm by using energy. But in cold water, swimming accelerates heat loss. Not one survived. However, their absence provided the space for Bennett to crawl on board. Even inside the float, the conditions were awful. The men were standing in about 4 feet 6 inches of bitterly cold water. For some, it was not much below their chins.

Bennett realised that he was the most senior man on board and quickly took charge. He collected some floating bits of wood to use for oars. There were a couple of paddles left, too, and Bennett took one himself and struck out with all the energy he had left. He persuaded the men to sing to keep their spirits up, and urged them on – 'Another ten minutes and we'll be there. Come on, lads. Put your pound on.' Shipwright Phillips and the others kept the raft heading shoreward as best they could in the bleak conditions. But eventually it became impossible to use the paddles: the seas were too violent. And, in time, most of the paddles and pieces of wood were wrenched from numb hands by the powerful waves. Soon, there was only one left.

They hoped that they would shortly see rescue ships. But there were none in sight. It was perhaps fortunate that these men did not yet know that the first rescue ships were not sent out until almost an hour from the original explosion.

In spite of their efforts, their body temperatures were continuing to fall. The winds and water were bitterly cold; the combination meant that it felt, literally, freezing. Squalls of rain soaked them from above and huge waves swept over and around them, again and again.

Bennett looked around at those on his float. One by one, they were dying of exposure and shock, even the youngest and fittest. Those in the water faded, gave up and drifted away. On board, it was little better: 'They were clustered around – dying as you looked at them.' A few more of the dead were thrown over the side, to make more room for the living. The ones who were still alive were the ones who were paddling.

It was now 9 p.m. – almost an hour since the ship had sunk. It was too cloudy to see the sun go down, but it was getting darker. They knew that by around 9.20 p.m., the sun would have set. By 10.30 p.m., even the twilight would have been lost. Each time the surging seas lifted their tiny float above the waves, they eagerly scanned the horizon. Surely help would not be long in coming? But there was still no sight of ships. Their only hope appeared to be to save themselves.

As they looked east, they could tell that they were not much closer to reaching land. Instead, the strong waves and tide were blowing them down the coast. They could see Marwick Head, but drifted straight past it. They could never have got up the steep cliffs there in any case, but after passing them they could see the protected shoreline of Marwick Bay, with its gently sloping beach. Here, they could have got ashore, but they were still much too far out to sea.

The only saving grace was that the raft had not so far capsized. But it offered little protection from the dreadful conditions. The cylindrical parts were under the water, dragged down by the weight of the men.

Shipwright William Phillips, age thirty, was one of those still alive. Next to him was a soldier, one of Kitchener's servants, who asked desperately if they would ever reach land. Phillips was as positive as he could be: 'Yes. Look! We are already halfway in now.' But the soldier had given up – 'I don't think so, mate' – and he died moments later, as if falling into a deep sleep. Not long afterwards, a big butcher, well over 6 foot, became delirious and died in Bennett's arms. At the other end of the raft from Phillips was a young lad, Reginald Sexton, a signal boy and the smallest member of *Hampshire*'s crew. He was aged only seventeen. He sang 'Tipperary' to cheer up the rest of the survivors. But within an hour he, too, was dead from exhaustion. He fell off the raft and disappeared under the waves.

An almost overpowering desire to sleep was now felt by all the men. But those who fell asleep never woke up. The rest thumped each other on the back to remain conscious. One dead man stood upright for the whole journey, with other dead men floating around him. Another died in the arms of 26-year-old Leading Seaman Charles Rogerson.

It was now past 11 p.m. They had been in the water for almost three hours. Perhaps the wind was not quite as strong, they thought. But the sun had set and the twilight was gone. It was dark and the cliffs were almost invisible. The sky was covered in cloud. Not a star could be seen. A thick, drizzly rain started to fall. They were beginning to lose hope. Phillips noticed that the gulls were flying ahead of their raft. Their shrieks could just be made out, above the noise of the wind and waves. Was it a wailing signal of sympathy, he wondered, an attempt to guide them in towards safety? Or were these renowned scavengers simply waiting for a free hand to pick at the corpses?

Phillips found himself lying across dead bodies, his limbs completely numbed by the water, wind and bitingly cold air. He could no longer speak. By now, there were around thirty-five men on the raft, but only fourteen of these seemed to be alive. Phillips began to feel it was over – time to give up. He had tried his best. He had survived three hours in the water. But he could last no longer. Sleep, followed by death, seemed an easy and tempting release.

Those who were not already dead were mostly dying. Soon there would be no one alive. They had now lost every paddle and were simply drifting south-east with the wind and the tide, hoping for the best.

But Phillips, faced with the prospect of death, now suddenly found new reserves of energy. He was not going to give up. And neither was Bennett – a tough man, who had fought his way up to officer level from the least promising of backgrounds. Bennett and Phillips now made fresh efforts to encourage the others, reminding them how near to land they had seemed when the sun went down. Surely they would reach the shore soon? 'Come on, lads!' But in their hearts they must have doubted if survival was really possible. And the minutes seemed to pass like hours.

Unknown to Bennett and the other survivors on Raft 1, two other Carley floats had escaped the catastrophe and were also now being blown south-eastwards towards the shore. They were following Bennett's raft, on almost exactly the same course.

The most senior of those on Float 2 was Petty Officer Wesson. The 33-year-old Wesson was standing by the hammocks on the mess deck when the explosion hit *Hampshire*. He saw Kitchener heading up to the main deck, escorted by a naval officer. He evacuated the ship on the second of the larger Carley rafts, initially with forty other men.

Wesson put some of the men who had been wounded by the explosion on the grating in the bottom of the raft. He told those in the float to paddle away from the ship before she sucked them all under. They dragged others on board, raising their numbers to over eighty. As the waves rose and fell, they could see a wink or two of light on the mainland of Orkney. They knew the wind and seas were carrying them back to land, but could they make it?

Wesson took charge. He would now need every ounce of the experience he had built up over eighteen years of naval service. He ordered the fittest men to paddle, and to keep the paddles on one side of the raft, in order to keep it beam on to the wind.

Men died with appalling swiftness – of shock, of wounds sustained from the explosion on the ship, and of hypothermia. The raft was on numerous occasions swamped by the waves. As with the other floats, the sea and the cold had their impact. Some slipped off and disappeared under the water. Others died where they lay. Mark Nugent, the ship's 25-year-old assistant paymaster, died on the float, along with two warrant officers and the ship's carpenter, George Stallard, aged thirty-two.

A gunner, 45-year-old Herbert Jennings, cheerfully led the singing. Others half-heartedly joined in. Predictably, it was 'Tipperary', and he sang it twice. Not long afterwards, he slipped to the bottom of the raft and died. The ship's boatswain was swimming on the outside of the raft, but eventually he too had to let go and was soon drowned.

And then, disaster. Part of the rope netting under the middle of the second float gave way without warning. Stoker Sims saw a dozen men suddenly sink out of sight. Men grabbed at them to try to save some, but it was no use. They were gone. Sims himself hung on grimly to the side of the float. He was determined to live, but his wounds from the blast on board the ship were draining his strength away.

Over forty men had died now on the raft. But the wind was blowing those still alive on their slow way towards the land. Could the twenty who were still alive keep going long enough to reach it? On their seemingly endless journey, they passed a score of bodies floating in the water. A few were clinging to lifebelts and wreckage. Most were dead.

Some on the float became delirious from hypothermia and threw themselves into the sea, to certain death. They had started with so many on the raft. But by 11 p.m., barely fifteen of these were still alive.

Behind these fifteen men on Float 2, but out of sight in the darkness, was the final raft – the smallest of the three, designed to carry just eighteen men. This was now under the charge of Petty Officer Sweeney, an experienced sailor who had spent all his life from age fourteen in the Royal Navy. Sweeney was Quartermaster of the Watch when the explosion went off on *Hampshire*. He was standing by the captain at the time.

When the abandon ship command was given, Sweeney ordered the launch of this final Carley raft, getting into the float and casting off. He was soon joined by fifteen or twenty other men, including 24-year-old Leading Stoker Alfred Read. Read had to jump in – a distance of about 15 feet in storm-force conditions. They were a mere 50 metres from *Hampshire* when her bows dipped under the water and the ship took her final plunge into the sea.

The journey to shore on the third raft followed the same general route as the larger floats and was the same seemingly endless nightmare: one moment high up on the crest of a wave, and then plunging into a trough from which it seemed the tiny raft would never rise again.

Float 3 lacked the size and weight of the larger rafts, so that those on board had a much more turbulent time. Two injured ship's stokers on board died soon after the journey began, followed by a soldier, possibly another servant from Kitchener's party. A sailor who had been burnt by the earlier explosion now began to slip away. After an hour he exclaimed, 'Mates, I'm done,' and sank to the bottom of the float and died.

Not long afterwards, the tiny raft was thrown over by the huge waves. There was a desperate struggle by exhausted men to right the raft and scramble back in. Only six men made it back. They were utterly exhausted. With most of the men lost, this was now an even lighter raft, in the heaviest of seas. And now the very same thing happened. And again. Four times in total the raft was thrown over. Each time, those who clambered back into the float wondered whether they could summon up the energy to do this again. Once, Read found himself trapped right under the raft, struggling to breathe, but somehow he managed to get back to the water's surface and scramble back inside.

It was now 11.15 p.m. – over three hours since *Hampshire's* sinking. Not a single rescue boat had been seen. It was utterly black.

The three floats were heading in to shore. But most of the 160–180 men who had set out from the ship on these feeble structures were now dead; perhaps only forty or fifty were still alive, and these few were dying, one by one. Would any reach the shore alive, and if they did approach land, might they be dashed to their deaths against the rocky shoreline of this unwelcoming island? At 11.15 p.m. on 5 June 1916, it looked highly likely that every man of the 749 on *Hampshire* would be lost.

Around half an hour after *Hampshire* had sunk, those in the military on shore finally realised they were facing a major disaster – one of the most serious of the war. It was not merely that 749 lives were in serious danger, but that Britain's War Minister, carrying secret papers, was now either dead or fighting for his life in the North Atlantic waters. The first step taken by those in military command was to send out ships to the site of the sinking. But soon afterwards they realised that they needed to despatch shore parties to assist anyone who made it back to the land. And given that Kitchener's mission had been carrying secret papers, they needed to recover these if they could.

Before departing with his rescue vessels at just after 9 p.m., Captain Walker had telephoned Lieutenant-Colonel Brooke, Royal Marine Artillery, who was Fire Commander, Western Defences. Walker instructed Brooke to organise a search party from Ness Batteries in Stromness.

Colonel Brooke sent off a rescue party in the two available cars. They left just after 9.15 p.m., and included Lieutenant Bossier, Surgeon Pickup, a sergeant and eleven marines. They took ropes, blankets and other items. They set out for Marwick Head, but as they approached there they were diverted further south, to search the shoreline from Outshore Point, back towards the Bay of Skaill.

Meanwhile, at Birsay, at around 8.40 p.m., a local farmer called James Robertson arrived on horseback from the south side of Marwick Head. Sub-Lieutenant Spence spoke briefly to him before he rushed to the post office. Robertson reported seeing four boats or rafts leave the ship and noted that they had last been seen south of Marwick Head at around 8.30 p.m. – just over forty-five minutes after the explosion on *Hampshire*. The details of this report were also cabled from Birsay to Stromness at 8.50 p.m. and reported to the Commander in Chief at 9.08 p.m. Jellicoe gave orders to warn all the inhabitants along the coast so that they could assist the rescue. A motorcyclist was sent out for this purpose. The authorities now knew that some men had got away. But was it too late to save them?

At Birsay, they were doing their best to get useful information back to inform the searches. Corporal Drever ran back to the beach to Sub-Lieutenant Spence: 'The Admiral wants to know what the wind direction is and can any boats land along the west side of the island?' Spence replied that the wind was now north-north-west, and that the only places boats could land safely would be the Bay of Skaill or Hoy Sound. Drever rushed back to the post office. At

10.07 p.m., Birsay wired, 'Wind NNW along the shore, boats could land Bay of Skaill or Stromness, sea rough.'

Vice-Admiral Brock had by now stopped all communications between Orkney and the outside world 'until further notice', and had ordered Colonel Harris, the officer commanding troops in Kirkwall, to head to Birsay by car to collect information and organise help. Declining assistance from those with local knowledge, Colonel Harris left with Commander Bertram Nicholson, commanding the Northern Patrol, at around 9.20 p.m. They needed to act with speed.

The journey from Kirkwall to Birsay was just eighteen miles by road. The weather was bad, but otherwise the route was straightforward and over low-lying land. However, local road signage had been removed because of the war. Harris and Nicholson took a staggering two hours to reach Birsay. They arrived just before 11.30 p.m. No explanation was given for the delay, but it seems certain that they got lost.

Fortunately, by this time, local residents and Territorials were already searching the coastline as far as Marwick Head. Some, from Marwick, were searching further south. At Birsay, the tardy Colonel Harris made a quick assessment of the situation, talking to Gunner Angus and to a local farmer. Sub-Lieutenant Spence was still on watch on the seafront, aghast that it was taking so long to get the rescue ships out – Spence had seen the first ships reaching the site of *Hampshire*'s sinking only shortly beforehand. The wind was now moderating and had veered back to the north. But the night was dark and rain was pouring down.

Talking to Harris, Gunner Angus was clear that he had seen a large, four-funnelled cruiser steaming north at about 7.40 p.m. After observing her for a short time, he saw two explosions in the fore part of the ship. He told Harris that he had immediately re-ported to the NCO in charge, Corporal Drever, who was in his billet a short distance away. Drever rushed out to look at the ship and then went to the post office to report to Artillery Kirkwall. Angus said that the ship sank just ten or twenty minutes after the second explosion. Harris then briefly spoke to Farmer Robertson of Quockquoy, Palace, Birsay. He was the man who had come down from Marwick Head and reported seeing four boats put off from the ship. These were now drifting to the south towards Marwick Head. Harris did not stop to talk to other local residents, even to Sub-Lieutenant Spence. He sent a message back to headquarters. It was handed in at Birsay Post Office at 11.25 p.m.: 'Two Vessels now in position where cruiser sank. Four boats from sunken vessel seen to the south of Marwick Head.'

Colonel Harris realised from what he was told that the direction of the tide and winds would be likely to blow any boats or life-rafts far to the south. The most obvious landing point seemed to be at the Bay of Skaill, a large, semi-circular bay around half way down the west side of Orkney. The bay had a small shingle beach on which it might be possible to land. That is where Colonel Harris now headed.

Staggeringly, it took Harris until 1.45 a.m. to travel the five miles to the Bay of Skaill. When he arrived, it was almost four and a half hours since he had been sent on his urgent mission. Harris achieved little at the Bay of Skaill and headed back to Kirkwall, arriving at 4 a.m. He had taken seven hours to achieve nothing of real value.

Fortunately, Captain MacKay of the Orkney Royal Garrison Ar-tillery (Territorials), whose family owned the Stromness Hotel, had already had the same idea about sending men to the likely landing points of the rafts. MacKay moved with rather greater speed and efficiency than Harris. At 10.30 p.m., he had taken a small rescue party of Territorials from Kirkwall to the Bay of Skaill, dropping two men off on the way to search the area just south of the bay. Other parties of local men were also searching further south.

Meanwhile, the Stromness party, under Lieutenant Bossier, had divided in two at Outshore Point, halfway between Marwick Head and the Bay of Skaill. The main group started to search along the cliffs to the south, while the cars headed off to the Bay of Skaill with two men who would be dropped off and would then head back northwards to link up with the other group. At last, the onshore rescue efforts were beginning to be more effectively managed.

Out to sea, the details of the modest and generally tardy rescue efforts were unknown to the two-score survivors who were still alive on the three rafts. It was 11.45 p.m. On Bennett's Raft 1, there were still around fifteen men alive. On Wesson's Raft 2, there were a similar number of survivors. On the small raft that Sweeney was now in charge of, just five or six men were alive.

On Bennett's raft, there in the blackness, Phillips and the rest were again beginning to give up hope. They had been in the water for almost four hours – at least twice the usual life expectancy in seas this cold and rough. Phillips could now feel the grip of death coming over him. He was foaming at the mouth. His legs and arms were completely numbed. He felt that any moment he would fall into a deep sleep from which he would never awake. The raft had started its journey with as many as eighty men in it or clinging to its sides. There were now twenty-four, but nine of these were dead. It seemed that it would not be long before the rest joined their fellow crew members in the quiet poses of death.

And then, suddenly, what was that? Phillips thought he could hear the sound of the waves crashing on rocks. Next, he could feel the raft grating on something – they were surely almost there.

Through the darkness, he could make out the unmoving shape of the shoreline. Bennett had seen the land too: 'Keep your strength, lads. We will need it shortly.'

The powerful waves were driving them towards land – but this was not a sandy beach or a rocky bay to clamber easily ashore on. When they were 40 metres or so from land, they realised with shock and fear that they were being blown towards cliffs 50 feet in height. Would they come so far, only to be smashed into rocks and con-cussed or drowned? Realising danger, sensing hope, the survivors now made every preparation for one last attempt to live.

They could not know precisely where they now were, but they were approaching Rivna Geo, a deep cleft in the cliffs extending some distance inland. Above this, if they could make it that far, was rough farmland, a couple of fields in width, and then habitation – a few solitary farmhouses squatting low against the Atlantic winds. Indeed, not far away now was the farmhouse from which the young Peter Brass had seen the explosions on *Hampshire* just four hours before.

They had survived this four-hour journey across mountainous seas and freezing waters. They were now approaching one of the most treacherous coastlines around Britain, in the middle of what was still a force 7 gale. The land was so close. But between safety and their raft were huge rocks and sheer walls of stone. Had they drifted slightly further south, they would have made land on the relative-ly sheltered and benign Bay of Skaill, with its mile of beach and shingle. But that choice was not available to them. Instead, Bennett saw a small opening at the end of some high cliffs. 'Let's make for that.' No matter. This was where their raft was being driven. A large wave washed them right up against the rocks and smashed them against a high cliff, and they were so close they could almost touch the land. Then the crest of the wave pulled back, taking them out to sea. Some of the men fell into the waters and were drowned. It was so far to come to die, just feet from safety.

Phillips felt desperate – the suspense of waiting for another surge to bring the raft back in without dashing them all against the rocks was overwhelming. They waited for the next wave, but the same thing happened – they smashed against the rocks but could not make land. They were so close, but would they all die here?

Another big wave roared in behind them. But, this third time, the direction of the sea was different, and instead of coming in against the cliff, the raft caught and hung for a while on some low rocks. They were now in the entrance of a narrow gap in the cliffs, with large slate-like rocks. This was at least a chance to get away, but the waves were still pounding around them. They might survive, or they might be battered to death on the rocks.

Bennett called, 'Jump out, lads.' The forward part of the raft was still packed with men, and Bennett expected to see them leap onto the rocks. But they didn't move. All were dead.

Instead, just six survivors crawled over the dead bodies to get out. First three and then another two made for the safety of land. Phillips threw himself onto a rock and remained, clinging on, expecting every second to be washed away. He lay there, watching the raft go back again into the sea. Exhausted, he and the others started to scramble up the cliffs. They were safe. But Phillips now lost consciousness and collapsed on a ledge. It was midnight. The first *Hampshire* survivors had reached land.

Five were now on shore, but just as Bennett was about to leave the raft, the sea sucked it backwards and he was so numbed that he fell while getting out and found himself in the water. He had to fight the tide three times from sucking him back to his death. His hands clawed at the slippery rock, ripping out his fingernails. He was trying to hold on, but the waters were pulling him back out. His energy was almost exhausted and he feared for his life. But at that moment Phillips and Cashman reached out their hands, grabbed his bleeding fingers and refused to let go when the sea again enveloped him. Bennett was safe. He lay on the rocks, gasping for breath, unable to believe he was alive.

The exhausted men dragged themselves clear of the water. Bennett was totally numb from the waist down and could not kneel, because his knees were cut up by the rocks. All his fingernails and toenails had gone, along with part of his big toe.

Bennett was now at the bottom of the cliff with Phillips and Cashman. He asked where the other men had gone and was told that Simpson, Rogerson and Bowman had already climbed the cliff unaided. Rogerson was perhaps in the best state of the six. His legs were numb, but otherwise he felt all right. He scrambled up the cliffs, stumbled across a couple of fields and found a cowshed in which to escape from the wind and rain. It was 12.10 a.m., Tuesday 6 June. The first survivor had reached the safety of both land and cover.

Simpson and Bowman followed, scrambling on the wet rock and falling back three or four times before making it to the top of the cliffs. On the windswept coast just north of the Bay of Skaill, a few farmhouses are set back from the sea, in the middle of fields. These fields run down to the ocean, but before they reach it are some rocky cliffs, not of great height but of sheer rock, and perilous to climb. This is where Raft 1 had landed.

Simpson and Bowman now headed for the nearest farmhouse they could see: Garson, the home of William and Mary Phillips and their twenty-year-old daughter Mina. The family were all in bed when, just after midnight, they heard a loud knocking at the front door. A voice from outside shouted above the wind, 'Can you help us? Our ship has hit a mine. We need help.'

The family rushed downstairs and opened the door to Jack Bowman, who stumbled inside, exhausted, soaking wet and bitterly cold. William Phillips quickly lit the fire while his wife looked for some warm clothes. And then, just a couple of minutes later, there was a second knock and they opened the door to find seventeen-year-old Dick Simpson, 5 feet 6¾ inches tall, with brown hair and a youthful complexion. Simpson had lacerated wounds to his feet where other men had stood on him in the raft. Both men warmed themselves in front of the fire and changed into dry clothes. A breakfast was prepared for them. They were doing all right. They were going to recover.

As Simpson and Bowman were recuperating in the farm, a group of rescuers – the marines from Fort Hoy – were making their way along the clifftops nearby, looking for survivors.

At Rivna Geo at just after midnight, the searchers on land heard a strange sound above the roar of the waves and the wind. They shouted out and heard the noise of answering voices. When they looked down below, careful not to lose their footing on the slippery rock, they could see that the voices were coming from a raft close to the cliff. They had found Bennett's float. There had been at least twenty-four men on board. Eight were still, barely, alive. Ten were dead.

At the base of the cliff, Bennett, Phillips and Cashman were not yet out of danger. But at least they could hear the calls of the rescue party above them and make out the shapes of those who had come to save them. Their relief was overwhelming. But they still had to scale the cliffs.

Phillips was wearing a bright white shirt, and one of the marines spotted it. Phillips lost consciousness just after hearing the voices above them. Bennett passed out shortly afterwards, too. One rescuer was lowered by rope, with a couple of men on the clifftop gradually letting him down to his complete his dangerous work and then hauling the man and his prize back up to the clifftop. Hands reached out to pull the three survivors up the final few feet. Finally, they were safe.

The float they had come in on still contained men – some dead and some, perhaps, barely alive. Two of the rescuers, Gunner Worrell and Private Head, continued to carefully descend the cliffs to do their vital work. In these conditions it was simply impossible to stabilise the raft. But the rescuers weren't going to give up. They could see bodies in the float, though they did not know if they were alive. And they could hear one man still on board the raft who was shouting out for assistance. Eventually, they succeeded in grabbing him and dragged him up the cliff. But when they reached the top, it was too late – he was dead.

The waves now swept the float back into the sea and then, buoyed by the ocean swell and the high tide, it was driven back towards the land and eventually jammed between two rocks, suspended 20 feet up in the air. It was a perilously difficult task now to rescue those inside. Eventually, they cut the bottom from the float and let some of the bodies fall. When they were brought up from below and examined by the doctor, Surgeon Pickup, every single one was dead.

The rescue party could do no more here, and in any case Gunner Worrell and Private Head were exhausted and bitterly cold; they had to be left at the nearby farmhouse to recover. Helping the marines with the rescue efforts were the locals. Peter Brass, aged thirteen, had seen immediately that *Hampshire* was in trouble and had called his father, David. Mr Brass had warned the inhabitants of the other local farms and they had watched the progress of the rafts towards the shore, hoping they could help.

The marines and local residents now assisted the remaining survivors to safety. Bennett, Cashman and Phillips were taken to Pallast, the farmhouse of David and Davina Brass. Rogerson, having been found collapsed in the cowshed, was already there, moaning that his tobacco had got wet. They took off their soaking clothes, sat in front of a large fire, drank down some spirits and were then wrapped up warmly in bed. Bennett was surrounded by as many hot water bottles as could be filled. He remembers waking in front of a warm fire. He was trying to come to terms with the fact that he had survived a sinking ship for the second time in six months.

In total, just six men had survived of the eighty or ninety who had reached this float in the fifteen minutes after the sinking. Eighteen more bodies were still in the raft, lying on the rocks or stretched out on the clifftop.

It was four hours after *Hampshire* had sunk. Only twenty-four of those on board were accounted for. Out there in the waves were another 725 men, some dead, and a few – a very few – alive.

* * *

Like many of the men on Bennett's float, those on Wesson's had mostly given up hope – including Stoker Sims, still recovering from the burns he had sustained four hours before. Then, not much before midnight, and just as Sims was in danger of drifting off into a potentially fatal sleep, he was roughly shaken by his friend Lofty Farnden: 'Wake up. Wake up. Look – there are rocks!'

They could just make out that they were approaching – it seemed around 100 metres away – a cliff of some 40 feet in height. But with the waves smashing hard on the rocks, could they make land safely? It was almost exactly high water. The sea was surging up to the land, producing white surf all around. Wesson, Sims, Buerdsell and Farnden watched with bated breath to discover what their fate would be. The waves washed them gradually in closer to the land, but as the sea struck the shore it then retreated sharply, dragging the raft back out with it. They were getting nearer, noticeably nearer. But it was a slow process. And then there was an enormous bump – and the sound of wood grating on rock. The raft had part grounded. Some of the survivors leapt out immediately and were swept in closer to land by the waves behind.

Petty Officer Wesson clutched at a rock and held on for dear life as the waves hurled themselves at him. He thought that at any moment he would be washed away. He knew there wasn't much more fight in him. Lofty Farnden found himself thrown onto the rocks as the raft beached. There was a 12-foot wide stretch of calmer water between him and the base of the cliffs. Farnden dragged himself across this and started to climb up. Stoker Sims now plunged into the water and half swam, half crawled onto the rocks. He too had now reached safety. Almost immediately, he passed out.

It was 12.15 a.m. Survivors of the second raft had reached the safety of the shore, at Nebbi Geo. It was just 300 metres to the south of the landing point for Raft 1.

Above them were the same set of features that had met those from the other float: a sheer wall of rock, a few hundred metres of gently sloping farmland, and then the welcoming sight of four farmhouses, set apart in a north–south line, almost a mile from top to bottom and running down parallel to the coastline.

In this float were forty-seven men. Most, though, were already dead. Of the fifteen left alive, just five now made it to the shore.

Others drowned, died of exposure where they lay, or were smashed against the rocks and killed.

Four of the survivors, Wesson, Buerdsell, Farnden and Sims, now tried to scramble up the cliffs. For fit and rested men, it would have been a tough task in these conditions. But these four sailors were exhausted, and their limbs were frozen and lead-like. The flesh of their hands and knees was cut badly as they dragged themselves up the sharp rocks. At last, the cliff was less steep. They had made it.

Wesson lay for a while in the grass, exhausted, as the wind blew around him and the rain poured down. Then he got up. He saw a house in the distance, crawled towards it and tried to wake the inhabitants. After ten minutes of shouting and beating the door with the heel of his boot, it was finally opened. Wesson could now barely speak. He tried to explain what had happened but could not find the words. He stumbled inside and, after a hot drink, managed to tell his story. He had reached Linnahowe, the home of Mr and Mrs Whitelaw and their 25-year-old son James. Buerdsell also found his way to Linnahowe and safety. Sims and Farnden were now at the top of the cliffs, still looking for shelter.

After the first survivors from Float 1 had reached safety, thirteen-year-old Peter Brass had rushed to the surrounding farms to wake the other residents. Now he was on the way back from the northernmost farm, Pallast. Suddenly, he saw a figure in the darkness, stumbling across the windswept fields. It was Stoker Sims, utterly exhausted and in pain from his burns. Peter quickly guided Sims to Stockan, where Farnden was also taken. Both men were looked after by Mr and Mrs Harvey and their two young sons, Willie, aged fourteen, and Robert, twelve.

The rescuers were astonished to hear from some of the survivors that Lord Kitchener had been on board the ship. Some thought this might be a hallucination, brought on by hypothermia.

Rescue parties of crofters were now making their way down to the shore with ropes, to see if they could recover other survivors. It was around 12.30 a.m.

Meanwhile, the two marines who had been dropped at the Bay of Skaill with instructions to work northwards up the coast were gradually approaching the area of cliffs where Floats 1 and 2 had landed. They soon met a labourer, who told them that he had seen a survivor making his way towards a farmhouse and who directed them to the second raft, which had been lifted by the waves and had come to rest between ledges of rock at Nebbi Geo.

The rescuers had now found the second raft – Petty Officer Wesson's. In this, or around it in the sea, they could see large numbers of bodies. In the darkness, they could not count the numbers, but they would later find forty-two. They now were mostly dead or in the final stages of death. They discovered only one man who was definitely alive: John Downes, the 23-year-old captain's writer. He was exhausted and suffering badly from exposure. The rescuers dragged him to the top of the cliffs. But minutes after reaching the safety of land, he was dead.

It was 12.45 a.m. Ten survivors from Rafts 1 and 2 were now alive and safe. After this time, none of those from Rafts 1 or 2 who made land lived. They died where they lay in the rafts, or were smashed against the cliffs until they died of their injuries or drowned.

The gruesome task of recovering the bodies from Rivna Geo and Nebbi Geo now began. For the next five hours, the Stromness party engaged in the ugly duty of bringing out the bodies and laying them at a safe distance from the waves and the tide. They were helped by three local residents and by some trawlermen. At around

5.30 a.m., these rescuers were relieved by another group of marines. With great difficulty, the bodies were dragged one by one to the top of the cliff and laid out on the ground. By the early morning, they had brought up sixty-one bodies from the two rafts below.

But the search was not yet over. A third float had been spotted out to sea, and at 12.45 a.m. the rescuers were as determined as ever to offer speedy support to any others who reached land alive.

Young Peter Brass wasn't giving up either. After accompanying Stoker Sims to Stockan, he rushed to Linnahowe, the furthest south of the four farms in this area. Here, Peter met James Whitelaw and young Jim Swidler. He persuaded them to go to the Bay of Skaill, where they woke the local miller, James Linklater, and started a search along the shoreline.

Further to the south, Captain MacKay's party of Territorials had also worked hard throughout the night, searching the huge expanse of the Bay of Skaill. And that was where the third and final raft was to land, coming ashore at around 1 a.m.

It had drifted over a mile further south than the other floats, prolonging the time in the freezing waters. But the compensation was that instead of coming in against the steep cliffs of Northdyke, Raft 3 was blown in at the more benign spot of the Bay of Skaill, with its short sand and pebble beach.

Float 3 was, of course, the smallest of the rafts, designed to support just eighteen men. There were now just four men alive on board. As the float reached a safe distance from the shore, Sweeney and Read plunged into the water and half-swam, half-stumbled to the beach. Sweeney collapsed there, utterly exhausted. Read, having caught his breath for a moment, looked back at the raft bobbing backwards and forwards in the surf. He realised that the other two occupants were too weak to make the land by themselves. Bravely, he waded out through the waves, cursing his bad fortune in having to again face the bitterly cold water. He seized the first man he came to, who was clearly too exhausted to move. Read heaved him up and dragged him back to the shore. He then plunged back into the sea, returned to the raft and recovered another man, pulling him onto the beach as well.

For a few minutes all four lay, unmoving, on the sand and rocks. Read and Sweeney hardly dared to believe that they had survived. But they knew they needed to escape from the bitter winds and squally rain if they were to be sure of living. They left the other two exhausted, semi-conscious survivors just above the beach and stumbled inland, managing to find a nearby boathouse, in which they collapsed.

Not far away now, the local people and Territorials were searching this stretch of coastline for their raft. Eventually, on the south side of the bay, they found it, now overturned on the beach. There appeared to be no survivors. They continued to search and 200 metres further on, where the cliff begins to rise, they found an upturned boat in the water, but it was impossible to get near it.

And then, turning back to the north, and in the first light of morning, they saw two bodies, slumped on the grass near some railings just above the beach. One was the captain of the marines, Cyril Hazeon, and the other was a young boy, an engine room artificer, almost certainly nineteen-year-old William Salisbury. They were quickly checked for signs of life. But it was too late. Exhaustion or exposure had claimed them.

The search party continued their grim work and soon afterwards, at around 2 a.m., were rewarded by finding the last two survivors, Read and Sweeney, in the boathouse. They were quickly taken to the nearest farm, Garricot, where they were cared for by 78-year-old James Marwick and by Mrs Beatten and Miss Spence.

That night, there had been 749 men on *Hampshire*. Twelve survivors had now made it to land and were being cared for in the farmhouses that bordered the sea.

Sixty-three men had been found on or around the rafts but were now dead.

Out there in the Atlantic, there were still 674 men unaccounted for.

And one of these men was the Secretary of State for War, Lord Kitchener himself.

THE SEARCH AT SEA

'Complete destruction. There appears nothing more to be done.'

COMMANDER OF HMS *OWL*, 4.25 A.M., 6 JUNE 1916

At around 10.30 p.m., the first rescue ships reached the site of *Hampshire*'s sinking. These were the destroyers *Unity*, *Victor*, *Midge* and *Owl*, followed by *Jason II* and *Cambodia*. The sun had set an hour ago. It was now almost completely dark.

The ships' captains knew that the twilight of the new morning would not assist them with their work until at least 2 a.m. And the sun would not be up fully until just after 3 a.m. In waters as cold and rough as these, submerged men would likely remain conscious for only thirty to sixty minutes. Death would be expected in one to two hours, at best. Those delays in calling out the first rescue vessels really mattered.

Those who had failed to make it onto the three rafts had already been fully submerged in the water for two and a half hours. Could any still be alive? And if they were alive, could they now be found in the darkness and in the turbulent seas? When the explosion on *Hampshire* had occurred, there was still over an hour and a half until sunset. But so much of that precious time had been lost in miscommunication, muddle and delay. The price to be paid was now, as the search began in pitch blackness.

Sailors on board HMS *Unity* were the first to find evidence of the earlier calamity, sighting wreckage in the waves at 10.30 p.m. *Unity* had been one of *Hampshire's* two escort ships earlier in the evening. Her sailors surveyed the scene in deep gloom and with a heightened sense of responsibility. Later, they would pull three dead from the waves. The other ships were now searching too.

Flying Kestrel, with Captain Walker on board, reached Marwick Head at around the same time as the destroyers and also began the search for survivors and bodies. Marwick Head is to the south-east of the spot where *Hampshire* sank, and Walker hoped to pick up the men who would have floated in that direction in the wind and waves.

There was still a heavy swell, persistent rain and strong winds, blowing between force 7 and force 8 – hardly the ideal conditions for a sea search. The only objects that could be easily made out in the waters were the other ten search vessels. These would be joined by five more destroyers at around 3 a.m.

Realising the seriousness of the situation, Admiral Jellicoe sent an urgent message from his flagship, *Iron Duke*: 'Use searchlights freely. Send destroyer north of the wreckage.' Lights would not usually be used at night, for fear of attracting the attention of enemy vessels. But Jellicoe knew that he had to take every possible risk to rescue Lord Kitchener, and as many of his mission and *Hampshire's* crew as possible.

At 11.50 p.m., HMS *Owl* reported to fleet headquarters: 'Much wreckage off Marwick Head.' At 12.15 a.m., she sighted a capsized boat. Perhaps this was the fourth craft observed earlier by one of the farmers from the land? An hour later, *Owl's* crew found a number of bodies in the water.

But in spite of the searchlights, the eleven vessels could find no survivors, and few even of the dead. And they had so far failed to find the four rafts, or boats, which had been reported as having carried survivors from the ship back towards the shore.

The military authorities now had a mini-armada of ships – sixteen in all – involved in the search, but there was a long pause before the reporting of more finds. Working in the dark was difficult at the best of times, even with searchlights. But in these stormy conditions, the task seemed impossible. And perhaps many of the men had simply drowned. Those without life vests would likely quickly disappear beneath the waves.

Eventually, in the light of the early dawn, the crew of the steam yacht *Jason II* saw the flash of a flare hanging in the sky, just off the Bay of Skaill – six miles from where *Hampshire* had sunk. They headed in the direction of this signal and soon came upon bodies in the ocean. At 3.32 a.m., the captain of *Jason II* sent a brief message to Longhope: 'Floating bodies near Rowhead. Too much sea still running to use boats.' They pulled a dead petty officer and a marine out of the water. But the sea was simply too rough to pick up the other bodies. Instead, *Jason II* headed north along the coast, hoping to find survivors. The vessel made two sweeps but saw no one. The wind had by now fallen back a good deal, but a powerful surf still beat against the cliffs. The captain concluded that no one could safely land on this stretch of coast – only at the Bay of Skaill or Marwick Bay. He was wrong: this is where Floats 1 and 2 had landed four hours earlier.

Jason II now turned south and headed back to the Bay of Skaill to try to find the other bodies, sighted earlier. They came across a wrecked boat which looked as if it had been smashed up while being lowered. It was difficult to tell whether it was the captain's galley or a whaler. And the sea was too rough to pick the pieces of boat out of the water. But the vessel was broken amidships and debris was floating near her. They also fished out an officer's hat, with Captain Savill's name inside it. It was the first time that those on the ships knew that the sunken vessel was *Hampshire*. But there were no clues as to whether Savill had got away from the ship.

With daybreak, eager eyes on all the ships looked down into the choppy seas, shielding faces against the wind and spray. At best, they hoped to see bodies or wreckage. By now, only an optimistic few could hope to find anyone alive. It was eight hours since *Hampshire* had sunk. All those on the rescue ships knew that no man could survive this long in waters so cold and rough – two or three hours would be a rare achievement.

And now, with the light of day, it was finally possible for the ships to do their bleak work. At 4 a.m., with the winds dropping back to force 5, a sailor on HMS *Oak* cried, 'Black object on the port side, sir.' Looking out, they could see that the ship was surrounded by a mass of floating bodies. Boats were lowered to fish the corpses out, and other vessels came to assist. The decks were now covered in bodies, including that of a surgeon lieutenant.

At around the same time, *Flying Kestrel* passed an extensive oil spill, and shortly afterwards came upon a large number of bodies bobbing up and down in the waves. They brought as many as possible onto the ship. All were long dead. There were thirty in total, including Commander Dasent, aged thirty-seven, and 29-year-old Lieutenant-Commander Stewart.

HMS *Owl* found two more bodies at 4.25 a.m. Again, there was not a single living soul to be seen or heard. *Owl*'s commanding officer sent back a grim message to headquarters at Scapa Flow: 'Complete destruction. There appears nothing more to be done.'

HMS *Victor* had picked up four bodies by 5 a.m. and HMS *Oak* hauled in another fourteen corpses at around the same time. At 5.58 a.m., *Opal* signalled that she had also brought bodies on board. Later, it was confirmed that these included Arthur Cossey, the engineer commander of *Hampshire*, along with a warrant officer, a stoker and six other men. HMS *Napier* recovered a single body at 7 a.m.

At 7.32 a.m., the first identified body from the Kitchener party was recovered: it was nineteen-year-old Second Lieutenant Robert Macpherson, the Russian-language interpreter. Macpherson was recovered by HMS *Oak* and was recognised instantly from his tartan trousers. The news was quickly relayed to Admiral Jellicoe.

Jellicoe hadn't slept that night. Instead, he was waiting for updates from his ships, desperate for news of survivors and particularly of Kitchener. At 8.10 a.m., the Commander in Chief felt he could no longer delay a painful duty. Kitchener did not seem to have made land. And, at sea, the rescue boats had failed to bring in a single survivor. As for the few survivors who had made the shore, news of their successful recovery had yet to be reported. It was now twelve hours since *Hampshire* had sunk. Jellicoe sat sombrely at his desk and wrote out a top-secret urgent-priority message, to be sent off immediately to the Admiralty in London:

Deeply regret to report that 'Hampshire' with Lord Kitchener and Staff on board was sunk by mine or torpedo off Brough of Birsay, west side of Orkneys, at about 8 p.m. last night. Four boats were seen to leave the ship by shore observers. A heavy sea was running, wind NNW. Destroyers and patrol vessels proceeded to scene at once and parties were sent to watch along coast, but up to present only some bodies and a capsized boat found. I greatly fear there is little hope of there being any survivors, as whole shore has been searched … shore parties have not yet reported.

The tragic message was sent. Jellicoe knew the shock and horror that it would cause in the Admiralty, in 10 Downing Street and throughout the Empire. He awaited the response, which he knew would not be long in coming.

And then, for Jellicoe, there was, at last, the first good news of the night. At 8.48 a.m., a telegram: 'Fire Commander Hoy reports thirteen survivors landed at various points and are now being cared for at local farms…' Jellicoe, read on, hoping for the best. But it was not to be: 'No officers among them. Many bodies on the shore now being recovered. Bodies will be sent to Stromness. Request instructions as to disposal of bodies.'

Of course, every survivor was important. But there was no use pretending they were equally regarded. After the disappointment of Jutland, the last thing Jellicoe and the British nation needed was the death of their wartime commander and national figurehead.

Now it was clear that no survivors were likely to be found at sea, the rescue vessels started to return with their grim cargoes. At 9.52 a.m., Captain Walker on *Flying Kestrel* signalled that he had brought thirty bodies to Stromness. These included four officers. Most had no identification discs, but they had already confirmed 29-year-old Lieutenant-Commander Stewart as amongst those recovered.

Kitchener was clearly not one of those found – no identity discs would be needed to recognise one of the most famous people in the kingdom. Having landed the bodies, Captain Walker then headed for the Bay of Skaill to interview the survivors. At 11.22 a.m., *Flying Kestrel* left Stromness without him, but with thirty-one bodies on board, destined for the hospital ship *Soudan*.

Later that day, Colonel Fitzgerald's body was identified on *Soudan*. He was recognised from his uniform, his name on his underclothing and by personal items on the body. The medical officer on board, Dr C. F. Beinbridge, judged that the cause of death was probably drowning. The corpse of Kitchener's closest friend and adviser appears to have been picked up by *Flying Kestrel* soon after she reached the area where *Hampshire* sank. It seems unlikely that the body of Kitchener would have been far away. It is a reasonable assumption that the faithful Fitzgerald was with his master until the bitter end.

On land, Colonel Harris left Kirkwall for the Bay of Skaill at around 8 a.m. He took with him four lorries and about forty-five Territorials, to assist in collecting and removing the bodies that were being brought up from the recovered rafts or had washed up on the shoreline. Once they reached the coast, the troops began the bleak task of searching for and identifying the dead and collecting any possessions. It was a gruesome job that made grown men flinch. Many of the bodies were in a bad state, having been dashed up numerous times against the rocks.

At Rivna Geo and Nebbi Geo, the remaining bodies were carried up, one by one, and laid out on the clifftops. At the Bay of Skaill, they used the grass banks behind the beach for the same purpose. For those who witnessed it, including the local farmers, it would never be forgotten. The troops did their best to keep locals away from the scene, in respect for the dead and to shield civilians from the ghastly sights.

Some seventy-five bodies in all were recovered, and without stretchers to move them it was hard work. Eventually, the bodies were loaded on a light truck to convey them to the larger naval lorries parked on nearby roads. They had to cross fields and rutted cart tracks, and the trucks often sank into the soaking wet ground.

Farmers' carts were eventually requisitioned to convey the rest of the dead to the road.

The bodies were placed aboard the lorries with as much respect as circumstances allowed. The first vehicle left for Stromness, fully laden with the dead. Soon, it returned, and took another full load back. A second lorry made one more trip.

In the evening, the hospital ship *China*, moored at Longhope, signalled that large numbers of bodies were being brought in by destroyers and other craft. *China* was given orders to lay the bodies out in lines on the poop deck, under awning. Nothing on the bodies was to be taken or tampered with. An identification party was assembled from the Paymaster's department of HMS *Cyclops*, and from the ship's police and other units, and this was quickly sent to *China* to do its necessary but unpleasant work. When the identification party reached *China*, it was a miserable night, with high winds and rain. But the men had clear orders, which were to be followed by the book. They were tasked with searching each body, looking for names on clothing and other forms of identification, and removing any jewellery and personal items, which were to be sent on to relatives.

The commander of the identification party, Rear-Admiral Prendergast, the officer in command of shore-based personnel at Scapa, soon noticed the bodies of the two military officers. One was wearing tartan trousers and had already been identified as Second Lieutenant Macpherson. The other was quickly established to be Colonel Fitzgerald. Prendergast was told that all the bodies picked up in the water by ships were supported by lifebelts, life buoys or pieces of wreckage. None were recovered from boats.

The bodies had to be counted, identified as far as was possible, and the details sent on to senior officers and the Commander in Chief. But on 6 June, the first priority had to be the survivors: who were they and what could they reveal about the fate of *Hampshire*, and particularly of Lord Kitchener?

Each survivor was formally interviewed by Captain Walker, beginning at around noon on 6 June. This took place at the farms where the men had come ashore, since they were still recovering from their ordeal. Walker carefully summarised their accounts and sent the information in to the naval authorities.

Around the same time, 12.25 p.m. on 6 June, Colonel Harris scrawled down a short note to himself:

Colonel Brooke tells me that one of the survivors (name unknown) has been talking about Lord Kitchener. He says he [Kitchener], with various others, got away in a boat which was swamped shortly afterwards. Man himself was not in the boat. I have told Brooke to tell man to keep quiet and to deny the fact that Kitchener was there. Survivors mostly got ashore in one raft. Most of the bodies are frightfully knocked about by being washed against the rocks and cliffs.

Lieutenant-Colonel Brooke later confirmed this claim in his own note of the rescue attempts, written on 8 June: 'One of the survivors informed the sergeant that he saw Lord Kitchener get into a pinnace with all his staff and almost directly after leaving the ship the boat capsized.'

It was an intriguing piece of information. But it completely failed to match the account given to Captain Walker by the twelve survivors. In these accounts, there was no indication from any survivor that Kitchener had been seen leaving the ship. And none of the survivors believed that any boats had succeeded in getting away from the ship.

The next day, after some photographs with their proud local hosts, all the survivors were collected together and taken by car to Stromness. A tug brought them to the depot ship HMS *Blake* in Scapa Flow. They arrived there at 3 p.m. and were given additional clothing and a medical inspection. A full interview with each survivor was planned.

It was now time for the naval authorities to make lists: of the survivors, of those whose bodies were found, and – the longest list of all – of those still missing.

Only one of the seventy-four crew under the age of eighteen was still alive: seventeen-year-old Dick Simpson, who came in on Raft 1. All the sixteen-year-olds on board were dead: Sidney Reynolds, William Brain, Percy Colbeck, Arthur Davis, George Mafeking Evans, William Evans, Bernard Flanagan, Henry Gildersleeve, Ernest Joels, William Lawler, William Oulton, Frank Potter, William Powell, James Rigby, William Smith, Charles Wheeler and William Wheeler.

There were numerous other tragic stories. Brothers William and Albert Pettett, both stokers, aged twenty-one and twenty respectively, were lost. They had consecutive service numbers and had signed up on the same day. Able Seaman Ralph Buckingham, aged twenty-one, was missing too – never to be found. His mother was notified of his death and a couple of days later received a letter he had written after the Battle of Jutland.

Thomas Hill had died too. He had enlisted in the Royal Navy but been dismissed for theft in 1897. He re-enlisted in 1903, using his brother's name of Reginald. The third Hill brother was notified of 'Reginald's' death, only to discover later that it was Thomas who was really missing.

Stoker 1st Class Thomas Harwood, aged thirty-two, was dead

too. He had the bad fortune to join *Hampshire* just twelve days before she was sunk. The sister of Stoker Jack Beechey, aged twenty-one, could at least continue to treasure the pendant cross that he had given her on his last leave home.

Like Jack Beechey, most men would never be found. The bodies of some floated long distances. Lieutenant Humphrey Matthews, the gunnery officer who shouted 'Make way for Lord Kitchener', was washed up far south at Thurso, on the mainland of Scotland. His watch was still on his wrist, stopped at 8.02 p.m.

But of the Field Marshal, the War Minister, Britain's greatest military hero since Wellington, there was no sight. The Admiralty quickly accepted the inevitability of his death. Their focus now was on containing further damage. They had already sent an urgent message to Jellicoe: 'Lord Kitchener had number of most secret and important official documents. Any wreckage floating about should be examined and precautions be taken to watch the coast for wreckage drifting in.' Jellicoe confirmed that such measures were already being taken.

And the very day after *Hampshire* had sunk, printed notices were distributed on Orkney and on the north coast of the mainland, offering a reward for the return of the mission's secret documents:

Reward: Lost Overboard at Sea. 4 Despatch Cases. (1.) Brown leather DESPATCH CASE about 17 inches by 12 by 5, with 3 initials on the top also some smaller writing. (2.) Black leather DESPATCH BAG with straps about 18 inches by 12 inches, with brass lock. (3.) Brown leather DESPATCH CASE similar to No. 1 but about 10 inches deep instead of 5. (4.) Wooden DES-PATCH CASE about the same size as No. 3 marked HQ in big black letters. The above have been lost at sea in the vicinity of

Orkney and contain correspondence which is only of value to the owner, who has authorised me to offer a reward of: £25 for a complete unbroken case. £1 to £20 for a portion of the contents. On delivery to the Senior Naval Officer, Thurso. F. E. E. Brock, Vice-Admiral, Longhope, 6th June 1916.

At 4.11 p.m. on 6 June, Jellicoe sent a further message to the Admiralty, updating them on the results of the search: 'Priority urgent. All hope of mission having been saved must be abandoned. Thirteen survivors of ship's company washed ashore on raft, one since died. Fear everyone else is lost. Some bodies recovered amongst them that of Second Lieut. MacPherson of Cameron Highlanders on staff as Russian interpreter.'

By 8 p.m. – twenty-four hours since *Hampshire* had sunk – there were still just twelve survivors. The bodies of over one hundred officers and men had already been recovered, and plans were in place to inter them in one common grave.

Jellicoe had to deal with the grim practicalities. He signalled the Admiralty, wanting to know if the bodies of Fitzgerald and Macpherson should be buried in dedicated graves on Orkney or returned to the mainland and to relatives. The next day, at around 1 a.m., Jellicoe had his reply. The relatives of Lieutenant Macpherson wanted him buried in a marked grave on Orkney. The body of Colonel Fitzgerald was to be brought to London. He would be buried close to his family home in Eastbourne. His would be the only body to leave Orkney.

Meanwhile, back on the mainland, not a glimmer of news had made it past the official censor. Late in the morning of Tuesday 6 June, Christina Simpson, mother of seventeen-year-old Dick Simpson, was at home in Tynemouth. A telegram arrived. What could it mean? She had two sons presently serving in the forces, as well as her husband, Ralph. She was proud of all three of them but worried every day about their safety. She opened the telegram. It was from Dick. Her heart missed a beat. It read, simply: 'All right. Don't worry.' But she did. What did it all mean? No news of *Hampshire*'s fate had yet been made public. Could it simply be a message sent after the recent Battle of Jutland?

Christina Simpson was not the only relative of a *Hampshire* sailor to receive a message that morning. Martha Reeve, wife of Yeoman of Signals George Reeve, also received one. Two days before, on Sunday 4 June, she had received a telegram and immediately feared the worst. She had opened it with shaking hands. But with relief she had read: 'Quite alright, inform Mother, George'. She had guessed that it was a reference to the Battle of Jutland, and now knew that her husband of just six years had survived. Nonetheless, it took her some time to recover from the shock and fear of receiving a message which she immediately guessed was bringing the worst possible news. Now, on the morning of Tuesday 6 June, she received a further short letter from George, explaining that British losses at Jutland had been severe but confirming that he was safe. It was written on Saturday 3 June, as soon as *Hampshire* had returned to Scapa Flow. It was signed off 'Your ever loving husband, George', with fifteen kisses.

That afternoon, hugely relieved and grateful, she sat down and wrote out a short reply to her beloved husband, from both her and from their five-year-old daughter, Winnie:

Bradley Cottage, New Hey, Tuesday June 6ᵗʰ/16.
My Dear George,
    I have just received your short note so am trying to get in a reply in

the dinner hour. What a blessing you are safe and how thankful I am. I won't weary you with saying how it affected me and you will have enough on your mind and my worry is nothing compared with the sorrow it will have brought into hundreds of homes...

Thanks very much for sending the telegram. I could scarcely open it ... I suppose you will send me a longer letter when you can spare the time ... I wish I could see you if it was only for an hour, just to satisfy myself that you are quite alright, but I must possess my soul in patience and be thankful for present mercies. I can't write any more now, send me another letter when you have recovered a little. Hoping this will find you quite well. We remain with fondest love your ever loving wife and daughter. XXX Nellie X Winnie XXX.

But her relief was to be short-lived. A few days after posting the letter, it was returned to her. Stamped on the top left-hand corner of the front of the envelope was a chilling message: 'Return to Sender. Admiralty Instructions.' By then, she already knew the worst.

Even as she was writing her letter of thanks and relief, her husband's dead body was floating in the waves off Orkney. In the webbing belt on his body was a leather pocket, in which were the contact details for his brother, a lance corporal in the King's Own Yorkshire Light Infantry, as well as one of his proudest possessions: a small silver watch fob, awarded as a football competition prize. On one side was his name. On the other 'HMS *Hampshire*: Football League 1915 Winners'.

George Reeve's body wasn't recovered from the Atlantic waters for six more weeks. And it took until 20 November for it to be properly identified and for the Admiralty to write to his widow to tell her that he had been buried on 20 July, in the naval cemetery on the island of Hoy. They had now confirmed his identity by making checks with the brother whose name was found on the piece of paper in his belt, which had miraculously survived.

On 12 June 1917, just over a year after his death, Martha Reeve received a package from the Admiralty. It contained one cap ribbon, one leather purse, one pair of nail clippers, the scrap of paper with her husband's brother's name and service number, and his precious football medal – which she kept, treasured and passed on to her daughter, Nellie.

It was only one of the deeply sad stories of *Hampshire*'s loss. There were 736 others.

THE AFTERMATH

'Moored mines have been discovered today, 8th June, in the locality in which HMS Hampshire *was lost. There is therefore no doubt as to the cause of her loss. I cannot adequately express the sorrow felt by me personally and by the officers and men of the Grand Fleet generally, at the fact that so distinguished a soldier and so great a man should have lost his life whilst in a measure under the care of the fleet.'*

ADMIRAL JELLICOE, MESSAGE TO THE ADMIRALTY, 8 JUNE 1916

Thursday 22 June 1916, 8 a.m. Five miles out to sea, off the Brough of Birsay, close to where *Hampshire* sank.

Eight Royal Navy vessels, led by *Evening Star*, are on minesweeping duty, off Orkney. They are heading out to trawl an area almost twenty miles south-west of the northern tip of the island. Leading the left grouping of ships is the 25-metre, eighty-ton wooden drifter *Laurel Crown*. Working alongside her is *Fair Isle*. *Laurel Crown* was built in 1912 and seized by the Admiralty for minesweeping operations not long after war broke out.

John Coull, age forty-two, by trade a fisherman, is in command. He joined the Royal Naval Reserve ten months ago. There are only eight other crew, most of them also fishermen. George Petrie, aged thirty-two, is working as a deckhand. He joined up just five weeks ago. Alongside him is Charles Durrant. Charles is only seventeen – he was born in Aberdeen but lied about his age, subtracting two years from his date of birth, when he joined up in August 1915. In the engine room is 38-year-old Thomas Baker. He has three children: Ellen, Emily and George.

It is a fine day with a moderate swell, and it's a routine mission. *Hampshire*'s sinking was over two weeks ago and the area has been thoroughly searched for mines, with thirteen having been found in the week or so after the disaster, around 5 metres below the sea's surface at low water.

This is a new sea route for minesweeping operations: before the sinking of *Hampshire*, it was assumed that it would be too risky for German surface ships to lay mines so close to the shore. In addition, the risk from minelaying submarines wasn't properly appreciated. But after *Hampshire*, nothing can be taken for granted.

The group of ships has already travelled up the east coast of Orkney Mainland and rounded the north of the island. It has passed the site of *Hampshire*'s sinking and is heading south-west, out to sea, making 8½ to 9 knots. To the left are the huge cliffs of Marwick Head – an impressive sight. It has already been a long day and the crews are looking forward eagerly to an early lunch.

Suddenly, at 8.05 a.m., there is a massive explosion. Men from the other drifters rush to the sides of their vessels to see what has happened. Where *Laurel Crown* had been is a huge spout of water, soaring up into the air. Then, there is a large cloud of smoke. Through this, finally, they can see the ship disappearing into the waters below. Soon, air bubbles on the surface are the only sign of her former existence.

They look for survivors. There are none. They find only one body

– the remains of Thomas James Baker, the engineman – picked up by a small boat from the drifter *Pitgaveny*. What else is in the water? The men in the rescue boat sight another mine, moored just a metre or so below the surface and bobbing up through the swell of the waves. It is spherical, painted red, with four spikes on it. It is smaller than most mines they have seen before. This object is towed away into shallower water and safely blown up.

The minesweepers have just found more of *U-75*'s cargo of death. Now, fifteen of her mines are accounted for. But they do not know that Beitzen laid thirty-four such mines; according to his records, these were fixed at around 7 metres below the surface at high water, or around 5 metres at low water. The draught of HMS *Hampshire* was around 8 metres below the water line.

When *Laurel Crown* was blown to pieces on 22 June, the Admiralty already knew that fixed German mines were the likely cause of *Hampshire*'s demise. After her sinking on 5 June, the search for mines began three days later, when the weather had improved. Over the next week, the Scapa trawler sweepers searched the area of the north-west coast of Orkney Mainland. They swept slowly and carefully, at an average speed of just 4 knots, using a length of wire of 2,250 feet and a vertical depth of kite of 90 to 120 feet. On two occasions, the trawlers came into contact with a wreck, believed to be that of *Hampshire*.

On the very first day of the sweep, 8 June, they discovered mines – red, spherical, with four horns protruding from them. They were laid at a depth of around 8 metres, in 210 to 240 feet. There were four of them: two found close together, to the north of the *Hampshire* wreck, and two found to the south and west.

At 3.12 p.m. on 8 June, Admiral Jellicoe sent a secret message to the Admiralty in London. As well as enclosing various additional documents relating to the findings of the court of inquiry into *Hampshire*'s loss, he included a cover message:

> Moored mines have been discovered today, 8th June, in the locality in which HMS *Hampshire* was lost. There is therefore no doubt as to the cause of her loss. I cannot adequately express the sorrow felt by me personally and by the officers and men of the Grand Fleet generally, at the fact that so distinguished a soldier and so great a man should have lost his life whilst in a measure under the care of the fleet.

It was good timing. By 5.36 p.m., the Admiralty was cabling Jellicoe to say that the Cabinet wanted more information about *Hampshire*'s loss. They wanted to know what the court of inquiry, assembled speedily by Jellicoe, had concluded.

On 13 June, three more mines were found, further to the west, and on the next day five more were found close together, near to Marwick Head. The final mine of the thirteen was well to the north of the Brough of Birsay. Seven of these mines exploded on contact with the sweep, three were exploded by gunfire, two were sunk by gunfire without exploding, and one was sunk by gunfire and exploded on the bottom.

* * *

The day after *Hampshire*'s sinking, most of the twelve survivors were suffering from lacerated wounds caused by the rocks on which they had landed. Some were suffering from shock. Others had frostbite. They were being nursed in the farmhouses close to where they came on shore.

Seventeen-year-old Able Seaman Dick Simpson asked that a telegram be sent to his mother to let her know that he was alive. This was despatched quickly – before she was even aware that *Hampshire* had been sunk – and he kept his costs down by restricting it to just four words.

Dick then sat down to write a short letter, to be posted when he was able:

Dear Mother, I cannot put 'Mess 23' on top of this letter now, as the ship has gone to the bottom ... Well dear I suppose you thought I was gone, so I sent you a telegram to let you know I was safe ... The people are very kind to us giving us clothes, eggs, bed, everything we need ... Your loving son, Dick.

Outside the house, as he wrote, the bodies were still being brought up by the rescue parties and laid out on the clifftop. For the survivors, it was a particularly sickening and shocking sight. Amongst the dead were many recognisable faces: these were the men they had worked, eaten and laughed with on *Hampshire* over months, and in some cases years. Some were much-loved friends.

In the early afternoon, when the task of recovering the dead was complete, the survivors gave their brief interviews to the military authorities. And then, on 7 June, they were collected and taken to HMS *Blake*. That morning, a signal had been sent from the rear-admiral commanding the 2nd Cruiser Squadron to Vice-Admiral Brock, the commanding officer of Orkney and Shetland, to the captain and commander of *Duke of Edinburgh*, and to the commander of *Minotaur*: 'Immediate. A court of enquiry into the loss of HMS Hampshire is to assemble on board "Blake" forthwith.'

The captain of *Edinburgh* was appointed president of the inquiry, assisted by his own ship's commander and the commander of *Minotaur*. All survivors were to give evidence. Vice-Admiral Brock was ordered to send any other relevant information urgently to the inquiry president, on board *Blake*.

Before the inquiry had met, but on the same day, Admiral Jellicoe had sent a secret four-page report to the Secretary of the Admiralty in London, with his own updated appraisal of the disaster. It started in sombre terms: 'Sir, It is with the deepest possible regret that, in confirmation of my telegrams Nos. 61 and 63 of the sixth instant, I have to report the loss of HMS *Hampshire* on the evening of the fifth instant, whilst she was on passage to Archangel.'

In seventeen numbered paragraphs, Jellicoe set out his account, starting with Kitchener's arrival at Thurso at 11 a.m. on 5 June and ending with a description of the rescue efforts. Jellicoe's version of what had happened was a simple one. He had selected the western route around Orkney because it offered better protection from the north-eastern gale. The winds then shifted to come from the north-north-west, forcing the destroyers to return to port, 'at about 7 p.m.'.

Captain Walker had reported to Vice-Admiral Sir Frederick Brock shortly after 8 p.m. that a cruiser appeared to be in difficulties between the Brough of Birsay and Marwick Head. Brock asked that ships be held in readiness to be sent out. There was, however, no mention of the fact that Brock had held Walker back from sending the vessels out immediately.

At 8.35 p.m., Brock and Walker had spoken again by phone. By now, they had news of a vessel down, and Walker had already ordered his rescue ships out. Jellicoe timed the explosion on *Hampshire* at 'shortly before 8 p.m.', and suggested the ship had sunk in ten to fifteen minutes.

Destroyers were then swiftly sent out, and the rescue mission commenced. The search was also looking to recover secret documents, and the military authorities kept an eye on all beaches for that purpose. Jellicoe concluded that the cause of the sinking was not yet certain but commented that the seas were too rough for a submarine attack, and therefore, 'I am forced ... to the conclusion that the *Hampshire* struck either a moored mine or a mine which had drifted from the minefield to the westward of the Orkneys.'

Jellicoe's account had been given before the court of inquiry had even assembled. That afternoon, 7 June, the survivors arrived on the depot ship HMS *Blake* at around 3 p.m. They were still recovering: it was barely thirty-six hours since they had emerged from their four- or five-hour ordeal in the freezing waters off Orkney.

Before the inquiry could commence, each man was medically examined by Surgeon Pickup and a record was made of their injuries and the after-effects of their traumatic journey. Pickup placed all the men immediately on the sick list, noting that they were all suffering from some degree of shock and the results of exposure, as well as other wounds.

Stoker Sims was clearly in pain from burns to the face, sustained on the mess deck of *Hampshire* immediately after the original explosion. His face was already carefully wrapped in bandages.

The surgeon found that Bennett, Buerdsell and Wesson all had contused and lacerated wounds to the feet and knees from having to climb up the sharp rocks. Wesson also had lacerations to his right hand, which were already septic. Dick Simpson was recorded as having lacerated and abraded wounds to his feet, where men had trodden on him in the raft.

Charles Rogerson, William Cashman and William Phillips were all suffering principally from the first stages of frostbite in their lower extremities. Their toes had turned red and still felt cold and numb.

Samuel Sweeney, the oldest of the survivors, had suffered most seriously from shock. But he had no external injuries or frostbite. Finally, Walter 'Lofty' Farnden, Alfred Read and John Bowman were in the best shape. They had only slight shock and had no external injuries or frostbite.

Later in the afternoon, each of the twelve men had to appear separately in front of the hastily convened court of inquiry in the captain's cabin on *Blake*. It must have been a trying experience for many of the men, including seventeen-year-old Simpson and 41-year-old Samuel Sweeney.

The senior officers for the court of inquiry had already gathered on *Blake*. They had been sent various accounts of the disaster by Sir Frederick Brock, the vice-admiral commanding Orkney and Shetland. These included the initial statements taken from survivors on 6 June, summarised in one or two paragraphs for each survivor.

Finally, the inquiry began. One by one, each man was called and put on oath. Similar questions were asked of each. What was the likely cause of the explosion? What happened when the ship was evacuated? Did they see Lord Kitchener? How did they come to survive?

First to be called was Sweeney, a 5 foot 5½ inch veteran with twenty-six years' naval service. He was clearly still suffering from shock.

The captain of *Edinburgh* leaned forward: 'Are you Petty Officer Samuel Edward Sweeney, of HMS *Hampshire*?'

'Yes, sir.'

The inquiry had started. For Sweeney, there were now thirty-one short questions from the three members of the inquiry board. He replied briefly and crisply – sometimes in a word, at most in a couple of sentences. He was keen to get it over with and obtain some more food and much-needed sleep. What was his account? Well, he had heard a rumbling explosion, then another smaller one, immediately afterwards. He thought this was at 7.30 p.m. His best guess was that the ship had hit a mine. He thought the ship had only stayed afloat for ten minutes. He timed his rescue at 3 a.m., local time – 2 a.m., GMT. He had not seen Kitchener.

Petty Officer Wilfrid Wesson was next. He confirmed his duties as Captain of the Foretop. He timed the explosion fifteen minutes later, at 7.45 p.m. He heard only one. He was sure it was a mine. He had seen Lord Kitchener going up from below to the deck, with a naval officer. He thought the ship sank in twenty minutes.

One after the other, the survivors came up, until all twelve had given evidence. The last to appear was Warrant Mechanician William Bennett. He was the most senior survivor, of officer rank, but was still struggling to recover from his experiences. He gave detailed answers to the questions put to him.

And then it was over. Most of the twelve were transferred to the hospital ship *Soudan* on 8 June, and a day later were taken over to Leith on the tender *Magic II*. They then travelled by train all the way to Haslar Naval Hospital in Gosport. Only Warrant Mechanician William Bennett went a different route – to another hospital ship, before being sent on to Chatham Hospital.

The evidence had now been collected by the inquiry. What did this show? On the timing of the explosion, five men gave evidence: the earliest estimate was 7.30 p.m., and the latest was 7.45 p.m. Three estimates were very close – 7.38 p.m., 7.40 p.m., 7.45 p.m.

On the number of explosions, nine survivors reported hearing one only. Three survivors reported two or more. On the cause of the disaster, three men expressed no view. Nine guessed it must have been a mine.

Estimates of the period between the explosion and the ship sinking were given by five men. They ranged between ten minutes and up to half an hour. Most thought around twenty minutes. Two men had seen Kitchener after the explosion. None saw him get into a boat, and none saw any boats get safely away from the ship.

It did not take the court of inquiry long to report. Later that day, a typed letter of the court's conclusions, signed by all three officers, was on its way to the rear-admiral who had established the inquiry. Their letter was just over one side in length and consisted of only seven paragraphs. The three officers claimed to have carried out a 'full and careful inquiry'.

The conclusions were: *Hampshire* had struck a mine somewhere forward on the ship, and had sunk in fifteen minutes. The explosion had occurred sometime between 7.30 p.m. and 7.45 p.m. This was earlier than the estimate of just before 8 p.m. that Jellicoe had given the Admiralty that same morning.

The inquiry concluded that more men would have survived if *Hampshire* had possessed additional Carley floats. The final paragraph stated that nothing more was seen of Lord Kitchener after he was taken on deck.

There was no serious analysis of the route selected by Jellicoe, or the decision to continue the mission without the escorting destroyers. More surprisingly, perhaps, no comments were offered about the effectiveness of the rescue efforts, which had largely been arranged by Vice-Admiral Brock. But on 8 June, Brock forwarded to Henry Blackett, captain of HMS *Duke of Edinburgh* and president of the court of inquiry, two further written statements: one from Captain

Walker and one from Lieutenant-Colonel Harris. These dealt with the conduct of the rescue efforts on land and at sea. Brock did not say so, but these statements included some implicit contradictions of the evidence he had offered in a letter to Admiral Jellicoe late in the evening of 5 June, while the rescue efforts were still underway.

Harris's submission was a scrappy one-page typewritten note. This claimed that Brock had instructed him to travel to Birsay at around 9.20 p.m. on 5 June. Brock's letter claims this was actually 9 p.m. It's easy to see why Harris might prefer a later time – he had taken an inordinate amount of it to reach his destination at Birsay.

Captain Walker, commander of the Western Patrol Office, Stromness, provided a slightly more detailed note of around a page and a half. It was written on 7 June. Here, the differences in evidence are much more striking. Walker stated that as soon as he received the first message from Birsay, at 7.54 p.m., that a cruiser was in distress, he immediately ordered the yacht *Jason II* and the trawler *Cambodia* to go out to help. He is then clear that he telephoned Vice-Admiral Brock, who overruled him, deciding not to send out the ships at this time. This conversation took place at around 8 p.m. – almost exactly the time at which *Hampshire* appears to have sunk.

Only when the second telegram arrived, much later than the first, at 8.31 p.m., stating that the ship was down, did Captain Walker send out his own ships on his own initiative. He then called Vice-Admiral Brock, who at last ordered him to head out with all available vessels.

By then, a precious thirty-seven minutes had been lost. When the first message was received, *Hampshire* was still afloat – just. Now, her crew had already been in the freezing Atlantic waters, being battered by a force 9 gale, for a crucial half-hour. Many were already dead.

Walker himself left just after 9 p.m. in *Flying Kestrel* and arrived off Marwick Head a little after 10.30 p.m., the journey having taken some one and a half hours. But by now it was dark, making the search conditions impossibly difficult. If the ships had set off when the first message had been received, they would have arrived between 9.30 p.m. and 9.45 p.m., with almost an hour of twilight in which to search.

And, crucially, in these waters every minute really mattered. The body loses heat much faster in water than in cold air – by some estimates the heat loss is twenty-five times faster. In waters as cold as those on 5 June, most humans will become unconscious or exhausted in between half an hour and an hour and will be dead in between one hour and three hours. And these estimates do not allow for the storm-force conditions and the fact that many men had no lifebelts.

The survival time of the individuals on *Hampshire* would have varied based on age, swimming ability, cold tolerance, build, fat levels, will to live, clothing, access to flotation devices and a range of other factors. But it is a reasonable guess that most men in the water would have had between half an hour and two hours to live on that bleak June night. The delay in sending out the rescue vessels almost certainly meant that by the time the first of these reached Marwick Head at 10.30 p.m., almost every man now in the water would have been a dead man.

As for those on the floats, the predicted survival time of a man in waters this cold would be about four hours. This was exactly how long it took the first two rafts to reach the shore. No wonder so many of those on the rafts never made it to the safety of land: many probably died in that last hour, approaching the shoreline. Had rescue boats reached them just a little earlier, many of the sixty-three men found dead on the three rafts might have been saved.

As it was, the twelve survivors were lucky to have lived. Had their journey back been an hour longer, it is quite likely that all would have died.

In spite of the importance of this new evidence, after reading through it Captain Blackett wrote the next day, 8 June, to the rear-admiral commanding the 2nd Cruiser Squadron, concluding, 'The attached has been received from the Vice-Admiral ... but it does not afford any further information than that already obtained and, therefore, does not affect the decision given by the Court of Enquiry.' It was clearly not a time when awkward questions were being asked – especially not of those in authority.

A few days later, Vice-Admiral Brock carried out his own 'inquiry' into the actions of the Birsay lookouts and the delay in sending out the rescue ships. On 15 June, Brock sent a three-paragraph note of the conclusions he had reached to Admiral Jellicoe. He exonerated the Birsay lookouts of any blame for their initial unclear message: 'Taking into consideration the fact that the Territorials who were there were not trained men, I consider that they did all that could be expected under the circumstances.' He also suggested that even if the initial messages had been clearer, only 'several minutes would have been saved'. This looks like a serious underestimate. Perhaps Brock wanted to avoid a spotlight on his own decision to block Captain Walker from immediately sending his vessels out. In any case, that issue, unsurprisingly, receives no mention in Brock's letter.

In spite of his 'several minutes' claim, Brock admitted at the end of his note that these 'several minutes ... would possibly have resulted in the saving of some, if not many, lives'.

But the court of inquiry had now concluded. It was to be the only official review of the *Hampshire* sinking for a decade. But it was a cursory and incomplete inquiry at best.

Was Jellicoe right to change his original routing decision and send *Hampshire* on a westerly course around Orkney, in a channel not swept for mines, and even after the wind direction had changed? Was it responsible for Captain Savill to sail on without destroyer escorts in sea conditions where submarine attack was unlikely but mines were a real risk? Why had the lookouts at Birsay failed to send clear messages when they had seen the explosion and must have known how much trouble *Hampshire* was in? Why was the message 'Vessel down' not properly reported to the military authorities? And why did Admiral Brock dither for almost three quarters of an hour, preventing the speedy despatch of rescue ships? On these five vital questions, the court of inquiry had nothing at all to say.

Now the inquiry was over. And the survivors were on the way to hospitals in England, where all would recover. Meanwhile, the search for more survivors continued for the next few days. None were found.

What the search parties did find, and go on finding, day after day, were dead bodies. Almost a month after the disaster, the body of an able seaman was recovered and buried on Sunday 2 July, in the naval cemetery in Hoy. On 5 July, the one-month anniversary of the disaster, they picked up the corpse of Able Seaman Bennett. He was twenty-four years old.

On 6 July, there was another. And on the 7th, and on the 10th. On 11 July, they found 24-year-old Able Seaman George Bartlett. On 13 July, they found Leading Stoker Waterman, aged twenty-seven. His body had drifted in to the Bay of Skaill. They were all buried on the day their bodies were recovered, or the day after. On 19 July, they finally recovered the body of 28-year-old Yeoman of Signals George Reeve. It took them almost four months to identify him.

After late July, there were no more bodies. Of the 749 men on *Hampshire*, 569 had been swallowed up by the ocean. They would never be seen again.

The search continued for other objects from *Hampshire*, including the secret documents carried by Kitchener's staff. But in spite of the rewards offered, the despatch cases were never found, only a variety of small objects and a chest of drawers.

Of the eleven boats on *Hampshire*, the remains of just four were identified and recovered. A small, 16-foot dinghy was sighted and picked up by the patrol trawler *Arisino* on 6 June, off Hoy Head. Allegedly, there was the body of a sailor in the bow. Could this have been the 'fourth boat' spotted by the farmer James Robertson soon after *Hampshire* had sunk? We will never know.

The smashed cutter from *Hampshire* was found in the Bay of Skaill on the morning of 6 June. *Flying Kestrel* sighted the ship's pinnace near Stromness when returning at 8 a.m. on 6 June. This was later washed up in Hoy Sound and was subsequently taken into Longhope, and the remains eventually transferred to the Imperial War Museum.

A whaler, 27 to 30 feet in length, was also washed ashore, forty-eight hours after the disaster, in Thurso Bay on the mainland of Scotland. It contained three oars and had no bottom boards. Three feet of both bow and stern were missing.

On 20 June, a rough ledger from *Hampshire* was found by a search party on the beaches on the south side of the Bay of Skaill. With the ledger was a copy of the 'Boat's Signal Book', marked '3rd Cutter'.

On 18 July, Admiral Brock sent out a secret note to all the military authorities on and around Orkney, pointing out that as bodies from *Hampshire* were frequently washing up on shore, they had better plan for the eventuality that that of Kitchener himself might soon be found. If this occurred, the matter was to be kept secret and the body was to be placed in a metal-lined 'shell', which had been prepared and was being kept on board *Cyclops*. Should the Field Marshal's body be recovered, Vice-Admiral Brock himself would want to be immediately notified, but without any mention of the name; instead, the information would be communicated using a secret memorandum number and date.

But there was no Kitchener body. Would it ever be found?

THE TRUTH

'By the afternoon, it was blowing a gale from the north-eastwards.'
ADMIRAL JELLICOE, *THE GRAND FLEET, 1914–1916*, 1919

Waterloo Railway Station, London. It is 5 p.m., Friday 13 August 1926 – over ten years since *Hampshire*'s sinking.

The newly rebuilt station, with its twenty-one platforms and 200-metre concourse, only opened four years ago and still looks smart and new – with a grand Victory Arch over the main entrance, to commemorate those railway staff who died in the Great War.

The train from Southampton, a Southern Railway Company service, finally pulls in, belching out its black smoke. On the long platform is a small group who have been awaiting the train's arrival: a camera crew from Crystal Productions of 19 Charing Cross Road; Edward Ackrill, an undertaker trading under the name Thomas Hurry; and a journalist. With owl-like features, round rimmed glasses and a bald head, this latter has given his name to the others as Mr Fraser. But he is more usually known as the 45-year-old journalist Frank Power. And if that isn't complicated enough, Frank Power's real name is Arthur Vectis Freeman. We have met him before in the Kingsway Opera House.

Just five days ago, *The Referee* newspaper in England published an article by Power under the banner headline 'Kitchener's Grave Found: Great Soldier's Remains Brought to England'. It was modestly badged 'Copyright throughout the world' and started, portentously, 'It is with a profound sense of all that it means to the nation and to the Empire ... that I am able to announce my bringing to England the remains of Earl Kitchener of Khartoum.'

And now, the great moment has arrived. The doors of the mail carriage are opened, and there inside is what they have been waiting for: a sealed wooden case, 7 feet 4 inches long, 2 feet 9 inches wide, and with a depth of 1 foot 11 inches.

Written in pencil on the top is 'To Mr. F. Fraser, South Western Hotel, Southampton', and near this – also in pencil – 'Baikie and Co, West Castle Street, Kirkwall'. There is also a 'Carriage paid' railway label from Southampton to Waterloo, partly rubbed off. On one side of the box is a crude drawing – a picture of a coffin with a figure lying inside.

'This is it,' says Mr Fraser. 'Lord Kitchener's coffin. We recovered his body from Norway, where it washed up after the *Hampshire* sank.' The undertaker, Mr Ackrill, steps forward, unfolds a large Union Jack and carefully lays it over the coffin case. The cameraman from Crystal Productions switches his camera on and starts to film.

Behind them on the platform, the station porter tactlessly interrupts the solemn moment: 'Has this got a coffin in, then? If it has, there's extra to pay.' It is not quite the welcome home that one of her country's greatest ever military commanders and a former Secretary of State for War might have expected.

But rules are rules, even for the great and the good, and the employee of the Southern Railway Company is most insistent. The surcharge of £4 has to be paid by the undertaker before the coffin case is carefully loaded into a waiting hearse and taken to the private mortuary owned and used by Thomas Hurry Undertakers at 154 Waterloo Road – a modest resting place for a once national hero. At the undertaker's, the arrival of the coffin case is again respectfully filmed. Mr Fraser – we shall now call him by his journalistic name of Frank Power – is very insistent about where in the mortuary the case should be located.

Before he leaves, Power gives the undertaker clear direction on two further points: 'Under no circumstances should the case and coffin be opened except on my instructions. And, other than me, only two people have authority to view the case – if they turn up here they will have written permission from me, which you must check.' The next day, 14 August, in the early afternoon, the two men with authorisation from Mr Power arrive. One views the case briefly. The other takes a photograph of it.

Meanwhile at the Home Office, in Whitehall, urgent meetings are taking place following the sensational newspaper reports of the arrival in England of Lord Kitchener's body. Later that afternoon, Mr Ackrill receives a further visit to his offices in Waterloo Road. When he opens the door, he receives a shock. On the pavement in front of him are four men, two of whom are in police uniforms.

'Good afternoon. Are you Mr Edward Ackrill, the owner of this business? I am Inspector Walter Bumby of the Criminal Investigation Department of the Metropolitan Police. These gentlemen are Detectives Owen and Lount. This is PC Farenden, the acting coroner's officer. We believe you have a coffin case which is of public interest. We are going to need to look at the case and we are going to need a statement from you.'

A shaken Mr Ackrill invites the police inside and shows them the case. A detailed statement is taken from him and written down in longhand. Their work now completed, the four police officers have a further announcement to make: 'On the authority of the coroner, Mr Ingleby Oddie, we are seizing this coffin case and taking it to Lambeth Mortuary. We are sure you will understand the great public interest in this matter. You will also understand the law, and that a post-mortem on the body is going to be necessary.' Mr Ackrill is in no position to argue.

It is now 9 a.m. on Monday 16 August 1926. Power is at the offices of the *Daily News* in London. He has come to receive payment for three photographs of Lord Kitchener's coffin case, taken in Mr Ackrill's mortuary. He is meeting with John Hugh Jones, a director of the newspaper.

Before leaving, Power hands Jones an envelope and indicates that Jones should open it. Inside is a small piece of frayed khaki cloth. 'It's from Lord Kitchener's own uniform,' explains Power to a dumbstruck Jones. 'I myself cut it from Kitchener's tunic before sealing up the case containing the coffin. When the coffin is opened, with the remains will be found some part of Lord Kitchener's clothing and you will find that this piece of cloth corresponds with what is there.' He leaves.

It is now 10 a.m. on the same Monday morning – one hour later, at Lambeth Mortuary. Standing in front of the large coffin case are the coroner, Mr Oddie; Chief Constable Wensley; a group of police officers; and Sir Bernard Spilsbury – at age forty-nine, Britain's foremost forensic pathologist, whose evidence was crucial in solving the so-called Brides in the Bath murder trial of 1915, and in sending Dr Crippen to the gallows in 1910.

There is a great sense of anticipation. Is the body of one of the most famous ever Britons to be revealed for the first time since he was lost off the shores of Orkney over ten years ago? The hush is broken by the coroner, who gives orders that the case should be opened.

The screws in the wooden planking are slowly removed and the top of the case lifted off. The group of observers lean forward for their first glimpse of the contents. Inside the case is a polished elm coffin, without inscription. There is no packing material – just a narrow, flat, piece of wood lying by the left foot of the case.

The coffin is now measured: the outside dimensions are 6 feet 9 inches in length, width 27¼ inches at the shoulders and 14½ inches at the foot. The depth is 17 inches. 'Open it,' instructs the coroner. The lid is loose. It contains two round-headed screws. These are inserted into the lid but not fixed into the coffin.

Those present instinctively lean forward again. In the room, there is complete silence. When the coffin lid is lifted, there is… another lid. This time the shell is copper, and it encloses an inner wooden shell with its own lid, firmly screwed down.

They look carefully at what is holding the lid in place. There are fifteen screws – two at the head, one at the foot, and six on each side. Before the lid can be removed, the copper edge of the shell has to be bent back. Now, they will surely get to see the body of the great man, or what is left of it after ten years and a journey of hundreds of miles across the North Atlantic ocean.

After a final struggle, the lid lifts off. There is a strange odour – not what they had been expecting. The great Sir Bernard Spilsbury, hair slicked back over his head from a right-sided parting, leans forward to see – nothing. The coffin is empty. This is no body or anything resembling one. But what is this, at the bottom and lining all four sides? A sticky, dark substance – surely not blood or human material?

The coroner and police carefully and cautiously scoop up some of this dark material. It is pliable to touch. 'Tar, with pitch mixed in' is the conclusion. They look from one to another, baffled. Sir Bernard Spilsbury frowns. 'Take it all to New Scotland Yard,' says the chief constable. 'Oh, and find Mr Power. I think we need to have a talk with him.'

Mr Power had been paid £40 by the newspapers for his story. In interviews with the police, he stuck by the account he had previously provided. But the subsequent police investigation uncovered that the coffin had never been to Norway, as Power had claimed. Instead, it was purchased by Power on 2 July 1926 for £12. He had bought it while on Orkney for the unveiling of the Kitchener Memorial. It had come from a local supplier: Samuel Baikie of Stromness, who had purchased it in a disposals sale of surplus military items. It was rumoured to have been made for Lord Kitchener in 1916, in case his body was recovered after the sinking of *Hampshire*.

After Power had secured ownership of the coffin and its case, it had travelled from Kirkwall Pier on Orkney to Leith Docks on 27 July. From Leith Docks, it was sent on to Forth Goods Station in Newcastle upon Tyne. It then travelled by train all the way down to King's Cross Station in London, arriving on 7 August. On 10 August, it made another train journey to Waterloo Station, and from there on to Southampton, before finally returning to Waterloo on 13 August for the reception provided by Power and the film company. It was, by now, a very well-travelled coffin. But it had never been anywhere near Norway, that much was clear.

Nor had Mr Power ever recovered a body from Norway, as he had claimed. A report from His Majesty's Consul at Bergen, relayed to the Foreign Secretary, Austen Chamberlain, on 13 August, ridiculed Power's claims. Under the heading 'See Stavanger and

Die: An Amusing Funeral', the Consul reported that Power and his film crew had travelled to Norway and filmed a 'faked' funeral procession. They had arranged for a coffin, draped with the Union Jack, to be carried to the quay in Stavanger. But, reported the British Consul, 'on the road to the quay, laughter and risky jokes were to be heard from the public, and the hotel boy, who was carrying the coffin on board, had difficulty keeping his countenance'. The British Ambassador in Oslo was less amused and more scathing – 'a revolting farce'.

Power, then, was a hoaxer and a fraud. Police enquiries revealed that he was adjudicated bankrupt – under his real name of Arthur Vectis Freeman – on 27 April 1923. Since then, he had struggled to find work. He had adopted the name Frank Power from the long-deceased correspondent of *The Times* who gained national renown during the 1884 siege of Khartoum. He had deceived *The Referee* newspaper. He had duped many members of the public. He had hoodwinked a number of gullible parliamentarians. He had disturbed and upset many of the relatives of the dead – including the Kitchener family. The Metropolitan Police now referred the matter to the Director of Public Prosecutions. But the case was dropped. The authorities wanted no more distracting and unhelpful publicity. They were content now that Power's credibility was destroyed. So, he was allowed to go free. But it was the end of his profitable mischief-making.

The 'Kitchener coffin affair' had been just one of the many hoaxes, conspiracy stories, half-truths and rumours that had surrounded Kitchener's death since *Hampshire* sank on 5 June 1916. It was becoming increasingly obvious that most had little basis in fact.

After the opening of the 'Kitchener coffin' in August 1926, the allegations from Frank Power could never be taken seriously again.

In the same month, after the tenth anniversary commemoration of *Hampshire*'s sinking, the Admiralty finally published its own detailed White Paper of some twenty-seven pages, which aimed to lay to rest the controversies of the previous ten years and uphold the Admiralty and the government's own explanation of the sinking.

In spite of the Admiralty's careful efforts, and the discrediting of Power, the Kitchener conspiracies still had further to run. There were yet more individuals, often with their own private agendas, who came forward with increasingly fantastic claims. And while the government remained determined to keep the Kitchener files under lock and key, there was always a suspicion that they must be hiding something that the government wanted hushed up.

In 1932, Fritz Joubert Duquesne, a Boer and a German spy, claimed to have assumed the identity of a Russian count, Boris Zakrevsky, and joined Kitchener in Scotland to travel with his mission on *Hampshire*. Duquesne asserted that he had boarded *Hampshire* with Kitchener and had signalled a German submarine shortly after departing Scapa Flow to alert them to Kitchener's presence. According to Duquesne, the German U-boat then torpedoed *Hampshire* and picked him up from the sea. It was clearly a ridiculous story, without a shred of evidence to support it. However, in the 1930s and 1940s, this man actually ran the Duquesne spy ring, and was captured by the FBI, along with thirty-two other Nazi agents, in the largest espionage conviction in US history.

In 1959, another journalist of dubious integrity, Richard Deacon, with yet another pen name – this time, Donald McCormick – sought to breathe new life into the conspiracy stories with his book *The Mystery of Lord Kitchener's Death*. The McCormick book rejected most of the now discredited Frank Power theories, but sought to replace these with more baseless conjecture of its own. For example,

McCormick claimed that intercepted British signals had caused the laying of the mines that had sunk *Hampshire*, and that there had been an IRA conspiracy. Neither theory had any serious evidence to support it. Nor did there seem much serious evidence for his boys-own account of secret intelligence about *Hampshire* being relayed by spies in a Turkish baths off the Strand.

The Public Records Office (now the National Archives) waited until 1967 before releasing most of the forty Kitchener files. But, stirring suspicions amongst the suspicious, a number of these were held back and dribbled out over the next forty-seven years, with the final file being released in 2014. There could hardly have been an approach better calculated to allow the myths and mysteries around Kitchener's death to continue.

However, after Power's 'Kitchener coffin' shambles, the conspiracy stories were never again to achieve quite the same traction and credibility in serious circles. And the government's 1926 White Paper effectively demolished most of the more plausible alternative stories about the sinking.

There was no evidence that the British Cabinet conspired to dispose of their Secretary of State for War, even though many of them felt that he had outlived his usefulness and needed to be replaced.

It was not possible that those in Germany who sent *U-75* on her mission could have known of Kitchener's travel plans, either before the mission or when the mines were laid. Indeed, *U-75*'s orders were finalised even before the details of the Kitchener mission were agreed.

There was no credible evidence of spies on board *Hampshire* or of bombs being planted on board by the Germans, Irish nationalists, ex-Boers or anybody else. Instead, there was a minor incident in a Belfast dock six months before Kitchener embarked on

Hampshire, which was blown out of all proportion by ship's gossip and media fantasy.

There was no evidence to suggest that *Hampshire* had been destroyed by anything other than a mine strike, and plenty of mines were found in the seas close to where she had sunk.

Kitchener had not survived *Hampshire*'s sinking, nor had his body been washed up in Norway. It is true that there was a small volume of contradictory evidence about whether he and others had got away from *Hampshire* in a boat, which may soon after have been 'swamped' and capsized. But this amounted only to a single, poorly documented claim apparently made by an unnamed survivor to a sergeant of the marines soon after the survivors reached land, besides the sighting of 'four boats', rather than the three floats, by a single farmer, from Marwick Head. There were also the remains of the four boats later found in the water. But, under questioning and over succeeding years, none of the twelve survivors could or would corroborate this theory. And in the absence of their eyewitness support, it seems right to prefer the evidence suggesting that Kitchener, accompanied by Fitzgerald, went down with the ship.

Contrary to long-running local claim and speculation, there is no serious evidence that Orkney residents were prevented from offering assistance to the rescue efforts. Some might have been kept away from the dead bodies on the shore, for obvious reasons. But that was a quite different matter. And it simply wasn't correct – as some had claimed – that the rescue ships were not sent until the day after *Hampshire* sank. Nor was it true that attempts to launch the Stromness lifeboat were prevented. The lifeboat simply wasn't called upon – almost certainly an error of judgement, but not part of a conspiracy.

As for the messages in bottles found around the shores of Britain and beyond, these were almost certainly hoaxes and in any case shed little or no light on how *Hampshire* came to be lost.

The more extravagant conspiracies which followed Kitchener's death were stoked by a combination of half-truth, gossip, tittle-tattle, mischief-making, media opportunism, journalistic exploitation and deceit, and by the half-baked theorising and headline-chasing of lower-grade politicians.

But if Mr Frank Power and a number of MPs should have been hanging their heads in shame, what about the government's official narrative about the loss of *Hampshire*? Why was the inquiry so cursory, and why were the official documents on *Hampshire*'s sinking kept secret for so long? Relatively innocuous files documenting the police interviews of Frank Power and detailing how the government sought to combat the conspiracy stories were not released until the years 1983 and 2000 respectively. And it took until 2014 for the last two files concerning Kitchener, held at the National Archives, to be published – one about the Kitchener Memorial, the other about his will. There is nothing in any of the files published which it was sensible to keep secret for so long.

The refusal to publish the results of the inquiry and the long delays in declassifying the Kitchener files reflect, in part, the usual desire for secrecy by governments who do not wish their actions to be open to scrutiny and criticism. And, of course, during wartime, the case for secrecy – whether for good or bad reasons – is hugely reinforced.

But was there something more serious than this? Were those in power trying to cover up some of the mistakes made? Had the wild conspiracy stories in fact helped the Admiralty and government to avoid confronting some of the real mistakes that were made on 5 and 6 June 1916?

The Admiralty's case was that Kitchener's death, and those of the 736 other men who died with him on *Hampshire*, had been a terrible and unavoidable tragedy of war, about which little could be done. No one had blundered. There were no errors. Nothing could or should have been done differently. And there were no lessons to learn – other than the need for ships to carry more Carley floats. A careful reading of all the evidence shows that this is too complacent by far. The military authorities made a number of serious errors which led directly to *Hampshire*'s demise and in particular to the very high loss of life.

Indeed, the British military and political authorities should perhaps have been grateful for the absurdly overstated conspiracy stories. These distracted attention from very real causes of concern: five blunders made by the British military authorities and one by the Russians. Kitchener did not die as a result of any conspiracies, but there were a number of cover-ups related to his demise.

Let us start with the Russian issue: over the extent to which the visit was kept confidential. The government's White Paper claimed that 'the secret of Lord Kitchener's Mission was strictly guarded at the Admiralty'. That carefully written claim was accurate as far as it went, but it told only half the truth.

No doubt in the Admiralty and London, the usual confidential niceties were respected, notwithstanding the alleged tendencies of various Cabinet members to brief their wives and mistresses. But this secrecy seems not to have been respected in Russia, where Kitchener's visit was widely known about by late May. Indeed, a contact of Sir George Arthur's, in Russia at the time, asked him in advance about Kitchener's visit, even though he should have known nothing about it. This ought to have been a concern in London, as it was understood that the Germans had an effective spy network in

Petrograd and in other major Russian cities. Perhaps there was little the British government could do about this, however, and there is no evidence that the Germans put in place any military actions that were directly targeted against the Kitchener mission. The mines laid by *U-75* turned out to be a lucky strike, and were aimed not at Britain's War Minister but against a Royal Navy fleet which the Germans were determined to tempt out of port to its destruction. So there was certainly a failure in Russia to keep the Kitchener visit confidential, but this had no consequences.

Now we come to the five British blunders, which did have serious consequences, and which neither Lord Jellicoe nor the Admiralty wanted to acknowledge.

The first mistake was the decision Admiral Jellicoe took on the routing of *Hampshire*. The original plan had been to send Kitchener on the usual warship route up the east coast of Orkney Mainland. This was regularly swept for mines. On 5 June, sometime before 3 p.m., Jellicoe changed his sailing instructions, routing *Hampshire* to the west of Orkney instead.

In his memoirs, Jellicoe claimed that 'by the afternoon, it was blowing a gale from the north-eastwards'. This was simply not true. The government's 1926 White Paper repeated the untruth, claiming that 'by late afternoon, the gale had shifted from North East to North'. In fact, by the time Jellicoe and Kitchener had sat down for lunch at 1 p.m., the wind had moved around from north-north-east and was blowing down directly from the north. This remained the case until 5 p.m., just as *Hampshire* set sail, when the wind had moved round further to blow from the north-north-west.

Jellicoe gave a second reason for favouring the westerly route: namely, that it was 'practically impossible' that it would have been mined. That may have been Jellicoe's view at the time but it turned out to be complacent and wrong. Nor was there much evidence for it: indeed, this westerly route had not been swept for mines.

The government's White Paper repeated Jellicoe's bogus claims about this westerly route, noting that 'the route close to the west coast of the Orkneys was not, in actual fact, a usual warship route ... At the date when the *U-75* was directed to lay these mines ... nothing was more improbable than that any warship would ever strike upon them.'

To claim that 'nothing was more improbable' seems breathtaking in the light of what occurred. But it was also not factually accurate to claim that warships never used the western route up Orkney: indeed, two cruisers, two minelayers and four destroyers had used the route in the short period from 28 May to 5 June.

Jellicoe sent one of the most important members of the British government on a sea voyage on a route chosen on the basis of out-dated weather assumptions, through waters unswept for mines, on the basis of groundless hunches about the low risk of mine presence.

The authors of the White Paper were keen to make the case that bad luck had sealed *Hampshire*'s fate. They claimed that *Hampshire* only hit the German mine because she passed over it at low water: 'The *Hampshire* herself [could have passed over the mines] during most of the twenty-four hours and in most weathers.' This was also untrue. The mines had been set at a depth that would allow smaller vessels to sail unharmed over them but which would assuredly det-onate in the presence of large vessels such as *Hampshire*, with her 8-metre draught.

Jellicoe had, at least, provided *Hampshire* with two escort de-stroyers, to help protect against attack and to provide support in case of a disaster. Unfortunately – the second British blunder – these destroyers were sent back by Captain Savill, on the grounds that they could not keep up with his ship in the stormy conditions. Savill did not, it is fair to say, have the discretion to cancel or delay his mission. He had also been ordered to make a speed of 18 knots. And Kitchener and Jellicoe together must bear full responsibility for the timing of *Hampshire*'s departure: they could have waited for better weather, but they chose not to.

But when Savill sent *Unity* and *Victor* home, he was taking a gamble – a gamble that speed without an escort was worth more than slower progress with them. Was this a sensible risk to take? The weather was so bad that the risk of submarine attack could be and was considered very low. But if the ship was sunk by either a torpedo or a mine, without escort ships it was surely obvious that the loss of life would be severe. Savill lost his bet – and his gamble cost the lives of hundreds of men.

What else had gone wrong? The third big British blunder was made by the small team of Territorials in Birsay who saw that an explosion had occurred on *Hampshire* and that she was in grave danger, but who failed to get an accurate and timely message to the naval authorities on Orkney. This cost almost forty minutes of delay and ensured that by the time the search vessels reached the area of the sinking, it was too dark to see people in the water.

The reasons for this failure of communication are difficult to establish. Gunner Angus had seen the explosion on the ship. He had immediately notified his superior, Corporal Drever, who had gone to the beach to view the disaster himself. Can they really have failed to discuss the explosion together, and was the smoke still not visible? How could Drever have sent such an ambiguous message – 'Battle cruiser seems in distress…' – when it was perfectly obvious that something far more serious had occurred? It is true that Drever tried to remedy his error shortly afterwards, by seeking to add the words 'Vessel down' to his message. But he was then let down by an emotional postmistress in Birsay and some apparently unimaginative telegram operators in Stromness. No matter. It was his job to get his message clearly and urgently transmitted. He failed to do so.

When the failures at Birsay were later investigated by Vice-Admiral Brock, he concluded generously that those on the ground had done their best: 'Taking into consideration the fact that the Territorials who were there were not trained men, I consider that they did all that could be expected in the circumstances.' He blamed neither the Territorials nor the postmistress, nor the operators who received both the first telegram warning and the later message that the ship had sunk. But the author of the first draft of the 1926 White Paper was rather blunter in private correspondence, referring to 'the bungle between the lookout and the post office people at Birsay and Kirkwall'. It was a harsher but fairer assessment, but it did not make its way into the government's official narrative, which stuck to Brock's more complacent interpretation.

Perhaps Brock was inclined to such a view because he did not wish for the spotlight to descend on the fourth British blunder – his own. Brock was, of course, asked to hold the post-disaster inquiry into the rescue efforts that he was himself responsible for. Even if his charitable perspective on the performance of the lookouts and telegram staff is accepted, it cannot excuse the tardy and lacklustre response that he himself displayed to the messages he received soon after the sinking.

And here, on the crucial issue of the military response to the news that *Hampshire* had been sunk, the 1926 White Paper is positively misleading. It records Captain Walker, who was dead by the time the White Paper was released, calling Vice-Admiral Brock and reading him the Birsay telegram, and says he 'asked whether he should send out the two vessels'.

In fact, Captain Walker's clear evidence, given to the court of inquiry just two days after the sinking, was that 'I ordered the yacht *Jason II* and trawler *Cambodia* to get away at once'. Captain Walker then telephoned Brock and it is clear from his evidence that Brock overruled him and decided to hold the vessels back until further information was received – fully thirty-seven minutes later.

This discrepancy was picked up on while the White Paper was in preparation. The draft was sent to both Jellicoe and Brock for their comments. Brock replied asking for a redraft of the key section which involved him and the delay in sending out the rescue ships. This now read:

> The first action of the Commander of the Western Patrol, the late Captain F. M. Walker RN, was to order the Yacht 'Jason II' and the Trawler 'Cambodia' to be ready to put to sea at once ... and Captain Walker getting into communication with [Vice-Admiral Brock] ...read him the telegram from Birsay and asked whether he should send out the two vessels.

This is inaccurate. Captain Walker had already ordered the despatch of the two ships, rather than simply directing them to be made ready. It was Brock who ordered them to wait.

But by the time the White Paper was being drafted, Captain Walker was dead. And now Brock chose to leave in place the false claim that Captain Walker had 'asked whether he should send out the two vessels'.

The White Paper – astonishingly – concluded that Admiral Brock was right to have held the rescue ships back until further notice, on the basis that the battlecruiser 'in distress' might simply have been facing heavy seas and slowing up to 'secure some fittings'. The White Paper goes so far as to claim: 'It is obvious that this interpretation of the situation was justified by the Birsay report.'

But it is surely far from 'obvious' that Brock had made the right call. Indeed, if anything is obvious, it is that Walker made the right judgement and Brock the wrong one. Brock was fortunate that Captain Walker was no longer alive to challenge this false record. Brock also appears to have inserted another claim, not present in earlier drafts of the White Paper: 'Nor had the Vice-Admiral any idea previously that the "Hampshire" had not gone eastwards.' This claim seems extraordinary, for someone who was after all the vice-admiral commanding Orkney and Shetland. Was it really credible that Brock did not know that *Hampshire* was sailing around the west of Orkney?

Brock insisted on adding yet another paragraph designed to cover his back: 'As soon as Vice-Admiral Brock received the news that the "Hampshire" had gone down, he immediately communicated it himself to the Commander in Chief and all subsequent steps were taken in consultation with the Commander in Chief and the Chief of Staff.' Brock was taking no chances that he might have to accept some blame for the slow-moving rescue efforts.

What the White Paper failed to acknowledge was that it took Brock thirty-seven minutes after hearing about the original telegram of a 'battlecruiser in distress' to send out any rescue ships. This was another issue Brock had played down in his report about the rescue efforts, sent to Jellicoe on 15 June, where he claimed that only 'several minutes' would have been gained for the rescue efforts if the first telegram had met with a swift response.

What results did the delays caused by Brock and the Territorials at Birsay actually have? Like Brock, the White Paper sought to play down the consequences, arguing that 'in the actual circumstances in which the accident occurred, any such difference in time [of getting the rescue ships out earlier] could have had no practical result in enabling lives to be saved at sea'.

But is this true? The 37-minute delay in sending out ships meant that these were arriving in the disaster area at around 10.30 p.m., two and a half hours after the ship went down and as the light was disappearing. Every minute in the water led to more men dying. And we know from the experiences of the rescue ships that it was almost impossible to find men after the sun went down: almost all the bodies recovered were found after the sun came back up the next day.

Thirty-seven minutes' more time would have meant thirty-seven precious minutes more of searching while there was at least some light. More importantly, since survival times in water as cold as that the crew of *Hampshire* faced are only one to two hours, thirty-seven minutes might have been the difference between living and dying for some of those in the sea.

Who can know how many men this could have led to saving? Ten, twenty, fifty of those in the water around the *Hampshire* wreck? What we know is that if the rescue vessels had arrived thirty-seven minutes earlier, at around 9.45 p.m., there might still have been some men alive, and it would have been easier to find them.

What we also know is that over sixty men died on the three floats which made land, probably in the hour or so before reaching the shore and as the rafts were thrown up against the cliffs. Had the ships, including the lifeboat, been sent earlier, it is possible that these rafts would have been sighted in the sea, and some of the men rescued earlier.

It can only ever be speculation, but the delayed rescued mission may have cost the lives of fifty to a hundred men. Kitchener was unlikely to have been amongst those rescued – at his age of almost sixty-six, he would almost certainly have died more quickly than others, whether of drowning or hypothermia. But many other men might have lived.

The White Paper also claimed that had the ships reached the survivors earlier, it would have proved impossible to save them because of the rough seas: 'One survivor states that he remembers thinking while he was on the float that if any rescue ship – destroyer or otherwise – was to come alongside, he was quite certain that they would have been able to do nothing.' But the many rescue vessels could have easily lowered their small boats and their own Carley floats. The Admiralty report was now applying far too much whitewash.

The fifth and final British blunder was the failure to call out the Stromness lifeboat. The White Paper claimed that 'the lifeboat could never have reached the spot except under tow. Neither she nor any other vessel could have covered the distance in time to save any lives at sea.' But, of course, the lifeboat would not have needed to reach as far as the area where *Hampshire* sank – miles away. With rafts and men being blown to the south-east, the lifeboat could have helped pick up men around half the distance from Stromness to the area of the sinking. The lifeboat was used to going out in appalling weather, and was manned by men who knew this coastline better than anyone else. Failing to use such experienced local crew was clearly a serious mistake. Some of the sixty men who reached the shore on the Carley floats but who died before getting to safety might have lived had the lifeboat been sent out to save them.

So the conspiracy stories weren't true. But nonetheless major mistakes had been made. In Russia, the mission was not kept secret – but fortunately there were no consequences of this error. It was the five British blunders which cost Kitchener and the 736 others their lives. And at the Admiralty, there was no desire to ask the difficult questions. The official reports were published. The conspiracies could be safely rubbished. And the real questions could be ducked, with the secrets locked away safely in government vaults for decades to come.

POSTSCRIPT

*'He had flashes of greatness. He was like one of those revolving
lighthouses which radiate momentary gleams of revealing light
far out into the surrounding gloom and then suddenly relapse
into complete darkness. There were no intermediate stages.'*

DAVID LLOYD GEORGE ON LORD KITCHENER, *WAR MEMOIRS*, 1933

The body of Earl Kitchener has never been found. After the national mourning for his loss, his reputation suffered over the
course of the next few decades, as those politicians and military
leaders who survived the Great War were able to write its history.
Lloyd George, in his war memoirs, described Kitchener as a talent-
ed but flawed personality, and implicitly blamed him for the huge
losses of men and the lack of shells and equipment. Churchill, too,
was now safely able to shift the responsibility for the failure of his
crazed Dardanelles exploit onto Kitchener – pointing to the latter's
unwillingness to back his naval exploits with sufficient troops.

Kitchener had been in post at the beginning of the war and had
played a crucial role in laying the foundations for long-term success.
But he was dead well before his investments, not least in man-
power, bore fruit. Instead, he would be tarred with the same brush as

Haig and French: as British generals who had sent the 'poor bloody infantry' to pointless deaths against a wall of German barbed wire and machine-gun emplacements.

Meanwhile, in South Africa, the legacy of the concentration camps, and the peace settlement which consolidated 'white rule', were seen as a stain on the Kitchener record. Once regarded as the military saviour of his nation, the victor of Omdurman, Kitchener began to be seen as the eccentric, outdated, relic of an imperialist Britain – no longer a great man, just the front man of that great poster.

Though Kitchener was lost for ever, that early June night in 1916 the body of his closest adviser and personal friend, Lieutenant-Colonel Oswald Arthur Gerald Fitzgerald ('Fitz'), was recovered from the Atlantic waters and shipped back to England. Fitzgerald's was the only body to be returned to the mainland. His coffin was placed in St Matthew's Church in Westminster, where it was covered in floral tributes from friends and other mourners, before being taken to Victoria Station for the journey to the family home in Eastbourne. At Eastbourne Station, the coffin, draped in a Union Jack, was transferred onto a gun carriage drawn by six horses, and driven by officers from the Army Service Corps. The route to the church was lined by many mourners and well-wishers, as well as by soldiers, heads bowed and rifles reversed. A wounded veteran in a wheelchair was seen to support himself against a wall, standing to attention as the coffin went by.

The procession passed along the seafront to All Saints' Church, where a military funeral was held at 1.15 p.m. on Saturday 10 June 1916, just days after the disaster. The Bishop of Chichester officiated and the gathering included family, fellow officers, foreign dignitaries and one rather gaunt naval officer who had followed behind the coffin: Commander Kitchener RN, the brother of Lord Kitchener. All were wearing black armbands. There were large crowds.

After the service, those accompanying the coffin to the grave formed up outside the church and from there processed up the hill to Ocklynge Cemetery. They walked around the small church and down the main pathway through the centre of the graveyard, turning right after 40 metres or so to halt at the spot where a new grave had been dug.

Several volleys were fired in tribute by some forty soldiers, and then great shovelfuls of earth were thrown onto the coffin. Two horses, frightened by the rifle fire, galloped away from the noise, across a field behind the cemetery. Months later, Fitzgerald's family had a large white oval marble slab placed above the grave, perhaps 2½ metres in height. Towards the top of this gravestone is carved: 'In loving memory of Lt. Colonel Oswald Arthur Gerald Fitzgerald CMG, 18th King George's Own Lancers. Eldest son of Col. Sir Charles Fitzgerald KCB'. At the bottom of the gravestone, fading now but still visible, are the words 'Faithful Unto Death'. Perhaps they possess a double meaning.

Of the 749 men on HMS *Hampshire*, just twelve survived. Of the remainder, only 168 bodies were recovered: 124, including Fitzgerald, lie in named graves, but forty-four could not be identified and lie in graves marked 'A Sailor of the Great War: Known unto God'. All but Fitzgerald are buried in the Lyness Naval Cemetery on the island of Hoy, overlooking Scapa Flow.

Perhaps as many as 200 men managed to reach a boat or the three Carley floats, but almost all these drowned or died of hypothermia or exhaustion. There were no survivors amongst the fourteen men in Earl Kitchener's party. And of the officers on board, only Warrant Mechanician William Bennett survived, though many of the bodies of the others were recovered. As for the ordinary sailors from below ship, they were less fortunate. Of the 233 stokers, only two survived, and the bodies of only twelve more were recovered.

Amongst the 735 crew of *Hampshire*, most were young men, the average age being not much more than twenty-five. Some were very young, and almost none of these lived. There was only one survivor aged under eighteen: Dick Simpson. All of the youngest and most junior members of the ship's company died, including fifty with the rank Boy 1st Class, as well as the nine signal boys and the three boy telegraphists. And of these sixty-two boys, only nine bodies were ever found.

The families were notified as soon as reliable information could be collected – the relatives of officers first, as none were considered to have survived. There were some particularly sad stories. After receiving notice of his death, the mother of Able Seaman Ralph Buckingham received a letter from him proudly advising that he had survived the Battle of Jutland, just days before *Hampshire* sank.

There was some monetary compensation for relatives, but not much. The widow of 38-year-old Acting Petty Officer William Cake received a lump sum of £43 and a pension of £2 18s, paid monthly until her death in 1957.

Otherwise, life for the families just had to carry on. But there were some heart-warming stories, too. A 22-year-old *Hampshire* marine, Private William Innoles, was courting Florence Gilbert on home leave in 1916. He was lost on 5 June. But after his death, Florence married his brother, Harry.

Meanwhile, after recovering for a few weeks from their ordeal, the twelve survivors of the sinking were all transferred to other Royal Navy vessels and naval duties – their brief comradeship brought to an end, as only two were sent to the same ship.

Petty Officer Samuel Sweeney, at forty-one the oldest survivor, whose raft landed on the beach in the Bay of Skaill, was returned to Portsmouth and joined HMS *Implacable* at Orkney in April 1918. He was invalided out of the navy in January 1919 because of an old injury to his right hand. The navy had been his life for thirty years and after *Hampshire*'s sinking he had suffered more from shock than the other survivors. In October 1926, on the steamship *Teelin Head* in Belfast Harbour, he committed suicide, allegedly after murdering his wife.

His fellow survivor of the third raft was Leading Stoker Alfred Read, aged twenty-five. Read joined the cruiser HMS *Attentive* in April 1917, and as part of the Dover Patrol his ship was responsible for defending home waters against German destroyer and U-boat attacks. But he must have been continuing to suffer stress from his earlier experiences on *Hampshire*: on 1 July 1917, he returned to Portsmouth and was invalided out of service because of a nervous breakdown, then described as 'neurasthenia'. After the war, Alfred returned to his old job as a painter and decorator. He retired in 1956 and died the following year, aged sixty-six.

Petty Officer Wilfred Wesson, aged thirty-three, was the most senior crew member on the second raft, which landed at Nebbi Geo. He had suffered severe wounds on his feet and knees from climbing over the rocks to safety. Wesson served out the rest of the war on shore, but in October 1919 went back to sea in HMS *Comus*. He transferred to the Royal Fleet Reserve in 1923 and died in Portsmouth in 1946, aged sixty-three.

For Stoker 1st Class Walter 'Lofty' Farnden, also on the second raft, the rest of his naval service was less peaceful than that experienced by Wesson. Farnden, aged twenty-four in 1916, was, ironically after *Hampshire*'s loss, given mine clearance duties – first on the sloop HMS *Pansy* and then on the minesweepers HMS *Gentian* and HMS *Sunflower*. While searching for mines in the Gulf of Finland on 15 July 1919 – after the war had been over for almost a year – his vessel, HMS *Gentian*, exploded a mine and was sunk. Six of those in the engine room were killed, but Farnden survived. A court martial was held and the crew were acquitted of any blame for the ship's loss. Farnden later worked on Southern Railway, and died in Chichester in 1972, at the grand age of eighty.

With Wesson and Farnden in Raft 2 was Able Seaman Horace Llewellyn Buerdsell, aged just twenty. Buerdsell joined HMS *Sandhurst* in Scapa Flow after the sinking and served on other ships until he was discharged in 1926. After periods of unemployment in the 1930s, he became a house and ship painter. He died in Rochdale in 1977 – another long-lived survivor of Raft 2, aged eighty-one.

The final survivor of Raft 2 was Stoker Frederick Lot Sims, aged twenty-one. Sims was badly burnt on the face from the initial explosion on *Hampshire*. Photos of the survivors show the 5 foot 4 inch stoker heavily bandaged. Sims spent a couple of weeks in Haslar Naval Hospital in Portsmouth and remained in the city until April 1918, when he joined the cruiser HMS *Latona* on minelaying duties in the Mediterranean. He left the navy in December 1919. After demobilisation, Sims worked on the London trams and during the Second World War he was a member of the Home Guard. He left many accounts of his experiences on *Hampshire*. He was the last survivor of *Hampshire* to die – in Dacorum, Hertfordshire, in 1991.

Raft 1 had landed at Rivna Geo with six survivors. Warrant Mechanician William Bennett was another who had suffered severe cuts to his feet and knees while climbing the rocks to safety. He was sent immediately to a hospital ship and then to Chatham Hospital – the seriousness of his condition indicated by his absence from the survivors' photograph, which was taken a few days after the sinking. His mother was notified by the Admiralty of his death. A correction was sent out to the grief-stricken lady a few days later.

After *Hampshire*, Bennett was posted to the battleship HMS *Glory*. This was the flagship of a squadron based at Archangel to protect arms supplies that were being sent from Britain for the White Russian Army. Bennett was to reach Archangel after all. He stayed in the navy after the war and was eventually promoted to the rank of lieutenant. It is not known when he died.

Able Seaman John (Jack) Robert Bowman was the second youngest survivor of *Hampshire*, at age twenty. After the sinking, he joined fellow survivor Horace Buerdsell on HMS *Sandhurst* in Scapa Flow before being sent to the destroyer HMS *Rapid*. He remained in the navy for twenty years after his scrape with death in 1916, and rejoined during the Second World War. In 1938, he married. He died of cancer in Norfolk in 1968, aged seventy-two.

Leading Seaman Charles Walter Rogerson, aged twenty-six, another Raft 1 survivor, suffered first-degree frostbite in the lower part of his body from immersion in the bitterly cold waters. He spent a week in Haslar Hospital and was then sent to join the armed merchant cruiser HMS *Arlanza*. He was invalided out of the navy in April 1918, suffering from neurasthenia, the same condition Leading Stoker Alfred Read experienced. He lived only five more years, dying in Auckland, New Zealand, on 5 December 1923, aged just thirty-three.

Scrambling up the rocks with Rogerson had been Able Seaman Richard 'Dick' Simpson – the youngest survivor, aged just seventeen. Simpson was born on 4 August 1898, but when he joined up in June 1915 he gave his date of birth as 1896, to give the impression that he was already eighteen. It was a common practice amongst young men from poorer backgrounds who were keen to join up and do service, in a war that was originally not expected to last long. The military authorities, delighted to recruit more men, often turned a blind eye. Simpson was the last to leave hospital in Portsmouth. After surviving *Hampshire*'s loss, he was posted as a gunner on DAMS (defensively armed mercantile ships). He was not as fortunate as the other *Hampshire* survivors, who all lived out the war. On 14 August 1917, Simpson was a gunner on the 400-ton steamer *Thames*. The vessel was carrying pig iron from Middlesbrough to France. Just off the mouth of the Humber, the ship was attacked by the German submarine *UC-63*. The *Thames* was sunk with the loss of all ten crew and both gunners, including Simpson. The ship was initially listed as 'overdue' and Simson's anguished parents had to wait a long period before his death was finally confirmed. Simpson's mother, Christina, attended the dedication of the Kitchener Memorial in 1926, and stayed with the very family who had provided food and shelter for her son after his landing near Garson farmhouse.

Leading Seaman William Cashman, aged twenty-eight, was the fifth survivor on Raft 1. He had also suffered severely in the cold waters off Orkney and had to be treated for first-degree frostbite. He survived the war and soon returned to County Cork in Ireland, where he was born. He died in Cobh in 1965, aged seventy-seven.

The final survivor of Raft 1 was Shipwright William Charles Phillips, aged thirty. He had left school at fourteen and joined the navy as a boy shipwright, aged just fourteen years and three months. Like Cashman and Rogerson, he sustained first-degree frostbite in the lower parts of his body. He recovered his strength in Wales and later joined HMS *Minerva* off the East African coast. He left the navy in 1926 and died in Pembroke in 1946, aged sixty.

The sinking of *Hampshire* had little effect on the way the Royal Navy planned or operated. Brief consideration was given to ordering more Carley floats for warships, following the conclusion of the 1916 court of inquiry that more lives could have been saved with additional numbers. A response from the naval authorities noted that 'Carley floats ... are expensive – the large floats costing £104'. The Director of Stores estimated in November 1916 that it would cost £53,000 to supply the extra rafts needed. It is not clear if these were ever purchased.

What of those responsible for the death and destruction on *Hampshire*? What did the future hold for the crew of *U-75*, and her commander, Kapitänleutnant Curt Beitzen?

On 20 June, the Chief Censor at the Admiralty, in London, picked up an intercepted message from Reuters news agency. This reported that a German newspaper had just published a statement from the Kaiser, bestowing the Iron Cross 1st Class on Beitzen for the sinking of *Hampshire*. It was the first confirmation of which U-boat was responsible.

Beitzen continued to command *U-75* until May 1917. During that period, *U-75* could also claim success in sinking eight other ships, though none of these would rank remotely alongside her success in destroying *Hampshire*. One of the additional scalps *U-75* could claim was that of *Laurel Crown*, sunk in the same minefield which caught *Hampshire*. But there were seven others: a British Navy trawler in August 1916, a Russian despatch vessel in the same month, a British steamer in September 1916, a Danish sailing vessel and a Swedish steamer in November 1916, and two further vessels in April 1917 – a Russian steamer and a British naval trawler.

After this, in May 1917, Beitzen was rewarded with the captaincy of a new torpedo-attack submarine, *U-98*. He left *U-75* at a fortuitous moment, but many of his crew remained with her under the new commander, Kapitänleutnant Fritz Schmolling. On 13 December 1917, *U-75* was travelling to lay mines off the Dutch coast. But just off Terschelling she hit a mine herself and immediately sank. Her commander and eight crew lived, but twenty-three others perished.

What of Curt Beitzen, who had so narrowly escaped disaster? Could he now survive the war? In November 1917, he transferred from *U-98* to *U-102*. On or around 27 September 1918, with the war's end just six weeks away, *U-102* was near to the scene of the *Hampshire* sinking: just off Orkney, close to the island of Stronsay, on the very route that Kitchener might have followed had not the storm-force winds been blowing from the north-east when Jellicoe made his fateful routing decision on 5 June 1916.

We cannot know, but, so close to the sight of his greatest success, perhaps Beitzen was tempted to toast his extraordinary luck in killing Britain's leading military officer and War Minister. If so, his moment of celebration was short-lived. His submarine had to traverse the Northern Barrage – a jointly created US–British minefield, designed to stop U-boats from accessing the North Sea. Like *Hampshire* before her, *U-102* now ran out of luck. She struck an American mine, and Beitzen and all his crew were killed. He died barely 30 miles away from where Kitchener and the *Hampshire* crew met their end – and probably of the same cause, drowning.

What remains today of all this, over 100 years after the conflict ended? The wreck of *U-102* was located in 2006. The wreck of *Hampshire* lies where it sank – just 1½ miles off Marwick Head, at the north-west of Orkney. It lies upside down under just 65 metres of usually clear water, making it a favoured site for wreck diving. *Hampshire* is, of course, considered a war grave, so as of 2002 permission to dive has to be sought from the Ministry of Defence, and is rarely given.

The first known dives on *Hampshire* were in the late 1970s and early 1980s. The permission was granted for historical research; those involved were not allowed to salvage from the ship. Some of the divers employed claimed that they were told there might be hidden gold on board the vessel – they found none, but there are suspicions that treasure-hunting, and not historical research, might have been the motivation for some of this activity.

In spite of having no permission to salvage, a dive in 1983 resulted in a selection of items being taken from the ship and brought to the surface, including a number of guns and *Hampshire's* starboard propeller. These were seized on behalf of the MoD on landing, and they are now on display in local museums.

In 2016, on the 100th anniversary of the sinking, two special dives were permitted, to assess the state of the wreck. One used a remotely operated diving vehicle and brought back superb images of the upturned vessel, highlighting the catastrophic damage to the forward part of the ship. The other, during late May and early June, was by a team of expert divers. The photos from this dive show that the bows remained largely intact, with the main damage just behind this, caused by the mine and by the front of the ship striking the seabed before the whole ship sank and rolled over. The ocean surface around the ship is covered in munitions, including large numbers of 6- and 7.5-inch shells and a few torpedoes. Some of the ship's Mk VII 6-inch casement guns can also be seen around the wreck – one as far as 30 metres away.

More human items have survived, too, in the debris field around the wreck – crockery, lamps, bathroom tiles and toilets, and a number of white porcelain washbasins.

Parts of the sides of the ship have cracked open as the weight of the armour protection around the waterline has caused fissures in the ship's side. It is now possible to see into the engine and boiler rooms. The port propeller is still undamaged, in its shaft, and can be clearly made out. A section of the ship's plating, containing almost all of *Hampshire*'s name, can be found near the stern.

It might be hoped that *Hampshire*'s wreck could give us some clues about the explosion, or explosions, that sank the ship. Is there evidence of mine damage? Was there more than one explosion? Alas, there is no evidence of any mine strike left on this shipwreck, as the keel plating, frames and stringers from Frame 38 of *Hampshire* to the bow have all been destroyed. This area of the ship can give us no help in understanding what happened, because it is now one vast open space.* This is, perhaps, clue enough to the catastrophic nature of the explosion that sank the ship.

* * *

Those who died on *Hampshire* are not forgotten. The impressive Kitchener Memorial, 15 metres in height and formally unveiled in July 1926, stands proudly on Marwick Head, at the top of the 85-metre-high cliffs, dominating the landscape and looking out over the scene of the tragedy of 1916. It was built to commemorate Kitchener, and stands on the land which is closest to the point at which *Hampshire* sank. It is as solid and unflashy as the man it commemorates. The impression is of the unbreachable tower of a much larger castle, never completed. It is well made to withstand the ferocious Orkney winds, which sometimes gust so hard across

---

* I am grateful to Rod Macdonald, who dived HMS *Hampshire* in 2016, for this assessment.

the clifftops that walkers from the nearby car park are forced to retreat in the face 70 mph blasts, blowing in from the Atlantic and threatening to bowl them over.

In 2016, a new commemorative wall was built on the cliffside of the monument, with the names of all the others who died on *Hampshire* on that June night 100 years before. It is no longer, therefore, a memorial to Kitchener alone.

Orkney hasn't forgotten *Hampshire*, and nor have the relatives of those who died. In 2014, the grandson of Brigadier-General Ellershaw, the 44-year-old artillery officer who accompanied Kitchener on his voyage, scattered his mother's ashes in the sea near the *Hampshire* wreck, so that she could be near her father in death.

In 2016, the centenary of the disaster was remembered with a service held at the memorial and attended by over 600 people. Out at sea, the site of *Hampshire*'s sinking was marked by the presence of HMS *Duncan* – a Type-45 destroyer. On a beautiful, sunny, clear and calm June day, so different from that of 100 years before, HMS *Duncan* fired the first of two rounds to mark a two-minute silence. It was 8.45 p.m. local time precisely – exactly 100 years from the moment when *Hampshire* hit *U-75*'s mine.

As for Kitchener, even the recent dives have failed to produce the slightest trace of his brief time on *Hampshire*. His body, secret papers and personal effects are lost for ever in the Atlantic. All that survives of him is the body of Fitzgerald, the greatest friend of his life, returned to a graveyard in Eastbourne.

If Kitchener's body cannot be rescued from the deep, perhaps it is nonetheless time for a re-evaluation of the career and achievements of this remarkable man. Kitchener surely deserves more than the damaging stereotype of the mindless World War I general and the originator of Boer concentration camps.

At Omdurman and in South Africa, Kitchener showed that he could win potentially difficult wars against organised and determined local resistance. While the British superiority in firepower and training gave a massive advantage in both conflicts, there was nothing inevitable about these two victories, and it took Kitchener's meticulous planning and ruthless organisation to deliver success. As importantly, in both countries Kitchener showed that he could be a pragmatic man of peace, not just a narrow-minded disciple of war. After Omdurman, he skilfully avoided head-on conflict with France at Fashoda, and then proceeded in Khartoum and beyond to rebuild the country on peaceful principles and while respecting local beliefs.

In South Africa, it was Kitchener, as Commander in Chief, who sought and eventually secured a pragmatic end to the war, negotiating with the Boer leaders and seeking to persuade the civilian authorities and the politicians back in London to reach a settlement. A symbol of Kitchener's success was that South African troops were fighting alongside British forces just twelve years after the South African war concluded.

In India and Egypt, Kitchener planned carefully for the risk of future conflict, but he was also a reformer and an innovator. And in Egypt he proved himself to be a benign colonial leader who worked hard not just in his country's interests but to improve the lot of the Egyptian people.

In 1914, Kitchener took on his final, and most challenging, role, as War Minister. His military background, his personality and all his experience to date ill-equipped him to serve as a member of a political Cabinet, sharing information and winning over others to his perspective. He was highly sceptical of much of the Western Front strategy of Sir John French and Sir Douglas Haig, and arguably exercised too little control, failing to limit the huge losses of men and resources. Kitchener also went along with Churchill's absurd naval strategy in the Dardanelles, when this was never likely to succeed, and then allowed the escalation of this strategy into a full-scale land invasion – again, without the plan or resources to deliver success.

But Kitchener also made a major contribution to the eventual Allied triumph. He correctly anticipated, earlier than most of his generals and many politicians, that the war would be a long one. In the face of much scepticism, he delivered detailed plans to scale up Britain's midget-sized army into a multi-million-man fighting force. He helped to ensure that recruitment targets were met, and when this was failing to keep up with need, he pragmatically supported a move away from voluntarism to conscription, avoiding making this a 'military versus civilian' controversy.

On war strategy, Kitchener was neither a 'westerner' nor an 'easterner'. He saw early on that a breakthrough on the Western Front could not be achieved without building up a much more formidable force. But his wider strategic view of the war made him aware of the need for the western Allies to contribute militarily to keeping up the pressure on Germany, and helping to keep Britain and France's essential ally – Russia – in the war. It was that wider strategic sense of priorities that made Kitchener open to eastern ventures, including in the Dardanelles. He saw these as contributing to keeping the war going, and relieving pressure on Russia, but he always thought that the final resolution of the war was likely to be on the Western Front, in 1917 or 1918. In this, he was right.

Kitchener's problem in 1915 and 1916, when his reputation was on the slide, was that he was Secretary of State for War at a time when there were no easy answers. France and Britain did not have the strength to secure a western breakthrough. Nor was there a real opportunity to end the war in the east. Given this, activity was bound to have costs, but inactivity would be costly too. Could Britain and France have engaged in no offensive actions, when Russia was under such huge German pressure? What if Russia had been knocked out of the war and the German forces had been redeployed to the Western Front? That could have been the end for France. And was it really possible for Britain to veto for two years all attempts by the armies of France to recapture their own homeland, until Britain's New Armies were ready?

For Britain and France, there were no simple solutions to win the war in 1915 and 1916, either in the east or in the west. Kitchener was unfortunate enough to be war leader at such a time – almost anyone in this position would have their strategy and effectiveness called into question. Indeed, this was the same in all of the other major countries that were at war.

Kitchener, then, helped lay the foundations for success in the First World War, and had he avoided his date with death in June 1916, it is likely that he would have ended the war still a national hero, the architect of success for Britain in the greatest conflict that the world had ever seen. And then, perhaps, as he craved, he might have secured the position of Viceroy of India. It would have been a fitting end to his career, after which it seems likely that he and Fitzgerald would have retired to their shared estate in East Africa, remaining there for over half the year, certainly for the winters, and returning occasionally to the UK for Kitchener to collect new honours and be the focus of attention at magnificent receptions in grand country houses, where choice items of porcelain might be identified and removed – by agreement, or perhaps without.

But it was not to be.

SELECT BIBLIOGRAPHY

BOOKS

Sir George Arthur, *Life of Lord Kitchener* (three volumes) (London: Macmillan & Co., 1920).

Winston Churchill, *The River War* (London: Longmans, Green & Co., 1899).

Winston Churchill, *My Early Life* (London: Thornton Butterworth, 1930).

Alan Clark, *The Donkeys* (London: Hutchinson, 1961).

Arthur Conan Doyle, *The Great Boer War* (London: Smith, Elder & Co., 1900).

Herbert Du Parcq, *Life of David Lloyd George* (four volumes) (London: Caxton Publishing Co., 1912).

Paul Ferris, *The House of Northcliffe: The Harmsworths of Fleet Street* (London: Weidenfeld & Nicolson 1971).

Norman Friedman, *British Cruisers of the Victorian Era* (Barnsley: Seaforth Publishing, 2012).

Martin Gilbert, *Churchill: A Life* (London: Pimlico, 2000).

Viscount Grey of Fallodon, *Twenty-Five Years*, Volume II (London: Hodder & Stoughton, 1929).

James Irvine et al., *HMS Hampshire: A Century of Myths and Mysteries Unravelled* (Kirkwall, Orkney: Orkney Heritage Society, 2016).

Viscount Admiral Sir John Jellicoe, *The Grand Fleet, 1914–16* (London: Cassell, 1919).

B. H. Liddell Hart, *History of the First World War* (publisher unknown, 1934).

David Lloyd George, *War Memories* (four volumes) (Watford: Odhams Press, 1933–36).

Donald McCormick, *The Mystery of Lord Kitchener's Death* (London: Putnam, 1959).

Rod Macdonald, *Dive Scapa Flow – Centenary Edition* (Caithness: Whittles Publishing, 2018).

Sir Philip Magnus, *Kitchener: Portrait of an Imperialist* (London: John Murray, 1958).

W. C. Phillips, *The Loss of HMS Hampshire and the Death of Lord Kitchener* (Tunbridge Wells; London: Hepworth & Co., 1930).

John Pollock, *Kitchener: The Road to Omdurman and the Saviour of the Nation* (London: Constable, 2001).

Frank Power, *The Kitchener Mystery* (London: Rotary Press, 1926).

Walter Reid, *Architect of Victory: Douglas Haig* (Edinburgh: Birlinn, 2006).

Trevor Royle, *The Kitchener Enigma: The Life and Death of Lord Kitchener of Khartoum, 1850–1916* (Stroud: History Press, 2016).

Nigel Steel and Peter Hart, *Jutland 1916: Death in the Grey Wastes* (London: Cassell, 2003).

G. W. Steevens, *With Kitchener to Khartum* (Edinburgh; London: W. Blackwood & Sons, 1898).

Sir Ronald Storrs, *Orientations* (London: Ivor Nicholson & Watson, 1937).

A. J. P. Taylor (ed.), *Lloyd George: A Diary by Frances Stevenson* (London: Hutchinson & Co., 1971).

THE NATIONAL ARCHIVES

ADM1/8468/226: HMS *Hampshire*, Loss of.

ADM1/8960: HMS *Hampshire*, Loss of (released 1926).

ADM1/22774: Wreck of HMS *Hampshire* – requests to salvage (released 1982).

ADM53/49310: HMS *Midge*, Ship's log, June 1916.

ADM53/50165: HMS *Minster*, Ship's log, June 1916.

ADM53/52211: HMS *Napier*, Ship's log, June 1916.

ADM53/53040: HMS *Menace*, Ship's log, June 1916.

ADM53/53045: HMS *Oak*, Ship's log, June 1916.

ADM53/54247: HMS *Owl*, Ship's log, June 1916.

ADM53/66480: HMS *Unity*, Ship's log, June 1916.

ADM53/67364: HMS *Victor*, Ship's log, June 1916.

ADM116/1515: Bi-Monthly Minesweeping Statement, June–July 1916.

ADM116/1526: HMS *Hampshire*, Loss of.

ADM116/2323: HMS *Hampshire*, Loss of (released 1977).

ADM116/2324A: HMS *Hampshire*, Loss of (released 1980).

ADM116/2324B: HMS *Hampshire*, Loss of (released 1977).

ADM137/302: Jutland.

ADM137/1167: Records used for Official History of Orkney.

ADM137/1209: Records used for Official History of Orkney.

ADM137/1992: Grand Fleet Intelligence Office Pack.

ADM137/3056: Record of Director of Minesweeping.

ADM137/3138: HM Drifter *Laurel Crown*, Loss of.

ADM137/3621: HMS *Hampshire*, Loss of.

ADM137/3903: Papers concerning German submarines *U60–U90*.

ADM137/3913: Original History Sheets *U41–U80*.

ADM137/4069: Intercepted German Messages.

ADM137/4105: Reports of Enemy Submarine Activities received by NID.

ADM186/624: Naval Staff Monograph, October 1915–June 1916.

ADM186/628: Naval Staff Monograph, June 1916–November 1916.

ADM186/629: Mining Operations of German Submarines around the British Isles, 1915–1918.

CAB45/276: HMS *Hampshire*, Loss of.

HO144/6029: Film *The Betrayal of Lord Kitchener* (released 2000).

HW7/23: Paper prepared for Jellicoe.

IR59/49: Lord Kitchener's Will (released 2014).

MEPO2/2469: Metropolitan Police file on Frank Power (released 1983).

PC12/202: Lord Kitchener National Memorial (released 2014).

PRO30/57/53: Kitchener Papers, Kitchener to Haig, 12 February 1916.

PRO30/57/67: Russia: correspondence.

PRO30/57/76: Kitchener Papers, Asquith to Kitchener, 17 October 1915.

PRO30/57/119: HMS *Hampshire*, newspaper reports.

WO138/44: Field Marshal The Earl Kitchener of Khartoum files.

WO159/5: Strategic and political papers.

WO339/45565: 2nd Lieutenant Macpherson.

ORKNEY ARCHIVES

D1 843: The Loss of HMS *Hampshire* and Lord Kitchener 1916: Personal Papers of Fleet Paymaster V. Weekes.

NATIONAL LIBRARY OF SCOTLAND

Acc 3155: Haig Papers Box 6, Haig to Henrietta Haig.

AUTHOR'S COLLECTION

Letter from Leading Signalman George Reeve to his wife, 2 August 1914.

Letter from Leading Signalman George Reeve to his wife, 23 May 1916.

Post Office telegram from Yeoman of Signals George Reeve to his wife, 3 June 1916.

Letter from Yeoman of Signals George Reeve to his wife, 3 June 1916.

Letter from Yeoman of Signals George Reeve's wife to him, 6 June 1916, returned by the Admiralty.

Admiralty letter to Yeoman of Signals George Reeve's wife, dated 15 November 1916.

Admiralty letter to Yeoman of Signals George Reeve's wife, dated 12 June 1917.

Biographical note of Yeoman of Signals George Edward Reeve, undated.

OTHER PAPERS

Chris Rowland and Kari Hyttinen, 'Photogrammetry in Depth: Revealing HMS *Hampshire*' (2017).

James Turner, 'Make Way for Lord Kitchener: The Loss of His Majesty's Ship *Hampshire* on 5 June 1916', West Sussex County Council Great War Project (2014).

INDEX